The Joy

MW01506132

The Vichara Buddhist Monastery Vegetarian Cookbook

A Collection of Recipes from
The Vichara Monastery
10049 Ernst Rd.
Coulterville, CA 95311

vicharamonastery@gmail.com

ISBN 0-9893066-1-5

For a **FREE e-Book copy** of this cookbook's recipes,
visit **www.morriscookbooks.com/ebook** for instructions.

Printed in the USA by

CookbookS
MORRIS PRESS

800-445-6621 • www.morriscookbooks.com
P.O. Box 2110 • Kearney, NE 68848

Dedication

This book is dedicated to the memory of
Rev. Jay DuPont, Roshi,
founder and first Roshi of Vichara.
His influence and discerning taste buds
can be found throughout this cookbook.

Introduction

The Vichara Monastery Bell Tower

The Vichara Monastery

The Vichara Monastery is a small independent Buddhist monastery that is an offspring of the Zen tradition. It is located in the foothills of the Sierra Nevada mountains near Yosemite National Park. Vichara was founded in 1969 in Long Beach, California, by Rev. Jay DuPont, Roshi. The original meditation center had a small dining room where members could have a vegetarian meal. Most of our members take a vow of harmlessness, which is the basis for having a vegetarian diet. For many people it is only natural to not require animals to give up their bodies simply to provide us with nourishment. We opened the dining room, because at that time it was difficult to order a vegetarian meal at a restaurant. If you wanted a good vegetarian meal, you usually had to make it yourself. In 1972 this monastery was established near Coulterville, California. It was not long afterwards that the meditation center in Long Beach was closed. At the monastery we continued to use many of the recipes from the dining room in Long Beach in addition to developing new ones. This cookbook is a collection of some of those recipes. All proceeds from the sale of this book will go to support the Vichara Monastery.

Acknowledgments

DuPont Roshi always complained that I, the monastery cook, did not have any taste buds. I frequently used the wrong amount of salt and occasionally forgot it altogether. Herbs and spices were no different. If any of the recipes here are particularly unique, flavorful, and spicy, it is generally because of his taste buds and instruction. What seemed like endless criticism was balanced with an equal amount of praise and encouragement. Frequently he would dictate an entire recipe to me. I would prepare the meal as instructed, he would fine tune the seasoning and ingredients afterwards, and that would be it. I would write everything down, and the next time I prepared that meal it was from those original instructions. Some of these dishes I had never heard of before. I personally feel that he should be listed as a co-author, but I know that it would make him feel uncomfortable, and he would not approve. So my deepest debt of gratitude goes to my beloved teacher who put up with my klutzy cooking skills for over 30 years.

I would also like to express my greatest appreciation to everyone who helped with the preparation of this cookbook. It has been four years in the making, and I am sure that some of these helpers felt that the end would never come, and that their hard work would be for naught. But here it is! Surprise! Some people helped with putting recipes on the computer. Others tested recipes and provided helpful criticism, while others helped by providing financial support. Finally there are the proof readers who spent what must have seemed like countless hours looking for mistakes. They found literally hundreds of errors that needed to be corrected. It pains me to think of how this book may have turned out without their tireless search for my blunders. Each person listed below helped with at least one of the jobs mentioned above or as many as all four. They include: Rev. Helen Engledow, Nancy Kemp, Sylvia Kincaid, Beverly Marino, Lou Marino, Sylvia Beth Mobley, Pat Stacy, Debi Swarts, and Pete Wilson. I would also like to express my deepest thanks to Meredith Kemp who did the beautiful artwork on the cover and the chapter dividers. If I have left anyone out, please accept my deepest apologies for the omission.

The Free ebook

Each purchase of a hard copy of this cookbook includes a single free ebook copy of the recipes. The URL for acquiring the ebook is located on the title page. Please note that the ebook only includes the recipes and not the introductory pages or the chapter dividers. The ebook cannot be purchased separately from the hard copy.

The Empty Pot.

Why is an empty pot joyful? Because if you look closely, you can see that it is not really empty. It is full of potential. The empty pot is always prepared to go to work. It sits patiently waiting to be called upon to do its duty. It is a symbol of always being ready to begin a new task. This not only applies to the pot, but also any frying pan, saucepan, or skillet in the kitchen that heeds the call to cook. It humbly accepts, without discrimination, whatever food it is given to prepare. It also represents the end of the preparation of a meal, and does not require any recognition for a job well done.

Not Another Vegetarian Cookbook!

Yes, this is another vegetarian cookbook. A lacto-ovo vegetarian cookbook to be precise. We do use eggs and dairy products in our recipes. The timing may not be very good, because the shelves of bookstores are currently straining under the weight of an abundance of vegetarian cookbooks.

This book is a collection of recipes that has bee frequently requested by our members. You do not have to be vegetarian to enjoy most of these recipes. This is not an attempt to get people to become vegetarians. Of all the things that are difficult to change in our lives, changing eating habits is probably one of the most difficult. If that were not the case, we probably would not have as much obesity to deal with in the world. Besides, lots of people become vegetarian, and then for an assortment of reasons switch back to eating meat again. If you do decide to reduce the amount of meat in your diet, I hope that you will find some of these recipes helpful.

This also is not a health food cookbook. To take a vow of harmlessness does not require a person to eat only healthy food, whatever that is. The most popular recipe in this collection so far has been New York Cheesecake, not exactly a poster child for healthy eating. While there are a lot of healthy recipes here, it is up to you to strike a balance in your diet between healthy and not so healthy. I think the appropriate phrase here is "everything in moderation."

There are several recipes that include forms of imitation meat. Tofu, and textured vegetable protein (TVP®) in particular, can be used as meat substitutes. Some observers have asked, "If you want something that tastes like meat, why not just eat meat?" There are two answers to this question. First of all, some have had to adopt a vegetarian diet for health reasons. Secondly, many vegetarians are converts. They started out eating meat and then for various reasons decided to become vegetarians. Sometimes they miss the flavors and textures of some of the foods they had during their meat eating days. A good example of this would be chili. Replacing the meat in chili with corn, green beans, and zucchini just does not cut it for many people. Having chili with a meat substitute goes a long way towards satisfying that craving. It will never taste exactly like chili made with meat, but it will be close enough. We do not expect regular meat eaters to be fooled into thinking that this is real chili. That is not the purpose.

The Well Equipped Kitchen

How does the old saying go, "You're only as good as your tools?" That also applies to kitchen gadgets. Here is a list of items that are not mandatory but will make life in the kitchen a little easier. Some of these items are not recommended if you have small children, especially the deep fryer, mandoline, and electric food slicer. A frying pan and knife will work until the kids grow up.

• **Aebleskiver Pan:** This pan is required in order to make aebleskivers (see Chapter: Breads; Baking Powder Breads). It is usually a heavy cast iron pan that has 7 indentations for cooking the aebleskivers. Aebleskivers are spherical pancakes about the size of a ping pong ball that are made in Denmark. The pan is also ideal for making evenly rounded vegetarian meatballs.

• **Butter Slicer:** This tool consists of a small frame with wire strings spaced about 1/4 inch apart. Using a butter slicer makes it easier to serve butter at mealtime, but it also has another advantage. With most butter slicers, one patty equals 2 teaspoons of butter. Since 3 teaspoons equals 1 tablespoon, if you need 1 tablespoon of butter you just use 1 1/2 patties. For 2 tablespoons of butter you will need 3 patties of butter.

• **Small Condiment Dishes:** Although they are not used in the kitchen for meal preparation, they can be very handy when it comes time to serve a meal. These small dishes are ideal for serving jams. jellies, or dips on the side. This helps to keep your plate from becoming too crowded. Each person should get their own condiment dish. They are usually 3 to 4 inches in diameter and 3/4 inch deep.

• **Deep Fryer:** Not recommended if you have small children in the house. With its preset thermostat, it makes frying much easier. Some of the larger deep fryers have a basket and adjustable thermostat.

• **Electric Food Slicer:** This is most useful if you do a lot of bread baking. Bread that is evenly sliced is easier to work with for toast, and sandwiches, etc. It is also handy for shredding lettuce and cabbage. If you have to prepare a large quantity of tacos, tostados, or coleslaw, a food slicer makes the job much easier. Since they are fairly expensive, you may want to consider how often you would use it before you commit to such a large purchase.

• **Half Sheet Pan (18 x 12 x 1-inch):** This is essentially a large cookie sheet, but it is used mostly by businesses like restaurants. You can usually find one at a restaurant supply store. The traditional cookie sheet used in most homes is 15 x 10 x 1-inch. The larger size makes it possible to bake larger quantities at one time. The other advantage of the Half Sheet Pan is that it is made of much thicker and sturdier metal. This means that it will not buckle when placed in a hot oven like a cookie sheet does sometimes. Measure the size of your oven before you purchase a Half Sheet pan to make sure that it will fit.

• **Hard Boiled Egg Slicer:** Not only are these good for slicing hard boiled eggs, they also make quick work of chopping eggs for egg salad.

• **Large fine wire mesh strainer:** This looks like a large tea strainer. It comes in very handy for removing lumps from both dry and liquid ingredients.

• **Long Handled Metal Tongs:** If you do a lot of frying, you may want to consider a pair of long handled tongs. They make turning food easier and help to keep your hands a comfortable distance from the hot oil.

• **Mandoline:** This gadget has a blade on a slanted platform that allows you to slice vegetables extremely thin. Most Mandolines have removable inserts that make it possible to change the thickness of the slices.

• **Small Mortar and Pestle:** This is used mostly with herbs and spices. If possible, it is best to use whole dried spices when cooking and then crush them just before adding them to the pot. Crushing them between your thumb and forefinger is the easiest technique. This releases the oils and fragrance of the spices. A mortar and pestle makes it easier to crush larger quantities all at once. Since ground herbs and spices have been processed at some earlier date, they do not have has much flavor as the freshly crushed product.

• **Pizza Cutting Wheel:** In spite of its name, I don't especially like this tool for cutting pizza, because it hits the edge of the pizza pan. However, it is excellent for trimming tortillas and cutting Egg Roll wraps, among other things.

• **Pressing Cloth:** A pressing cloth is required for several of the recipes here. An old tea towel or dish towel will work, or you can make one from muslin cloth. Keep in mind that once something is used for a pressing cloth it should be reserved for that process. They usually become stained and are no longer suitable for their original purpose.

• **Pressure Cooker:** I am surprised that this has not received more attention recently because it is a great way to save both time and energy resources. Many soups are ideally suited for preparation in a pressure cooker.

• **Rice Cooker:** If you eat a lot of rice, this is a must. It will cook white rice, brown rice, and even barley. It shuts off automatically so that you do not have to be concerned about under/over cooking. It also keeps the rice warm until it is time to serve the meal.

• **Slow cooker:** Traditionally known by the commercial name Crock-Pot®. Used mostly here for cooking dried beans (pintos).

• **Spaghetti Pot:** Sometimes called a multipot or multiuse pot. The pot includes four parts: a stock pot, spaghetti basket, steamer basket, and lid. This makes draining pasta when it is done a snap. The steamer basket is not only excellent for steaming vegetables, but it can also be used as a mold for homemade tofu (see Chapter:Tofu).

There are more equipment suggestions on the back of some of the chapter dividers that are specific to that chapter.

A Few Words About Wheat Flour and Yeast

Flour is a staple ingredient that is frequently taken for granted. Since we use several different kinds of wheat flour in this cookbook, I thought that I would describe some of the different flours and how they are used. While all-purpose flour is what is most frequently used, the following is a list of flours that are referred to in this cookbook and how they differ from each other. I will stick with wheat flours, since there is another whole world of flours that exist from other sources. Some examples would be oat, chickpea, soy, rye, and buckwheat flours, just to name a few.

To get the light and airy structure of cakes, you want a flour with very little protein. But to form the dense chewy structure of bread, you want a flour with a lot of protein so that you can create as much gluten as possible.

Cake flour: (7 - 8% protein) Cake flour is a fine textured, soft-wheat flour with a high starch content. It has the lowest gluten (protein) content of any white flour. This flour is excellent for baking fine-textured cakes with greater volume.

All-Purpose flour: (10 - 12% protein) This flour is the flour of choice for most home bakers. It can be used in place of cake flour or bread flour by making minor adjustments. If you only have enough cupboard space for one variety of flour, this is the flour to use. I am sure that this flour outsells all other flours by a wide margin because of its universal appeal.

Bread flour (also called Hi-Gluten®, Hy-Gluten flour®, or baker's flour): (14 - 16% protein) Bread flour, with its higher gluten content is ideal for baking yeast breads. It is almost mandatory if you should decide to try some baking with a bread machine.

Bleached or unbleached flour: The three flours listed above can be either bleached or unbleached. Bleached flour has been treated with chemical agents to give it a whiter color. White flour naturally becomes whiter with aging, but with bleached flour the chemicals speed up the process. Unbleached flour is slightly heavier than bleached and is preferred for pastries and yeast breads. For many people, though, it is difficult to tell the difference in the final baked product. Those with refined taste buds say that food made with unbleached flour has more flavor than bleached. While bread flour is traditionally unbleached, you can still find some that is bleached.

Vital wheat gluten flour: (75 - 80% protein) Sometimes referred to as just gluten flour, this is the protein that has been extracted from flour without the starch. It is essentially just the protein from wheat flour in powdered form. Gluten is what gives flour its elastic and binding properties. Pure gluten is also used to make many imitation meat products. As you can see from its high protein content, you can add a little to all-purpose flour (1 to 2 tablespoons per cup) when making bread if you do not have bread flour. The gluten flour will improve the texture and allow the bread dough to rise more before baking. It is also used as a binding agent when making vegetarian burgers and vegetable fritters.

Whole wheat flour: (15 - 16% protein) This is the only flour listed here that uses the whole kernel of wheat. Since it contains all of the fiber (bran and wheat germ), it has more nutrients than any of the white flours. The high fiber content seems to counteract the elastic and binding qualities of the gluten. That is why it is frequently mixed with all-purpose flour, bread flour, or even vital wheat gluten when baking bread.

Active dry yeast: The bread recipes in this book use instant dry yeast exclusively, as opposed to regular dry yeast. Instant dry yeast can be added directly to your flour when making bread, whereas regular yeast needs to be added to warm water or another liquid and "proofed" (activated) before being added to the flour. Regular yeast also does not seem to rise as fast as instant dry yeast.

Twisted Egg Bread Loaf

Please Read Recipe Notes First

Some of the recipes will have a section of "Notes" at the end. Please read the notes first, before preparing the recipe. In spite of their location, they generally include information that is helpful or even vital to the preparation of the recipe. This format and location at the end was established by the printer. When notes are available, they generally include a list of items that you will need before you begin preparing the recipe. This frequently may include special utensils or unique ingredients.

Generic Terms and Corresponding Brand Name Suggestions

Here is a list of some generic terms and their corresponding brand names. Most of the brands are being mentioned because they were the first to become available or because they are the most widely available. There are new brands entering the marketplace at an alarming rate. So keep your eyes open, and don't be afraid to try a new variety.

• **Biscuit Mix:** *Bisquick® Original Pancake and Baking Mix:* The original biscuit mix that started it all. There are probably countless generic versions of this product available. Betty Crocker® also makes a gluten-free version of *Bisquick®*. There is a recipe for making your own biscuit mix in the chapter on Breads.

•**Browning Sauce:** *Kitchen Bouquet® Browning and Seasoning Sauce.* This is what is used most often to give gravies, etc. their dark brown color. There are several other brands of this type of sauce that will work just as well.

• **Hickory Salt:** *Spice Islands® Old Hickory Smoked Salt.* This is handy when you want to add a mild smoked flavor to a recipe, and liquid smoke would be too strong. There is a recipe for making your own that uses liquid smoke, in the last chapter, "This and That." There are many other companies that make a similar product, and some even use sea salt.

• **Imitation Chicken:** *Worthington®,* which is found mostly in health food stores,makes two different frozen imitation chicken rolls: 1 lb. Chik-etts and a 4 lb. Meatless Chicken Style. *MorningStar Farms®,* which can be found in most large markets, makes chicken patties which are available in the frozen food section.

•**Imitation Chicken Seasoning:** *McKay's® Chicken Style Instant Broth and Seasoning.* This is what we use most often when a chicken flavor is needed. This powdered soup mix is available in three varieties; Regular, Vegan Special, and No MSG Added. They also make a beef version. There are other brands of chicken seasoning that can be used, but this probably is the most widely available.

• **Onion Soup Mix:** *Lipton® Recipe Secrets® Onion Recipe Soup and Dip Mix.* When using this soup mix, stir the ingredients in the envelope or box to make sure that the dried onions are evenly distributed before measuring. This is sometimes labeled as *Onion Soup Base.*

• **Powdered Fruit Pectin:** *Sure-Jell Premium Fruit Pectin.* We use only the premium variety and not the *Sure-Jell For Less* or *No Sugar Needed* recipes.

• **Vegetable Bouillon Cubes:** *Herb-ox® Vegetable Bouillon Cubes.*Again, there are many companies that make vegetable bouillon; this just happens to be one that is widely available. There are also vegetable powders that can be used in place of the cubes.

• **Vegetarian Meat Substitutes:** There is an ever expanding variety of meat substitutes currently available. Many of them are vegan. Most can been found in the freezer section or the refrigerated section of the produce department of your local grocery store. Some stores also carry the canned versions of Loma Linda® and Worthington® products.

• **Vegetarian Sausage Links:** Both *Worthington®* and *MorningStar Farms®* make excellent imitation sausage links.

• **Vegetarian Sausage Patties:** Again, both *Worthington®* and *MorningStar Farms®* make excellent imitation sausage patties. Worthington also makes an especially good 1 lb. frozen sausage roll that can be sliced into patties called *Prosage®* (see following listing).

• **Vegetarian Sausage Roll:** *Worthington Prosage® Roll.* Because it comes in a one pound roll, it can be sliced, diced, or crumbled.This is a unique product for which there is no equal. The thing that makes it unique is its texture and seasoning. There are other vegetarian sausage products available, but none of them, to my knowledge, can be used in place of Prosage®. It also comes in links which are not quite as versatile as the roll.

Practical Trivia

Chile vs. Chili: The debate rages on. In North America many people use the two terms interchangeably. Chile is used to refer to a single chile or chile variety, as in Jalapeño chile pepper. Ground chiles refers to a single variety of dried chiles that have been pulverized. Chili, on the other hand, refers to the Texas bowl of highly seasoned beans and meat. Chili powder refers to the ingredient used to make a bowl of chili. Chili powder can contain a single variety of chiles for seasoning but generally contains other ingredients like cumin, garlic powder, cayenne, oregano, etc. A general rule would be that chile refers to a single pepper item and chili refers to a mixture of one or more different kinds of peppers and various other ingredients.

Herbs and Spices: Herbs are essentially the dried leaves of plants. Spices include all of the other parts of the plants such as stems, roots, dried fruit, and bark.

Powdered egg whites: Some of the recipes here require powdered egg whites. Since powdered egg whites have been pasteurized, they do not carry the risk of salmonella contamination that is possible with fresh egg whites.

Dried vs. fresh onions: Some readers may wonder why a recipe may include both onion powder and fresh onions. The simplest explanation is that they have a different flavor. When onions are dried and ground into powder their flavor changes considerably. This is also true of garlic and ginger.

Boiling Water Bath

Several recipes here call for the use of a boiling water bath. It is used in most of the recipes in Chapter: Jellies, Jams, etc. If you have done any canning, you can probably skip this section. If you have never done any canning before, then read this section carefully. You may already have some of the equipment that you will need in your kitchen. There is a list of suggested supplies on the back of the chapter divider for Jams and Jellies.

A jar lifter that is specially made for canning is a handy tool, but long handled tongs will work if used with caution. Special pots are made for water bath canning. If you are just canning jellies etc. in 1/2-pint jars, then all you need is a large pot that is at least 6 1/2 inches tall on the inside. You will also need a trivet to put in the bottom of the pot to keep the jars from directly touching the bottom (allow 1/2 inch). Most 1/2-pint jars are about 4 inches tall. You will need to cover the jars with at least 1 inch of water when sterilizing and processing and then have another 1 inch of head room to keep the boiling water from spilling out of the pot. Larger jars will require a larger pot.

Prepare the lids according to the manufacturer's directions. If you like, they can be sterilized in the pot along with the jars. Place your jars in the pot with the trivet in the bottom. Cover the jars with water and place over high heat. Bring to a boil and sterilize the jars by boiling gently for 10 minutes, adjusting processing time if necessary as directed in the Altitude Chart (see below). Turn off the heat when done and set aside until ready to fill the jars.

Once the food you are preparing is ready, fill the jars immediately by following these directions. Remove the jars and set on a dry towel while filling. Fill a jar with the food that is being canned. Leave about 1/4 inch headspace when filling the jar. Headspace is the distance between the top of the food in the jar and the top of the jar. Wipe the rim and the threads of the jar with a clean, damp cloth. Place a metal lid on top and lightly screw a metal band in place. Return the jar to the pot of hot water. Repeat for the remaining jars. Place the pot over high heat, bring to a hard boil, and cover the pot. Reduce the heat slightly to a gentle boil and begin counting the processing time called for in the recipe. Adjust the processing time if necessary as directed in the Altitude Chart (see below). Reducing the heat will help to keep the water from spilling on the stove. Remove the jars when done and place upright on a dry towel to cool. After the jars have cooled to room temperature, check to make sure that the lids have sealed properly by pressing the center of the lids with your finger. If a lid springs back, it did not seal properly and must be refrigerated to prevent spoiling. Let the jars stand at room temperature for 24 hours. Remove the bands and wash the jars to remove any food that may have spilled on them during filling. Pay careful attention to the threads of the jars. Store unopened jars without their bands in a cool, dry, dark place. Refrigerate the jars after opening.

Altitude Chart

Processing times are for sea level to 1,000 feet. For altitudes above 1,000 feet, increase the processing time as indicated below.

1.001 to 3,000 feet ....add 5 minutes.
3,001 to 6,000 feet ....add 10 minutes.
6,001 to 8,000 feet ....add 15 minutes.
8,001 to 10,000 feet ....add 20 minutes.

Table of Contents

240812-16

Salads

Salads

Most main dishes should be accompanied by a salad, even if it is only a small tossed green salad.

Equipment Suggestions

Two pieces of extra equipment that you may find helpful in the kitchen when preparing salads are the mandolin slicer and lettuce spinner.

More Salads

The following three recipes appear in Chapter: Main Dishes. You may want to keep them in mind when considering your choices for preparing a salad, especially if you are considering a larger than average salad.

Stuffed Tomato: This is essentially a large salad that is prepared as an entree. By using a small tomato and stuffing of your choice, you can also make an excellent small salad as a side dish.

Large Guacamole Tostado: Technically this is not a salad. But since it has so much lettuce and guacamole it would not take much to convince some people that it is a large salad ideal for eating on a hot summer day.

Large Summer Salad: This large salad is served as a main dish and could have just as easily been included in this chapter. It appears in the chapter of Main Dishes where, hopefully, it will have less chance of being overlooked.

SALADS

CLASSIC POTATO SALAD
(Makes 6 cups)

2 lb. red potatoes, boiled, peeled
    and cubed
2 hard-boiled eggs
½ c. diced celery
¾ c. mayonnaise
¼ c. sliced Spanish, pimiento
    stuffed, olives

¼ c. sweet relish
½ tsp. yellow mustard
½ tsp. celery salt
½ tsp. salt
¼ tsp. crushed summer savory
⅛ tsp. black pepper

Prepare potatoes and measure. There should be about 5 to 6 cups of cubed potatoes. Place the potatoes in the refrigerator and make sure that they are thoroughly chilled before assembling potato salad. Place the potatoes in a large bowl. Peel and chop the hard boiled eggs and add to the potatoes. Add the diced celery, mayonnaise, sliced Spanish olives, sweet relish, yellow mustard, celery salt, salt, summer savory, and black pepper. Gently fold the ingredients together with as few strokes as possible. Refrigerate until ready to serve.

Note: You can cook the potatoes in a microwave oven if you like.

TABOULI
(Makes about 6 cups)

1 ½ c. boiling water
1 c. bulgur wheat
2 lrg. ripe tomatoes, about 1 lb.
2 cloves garlic, peeled and
    minced, about 2 tsp.
1 ⅓ c. finely chopped yellow
    onion (8 oz.)

1 c. chopped Italian flat parsley
    leaves
¼ c. chopped fresh mint leaves
1 tsp. salt
¼ tsp. black pepper
½ c. olive oil
⅓ c. fresh lemon juice

Pour the boiling water over the bulgur and let soak for 1 hour. Drain excess water and place in a large bowl. Cut the tomatoes in half from top to bottom. Scoop out the seeds with a spoon and discard. Dice the tomatoes into small pieces. There should be 1 ½ cups diced tomato. Add the tomatoes, minced garlic, onion, parsley, mint leaves, salt, and black pepper to the bulgur. Stir together until well blended. Just before serving, whisk together the olive oil and lemon juice in a separate small bowl. Pour the olive oil mixture over the bulgur and stir until well blended.

Note: Also spelled tabbouleh and tabouleh. This colorful salad from the Middle East (Lebanon) provides a great break from some of the more traditional salads built around salad greens.

BROCCOLI SALAD
(Makes 4 servings)

BROCCOLI PREPARATION

¾ lb. broccoli crowns   2 tsp. salt

Rinse the broccoli crowns under cold water and drain. Cut the broccoli into pieces about 2½-inches long and 1 to 1½-inches wide. You should have at least 4 cups of broccoli florets when done. Fill a 3-quart saucepan three-quarters full with water. Stir in the salt and bring to a boil. Add the broccoli and cook for exactly 4 minutes from the time you add the broccoli to the pot. Drain the broccoli in a colander, place in a large bowl, and cover with plastic wrap. Chill the broccoli in the refrigerator for at least one hour or overnight and then use in recipe below.

ASSEMBLING SALAD

1 sm. sweet red or white onion
 (about 6 oz.)

1 med. sweet red bell pepper
 (about 6 oz.)

1 c. lrg. pitted black olives,
 drained

⅓ to ½ c. salad dressing of your
 choice

4 lrg. lettuce leaves

Cook broccoli according to directions above. Slice onion into rings about ¼-inch thick. Dice the red bell pepper into 1-inch pieces. There should be about 1 cup. Combine broccoli, onions, bell pepper, and olives in a large bowl. Pour ⅓ cup of salad dressing over salad and toss. Taste and add more dressing if necessary. Refrigerate until ready to serve. Serve on a bed of lettuce made from a single large lettuce leaf.

Note: You can use either a creamy salad dressing or a vinegar and oil dressing with this salad.

240812-16

TRADITIONAL COLESLAW
(Makes 1 quart)

4 c. finely chopped green
  cabbage, about 1 lb.
¾ tsp. salt
¼ c. grated carrot
2 Tbs. minced sweet onion (opt.)
¾ c. mayonnaise
1 Tbs. sugar
2 tsp. Dijon mustard

½ tsp. dried dill weed, crushed
¼ tsp. black pepper
¼ tsp. celery salt
¼ tsp. dried summer savory,
  crushed
⅛ tsp. nutmeg
pinch dried peppermint leaves

In a large bowl stir together the chopped cabbage and salt. Let stand for 10 minutes and drain any excess liquid. Add the grated carrot, optional sweet onion, mayonnaise, sugar, Dijon mustard, dill weed, black pepper, celery salt, summer savory, nutmeg, and peppermint. Mix well and chill. Refrigerate until ready to serve.

Note: You will need to purchase a cabbage that weighs about 1 ½ pounds.

MACARONI SALAD
(Makes 7 cups)

2 c. dry small elbow macaroni or
  shells (8 oz.)
½ c. diced celery
⅓ c. diced red or green bell
  pepper
¼ c. diced red onion (opt.)
2 hard boiled eggs, peeled and
  diced

1 c. mayonnaise
⅔ c. sweet pickle relish
1 tsp. salt
1 tsp. celery seed, crushed
¼ tsp. summer savory
½ tsp. yellow mustard
individual lettuce leaves
paprika

Cook the macaroni according to the package directions, drain, and allow to cool to room temperature. Place the macaroni in a large bowl. Add the celery, bell pepper, optional red onion, hard boiled eggs, mayonnaise, sweet relish, salt, celery seed, summer savory, and yellow mustard. Mix thoroughly and chill. To serve, place each portion of macaroni on a lettuce leaf and sprinkle a little paprika over the top.

TOSSED GREEN SALAD
(Makes 6 to 8 servings)

SIMPLE SALAD

1 head iceberg lettuce -- OR --   Your choice of salad dressing
1 head of leaf lettuce

Remove and discard the tough outer leaves of the lettuce. Rinse and drain the head of lettuce well. If you are using leaf lettuce, wash each leaf individually and drain. Break or tear the lettuce into pieces and put in a large bowl. Add about three ingredients from the following list to your salad. Pour salad dressing over top, toss, and serve.

ADDITIONAL INGREDIENTS

Diced tomato   Canned asparagus
Sliced cucumber   Marinated Fresh Mushroom (see
Thinly sliced dill pickle   following recipe)
Diced avocado   Cooked broccoli, chilled
Diced cheese   Cooked cauliflower florets, chilled
Sliced young zucchini   Cooked sliced carrots, chilled
Sweet onion rings   Cooked green beans, chilled
Diced jicama   Pickled beets, drained
Olives, Spanish or pitted black   Sliced hard boiled egg
Diced bell pepper   Home made croutons
Sliced celery

Here is a list of ingredients that you can add to your simple salad to make it a little more interesting. Try not to overdo it. Just add two to four items from the above list. This is also a good way to use leftover vegetables that are being kept in the refrigerator.

SIMPLE WEDGE OF LETTUCE - Makes 4 to 6 servings

1 head of firm iceberg lettuce   Salad dressing of your choice

This is essentially your no frills simple salad that can be served in place of the above tossed green salad. The head of lettuce should be very firm (i.e. solid). Remove the core and tough outer leaves. Cut in half from top to bottom. Rinse under cold running water and drain thoroughly. Remove four to six of the large outer leaves and reserve. Place a lettuce half on a cutting board, cut side down. Cut across the head of lettuce about one-half inch from the top. Save the top piece for another meal. Cut across the head again about one inch from the original slice, creating a wedge that is about one inch thick. Place on a salad plate that is covered with one of the large reserved lettuce leaves. Repeat once or twice depending on the size of the head of lettuce. The remaining lettuce at the bottom can also be saved for another meal. Repeat for the other half of the head of lettuce. Keep refrigerated until ready to serve. Pour salad dressing over wedge just before serving.

MARINATED FRESH MUSHROOMS FOR SALAD
(Makes about 1 cup)

4 oz. fresh white or brown cap
mushrooms

¼ c. Italian Salad Dressing (see
recipe later in this chapter)

Gently rinse off the mushrooms and pat dry. Slice the mushrooms from top to bottom into quarters. There should be about 1 ½ cups of mushrooms. Place in jar and add ¼ cup Italian Salad Dressing. Place lid on jar and gently shake. Allow to marinate at room temperature for 2 to 3 hours. Refrigerate until ready to use. Use as an addition to any of your favorite salads. Mushrooms are at their best when used within 24 hours. After that they tend to darken and get rubbery.

Note: You will need a pint jar with a tight fitting lid for this recipe.

SPINACH SALAD
(Makes 4 servings)

2 hard boiled eggs, sliced
2 c. fresh spinach, washed and
drained
2 c. leaf lettuce, washed and
drained
½ c. thinly sliced celery

2 thinly sliced red onion rings,
broken apart
1 Kosher dill pickle, thinly sliced
crosswise
Italian Salad Dressing

Cook the hard boiled eggs ahead of time and chill. Tear the spinach and lettuce into bite-size pieces. Place in a large bowl and add the hard boiled egg, celery, sliced onion rings, and dill pickle. Pour salad dressing over top and toss well. Serve immediately.

CARROT SALAD
(Makes 3 to 4 servings)

¼ c. raisins
1 c. grated carrots
2 slices canned pineapple, cut
into small pieces

2 Tbs. chopped walnuts
¼ c. mayonnaise
⅛ tsp. salt

Plump the raisins by soaking in ½ cup hot water for 5 minutes. Drain thoroughly. In a medium bowl combine the grated carrots, pineapple, walnuts, mayonnaise, and salt. Stir until well blended and fold in the raisins. Refrigerate for at least one hour or until ready to serve.

JAPANESE PICKLED CUCUMBER
(Makes 4 to 6 servings)

1 cucumber, about 12 oz.
¼ c. sugar
¼ c. water

3 Tbs. white vinegar
⅛ tsp. salt

Combine the sugar, water, vinegar, and salt in a small saucepan. Heat and stir until sugar is dissolved. Set this syrup aside to cool while preparing the cucumber. Peel the cucumber and discard the ends. Cut crosswise into very thin slices using a mandoline slicer or knife. There should be about 2 cups of cucumber slices. Pour the prepared syrup over the cucumber slices in a bowl. Refrigerate and stir after about one hour. Stir again before serving in small condiment dishes.

Note: A Mandoline slicer will help to cut the cucumber into very thin slices. These pickled cucumbers can be served as a small side dish in almost any Asian meal. They taste best when prepared about 2 hours before being served. They will keep for 2 to 3 days in the refrigerator. A small condiment dish is about 3½ inches in diameter.

PASTA SALAD
(Makes 4 to 6 servings)

6 oz. rotini or rotelli (2 c.), cooked
1 c. broccoli florets, cooked
½ c. sliced carrots (2 oz.), cooked
½ c. diced bell pepper (2 oz.)
½ c. cucumber slices
1 med. tomato, seeded and diced, about ⅔ c.
¼ c. diced celery

½ c. small Spanish olives, stuffed with pimiento
1 med. avocado, peeled and diced, about 1 c. (opt.)
⅓ c. diced sweet red onion (opt.)
Any salad dressing of your choice.
6 lrg. lettuce leaves

Cook rotini, drain, and allow to cool. Place in a large bowl and add broccoli, carrots, bell pepper, cucumber, diced tomato, celery, and Spanish olives. You can also add the optional avocado and red onion. Pour a modest amount of your favorite dressing over the top and toss until well blended. Serve on a lettuce leaf. This makes about 30 ounces by weight or 6 cups of salad.

Note: Vegetables that are diced should be cut into 1-inch pieces. Vegetables that are sliced should be slice about ¼-inch thick. All ingredients should be chilled before assembling salad.

240812-16

ITALIAN SALAD DRESSING
(Makes ¾ cup)

1 ½ Tbs. cider or red wine vinegar
3 Tbs. water
1 envelope Good Seasons®
   Italian Salad Dressing Mix

¼ c. extra virgin olive oil
¼ c. canola oil

In a cruet combine the vinegar, water, and envelope of Italian Salad Dressing Mix. Put the lid on top and shake well. Add the olive oil and canola oil. Put the lid on top and shake again until well blended.

Note: You will need a cruet or recycled salad dressing bottle. A half-pint or pint canning jar with a tight fitting lid will also work. This is the Italian dressing that we use here at the monastery. It does not follow the directions on the package, which tends to make a dressing that is a little more tart.

THOUSAND ISLAND SALAD DRESSING, SANDWICH SPREAD, AND DIP
(Makes 1 ⅓ cups)

SALAD DRESSING

1 c. mayonnaise
2 Tbs. ketchup

⅓ c. sweet pickle relish

In a medium bowl combine the mayonnaise, ketchup, and sweet pickle relish. Mix together until well blended. Store in the refrigerator until ready to use.

SANDWICH SPREAD AND DIP

Same ingredients as above

Lrg. fine mesh strainer

In a medium bowl combine the mayonnaise and ketchup. Place the sweet relish in a large strainer over the sink. Press the relish with the back of a spoon to remove as much of the pickling syrup as possible. Add the drained relish to the mayonnaise and stir until well blended. Removing the syrup in the relish makes this spread thicker than the salad dressing, which makes it easier to spread. Store in the refrigerator until ready to use.

Note: Although this originally started out as just a salad dressing, we changed it slightly so that we could also use it as a sandwich spread. It works especially well on Mushroom Burgers (see Chapter: Main Dishes). While there is an ongoing debate about the difference between Russian and Thousand Island Dressing, we use the terms interchangeably.

CREAMY ROQUEFORT DRESSING
(Makes 1 cup)

½ c. mayonnaise
½ c. fresh buttermilk
1 Tbs. white vinegar
1 Tbs. minced chives (opt.)

Dash salt
Dash pepper
½ c. Roquefort cheese, (2 oz.)

In a medium bowl whisk together until smooth the mayonnaise, buttermilk, white vinegar, optional minced chives, salt, and pepper. Break the Roquefort cheese into crumbles and stir into the dressing. Serve on your favorite salad.

Note: Blue cheese can be used in place of the Roquefort cheese. Please note that this dressing should be used within 1 to 2 days. It has a tendency to get much thinner when left in the refrigerator for a longer period of time.

MEXICAN SALAD DRESSING
(Makes ⅔ cup)

¼ c. mayonnaise
3 Tbs. vegetable oil

1 ½ Tbs. cider vinegar
2 Tbs. taco sauce

In a small bowl combine the mayonnaise, vegetable oil, cider vinegar, and taco sauce. Whip together with a whisk until well blended. Refrigerate until ready to use.

Note: This dressing is frequently used on tossed green salads that are served with Mexican food.

SIMPLE CREAMY FRENCH DRESSING
(Makes 1 cup)

½ c. Italian Salad Dressing
¼ c. ketchup

¼ c. mayonnaise

In a small bowl combine the Italian Salad Dressing, ketchup, and mayonnaise. Beat everything together with a fork or small whisk. Store in a covered container in the refrigerator.

Note: You can use the Italian Salad Dressing recipe from this chapter or any store bought variety.

240812-16

Sauces and Gravies

Sauces and Gravies

A tasty sauce or gravy can turn an ordinary meal into something special. The recipes in this chapter are sauces and gravies that can be used in a variety of different meals. Here is a list of more sauces in this cookbook that appear with their own unique dish.

Sauce	*Recipe*
Barbeque Sauce for Gluten	Gluten
Barbeque Sauce for Meatloaf	TVP Meatloaf & Tofu Meatloaf
Chiles Rellenos Sauce	Chiles Rellenos
Corn Dog Dip	Corn Dogs
Enchilada Sauce	Cheese Enchiladas
Thin Pasta Sauce	Rigatoni
Pizza Sauce	Pizza
Tostado Sauce	Guacamole Tostado

Equipment Suggestions

The only special equipment that might be helpful with recipes in this chapter would be a good bulb whisk. It will go a long way in helping to prevent lumps from forming in your sauce or gravy.

A Word About Thickeners.

There are basically two thickeners used throughout this cookbook; flour and cornstarch. When used as a thickener, flour is first heated in some a fat like butter or oil to create a thick paste that is generally known as a roux. Then whatever liquid is required is slowly added and stirred swiftly to help prevent the formation of lumps. The heat is slowly increased until the gravy begins to boil. The resulting gravy is usually cloudy.

Cornstarch, on the other hand, uses an almost completely different methodology. The cornstarch to be used is dissolved in an equal amount of water or other liquid, usually at room temperature. The liquid must not be hot. When powdered cornstarch is added to a hot liquid it will solidify almost immediately and create lumps that are virtually impossible to remove. The dissolved cornstarch is slowly stirred into the sauce before it begins to boil. If the sauce is boiling when you want to add the cornstarch, it should be removed from the heat before it is added. The cornstarch should be quickly stirred into the sauce and then returned to the stove to be heated until it boils. The sauce will not thicken completely until it begins to boil. Sauces thickened with cornstarch are not as cloudy as those made with flour.

SAUCES AND GRAVIES

CHEESE SAUCE
(Makes 1 ½ cups or 4 servings)

2 Tbs. butter
2 Tbs. all-purpose flour
⅛ tsp. salt

1 c. whole milk
1 c. firmly packed freshly grated
    cheddar cheese (4 oz.)

Place the butter in a 1-quart saucepan over medium heat. Stir until butter is melted. Stir in the flour and salt. Continue to cook the paste until it begins to bubble. Slowly stir in all of the milk. Beat with a whisk to remove any lumps that may form. Add the grated cheddar cheese and continue to stir over medium heat until all of the cheese has melted. Serve immediately. If the cheese sauce is allowed to cool, it may develop lumps when reheated. If that is the case, beat the sauce with a whisk again to remove as many of the lumps as possible.

Note: This cheese sauce is perfect for serving over cauliflower or broccoli. It is essentially white sauce with grated cheddar cheese added. It is simple yet delicious. Nonfat milk can be used in place of the whole milk with little effect on the final result. Cheese grated from a block of fresh cheese is preferred. Processed grated cheese sold in a bag may not melt as well.

BROWN GRAVY
(Makes 1 ½ cups)

1 Tbs. olive oil
1 ½ c. water or vegetable stock
½ tsp. instant coffee powder or
    granules
¼ tsp. salt

⅛ tsp. garlic powder
1 vegetable bouillon cube
2 Tbs. cornstarch dissolved in --
    2 Tbs. water

In a 1-quart saucepan combine the olive oil, water or vegetable stock, instant coffee, salt, garlic powder, and vegetable bouillon. Bring to a boil and simmer until bouillon cube is dissolved. Remove from heat and stir in cornstarch mixture. Return to medium heat and stir until mixture thickens and begins to boil. Keep warm until ready to use.

BROWN GRAVY WITH MUSHROOMS

Brown Gravy from above recipe.   ½ (6 oz.) can sliced mushrooms

Drain mushrooms and add to brown gravy. Heat gently until it begins to simmer. Keep warm until ready to serve.

FRESH MUSHROOM GRAVY
(Makes 2 cups)

4 oz. fresh mushrooms
3 Tbs. olive oil
3 Tbs. all-purpose flour
1 ¾ c. water
½ tsp. Kitchen Bouquet®
   browning sauce

¼ tsp. salt
¼ tsp. onion powder
pinch black pepper
pinch garlic powder

Gently wash the mushrooms and pat dry. Slice mushrooms ¼-inch thick from top to bottom and measure. There should be 1 ½ cups of sliced mushrooms. In a 1-quart saucepan combine the olive oil and sliced mushrooms. Cook and stir the mushrooms over medium heat for 5 minutes or until mushrooms are tender. Add the flour and stir to form a paste. Slowly stir in the water with a whisk to help remove any lumps. Add the browning sauce, salt, onion powder, black pepper, and garlic powder. Simmer gently for about 3 minutes. Keep warm until ready to serve.

COUNTRY GRAVY
(Makes 2 cups or 4 to 6 servings)

¼ c. butter
¼ c. all-purpose flour
1 Tbs. onion soup mix
2 c. water
½ tsp. hickory salt

¼ tsp. sugar
⅛ tsp. black pepper
pinch sage
pinch summer savory

Melt butter over medium heat in a 1-quart saucepan. Add flour and stir until a paste is formed that starts to bubble. Add onion soup mix, water, hickory salt, sugar, black pepper, sage, and summer savory. Stir until sauce is thickened and begins to boil. Beat with a whisk to remove any lumps. Keep warm until ready to serve.

Note: Serve over homemade biscuits or Fried Tofu Nuggets (see Chapter: Tofu).

240812-16

CHINESE BROWN GRAVY
(Makes 1 ¼ cups)

1 c. water or vegetable stock
¼ c. soy sauce
1 Tbs. peanut oil
1 tsp. sugar
¼ tsp. garlic powder

¼ tsp. onion powder
pinch dried hot chile pepper
2 Tbs. cornstarch dissolved in --
 2 Tbs. water
¼ tsp. sesame oil

In a 1-quart saucepan combine the water, soy sauce, peanut oil, sugar, garlic powder, onion powder, and chile pepper. Bring to a boil and simmer gently for 2 minutes. Slowly add the cornstarch mixture and stir until thickened. Keep warm until ready to use. Stir sesame oil into gravy just before serving.

SWEET AND SOUR SAUCE
(Makes 2 cups)

1 Tbs. peanut oil
½ sugar
½ c. ketchup
½ c. water

⅓ c. white vinegar
2 Tbs. cornstarch dissolved in ---
 2 Tbs. water

In a 1-quart saucepan combine peanut oil, sugar, ketchup, water, and white vinegar. Stir over medium heat until sauce begins to simmer. Remove from heat and stir in cornstarch mixture. Return to heat, stirring constantly until sauce thickens and begins to boil. Remove from heat and serve over your choice of dishes (stuffed won ton, etc.) or on the side as a dipping sauce.

TARTAR SAUCE
(Makes ¾ cup)

¾ c. mayonnaise
¼ c. finely chopped dill pickle

¼ tsp. cream of tartar
¼ tsp. garlic powder

In a small bowl combine the mayonnaise, dill pickle, cream of tartar, and garlic powder. Mix until well blended. Refrigerate for at least an hour. Serve in a small condiment dish as a dip for Frozen Tofu Nuggets and Tofu Imitation Fish Sticks (see Chapter: Tofu).

Note: This tartar sauce is made with dill pickles and not sweet relish so it is tangy and not sweet. Cream of tartar is used in place of the lemon juice that many cooks use.

CHILE COLORADO SAUCE
(Makes 1 ¼ cups)

6 dried New Mexico chile pods
(about 1 ½ oz.)
Water to cover pods
2 cloves garlic, minced
1 tsp. dried oregano, crushed

¾ tsp. salt
¼ tsp. ground cumin
1 c. water
1 Tbs. olive oil
1 ½ tsp. flour

Rinse the pods under running water. Split open and remove the stems, seeds, and ribs. Place in a 2-quart saucepan, cover with water, and boil over medium heat for 10 to 15 minutes. Allow mixture to cool and then drain and discard all of the water. Whirl the chili pods in a blender with the minced garlic, oregano, salt, cumin, and one cup of fresh water. Pour through a large wire mesh strainer into a bowl to remove the skins from the chili pods. Stir and press the chili pods against the strainer to recover as much pulp as possible. Discard the skins left behind in the strainer. In a small saucepan, heat the olive oil and stir in the flour to make a paste. When the paste begins to bubble, add the strained chile mixture from the bowl. Stir over medium heat until sauce thickens and begins to boil. Keep warm until ready to serve. Leftover sauce will keep for about a week in the refrigerator.

Note: You will need a large wire mesh strainer. This is a standard recipe for Red Chile Sauce which should not be confused with Chile Colorado that has chunks of meat. Some of the other chiles that can be used in this recipe: Chiles de Arbol, Chipotles, Pasillas, Anchos, and Japones are just a few.

GUACAMOLE
(Makes 1 ¼ cups)

2 lrg. ripe avocados (about 1 lb.)
1 ½ tsp. lime juice
¼ c. sour cream
½ tsp. salt

⅛ tsp. garlic salt
1 tsp. stemmed, seeded, and
minced Jalapeño pepper

Pit, peel, and mash avocados in a medium bowl. Add the lime juice, sour cream, salt, garlic salt, and jalapeño pepper. Mix well and taste. Adjust seasonings. Refrigerate until ready to use.

Note: This is a simple basic guacamole recipe without a lot of extra ingredients. Omit the jalapeño if you find it too spicy.

240812-16

GUACAMOLE SAUCE
(Makes 1 ½ cups)

2 lrg. ripe avocados (about 1 lb.)
3 Tbs. sour cream
2 tsp. fresh lime juice

¼ tsp. salt
¼ tsp. garlic salt
⅓ c. whole milk

Pit and peel the avocados. Cut into pieces and put in a blender. Add the sour cream, lime juice, salt, garlic salt, and whole milk. Whirl in blender until smooth. You may have to stop a few times and scrape the sides of the blender to get everything blended together evenly. The end product should have the consistency of yogurt. If too thick, slowly add more milk (about 1 teaspoon at a time) until the Guacamole sauce reaches the right consistency.

Note: This is not to be confused with regular guacamole (dip) in the previous recipe which is thicker. Guacamole Sauce is thinner and smoother than regular guacamole. It is recommended in the recipes for Bean Burritos and Taquitos (see Chapter: Main Dishes).

FRESH CHILE SALSA
(Makes 2 cups)

6 to 8 yellow hot chile peppers
2 med. tomatoes, diced into small
  pieces (about 1 ½ cups)
¾ c. finely chopped yellow onion

2 cloves garlic, minced (about ---
  2 tsp.)
½ tsp. salt
¼ tsp. chili powder

Remove stems from the yellow chile peppers and cut in half lengthwise. Remove seeds and chop into small pieces. There should be 2 tablespoons chopped chile peppers. Place in a medium bowl and add the diced tomato, chopped onion, minced garlic, chili powder, and salt. Mix well and serve as an accompaniment to just about any Mexican meal. Will keep in the refrigerator for up to 5 days.

VARIATION: HOT CHILI SALSA

1 whole Jalapeño chile pepper,
  stemmed, seeded and minced

For a spicier salsa, use the Jalapeño pepper in place of the yellow hot chili peppers.

SPAGHETTI SAUCE
(Makes 5 cups)

1 (28 oz.) can whole tomatoes, do not drain
1 c. diced yellow onion
¼ c. olive oil
2 cloves garlic, minced
½ tsp. dried oregano, crushed
¼ tsp. whole anise seeds, crushed
¼ tsp. coarse black pepper
¼ c. chopped fresh Italian parsley
2 Tbs. chopped fresh sweet basil
1 (6 oz.) can tomato paste
½ (4 oz.) can sliced mushrooms, drained
1 bay leaf
1 (15 oz.) can tomato sauce
½ tsp. sugar
¼ tsp. salt
¾ c. water
¼ c. Burgundy wine

Place the whole tomatoes in a large bowl. Mash with a potato masher until reduced to small chunks and reserve. In a 3-quart saucepan, cook and stir the onion in the olive oil until tender, about 6 to 8 minutes. Add the minced garlic, crushed oregano, crushed anise, black pepper, parsley, and basil. Continue to cook and stir for about one minute. Add tomato paste and stir continuously for one more minute. Stir in sliced mushrooms, bay leaf, tomato sauce, reserved mashed tomatoes, sugar, salt, water, and wine. Simmer over low heat for 45 minutes to one hour. Stir frequently to prevent sticking. Taste and adjust seasoning if necessary. Remove bay leaf and serve over spaghetti or any other pasta. If you allow ½ cup of sauce per serving, this makes enough for 8 to 10 servings.

Note: This can also be called Italian or pasta sauce because it has so many other uses besides being used on spaghetti. But here we are calling it Spaghetti Sauce to help reduce the chance of confusion. You can use ¾ to 1 cup finely diced eggplant or zucchini in place of the sliced mushrooms. Add to the pot at the same time as the onions.

PESTO SAUCE
(Makes 1 cup)

2 c. fresh basil leaves, firmly packed
2 cloves garlic, minced
3 Tbs. chopped flat Italian parsley
2 Tbs. walnut pieces or pine nuts
¼ tsp. salt
½ c. olive oil
½ c. grated Parmesan cheese

Place fresh basil, garlic, parsley, nuts, and salt in a blender. Pour olive oil over contents in a blender. Whirl blender until you have a smooth paste. Pour into a large bowl, add Parmesan cheese and mix until thoroughly blended. Fresh pesto sauce will keep in the refrigerator for one week or may be frozen for up to six months.

Note: This pesto may be used to season pasta, Spaghetti Sauce or any other dish where you would like the flavor of fresh basil.

240812-16

Soups

Soups

Equipment Suggestions

You may find that a pressure cooker or slow cooker is very helpful in preparing soup. The pressure cooker can cut the cooking time for soup by more than half. Not all soups benefit from a pressure cooker. Wonton and Matzo Ball soup are good examples. Some soup ingredients do not work well in a pressure cooker. Rice and barley have a tendency too stick to the bottom of a pan if not stirred, so when pressure cooking they should be cooked separately and added at the end. The same is true of pasta. Pasta would be cooked to smithereens in a pressure cooker.

The slow cooker, a.k.a. Crock Pot®, can be a big help if you work during the day and would like your soup ready and waiting when you return from work. I have not included any instructions here for either one of these aids because of limited space. There are plenty of cookbooks devoted entirely to each of these cooking methods. If you like one of the recipes here, then you can do a little research and convert the recipe to pressure cooker or slow cooker method.

Serving Size

The number of servings that a pot of soup makes can vary widely. Soup can be used as a side dish to go with a sandwich or it can be an entree served with a French roll and a salad. A single serving of soup can range from about 3/4 cup to two or more cups. That doesn't even take into consideration the fact that someone may want a second helping. Because of this dilemma, each recipe indicates how many quarts or cups it makes and not the number of servings. Hopefully this will be more useful in planning your meals.

Vegetable stock

Some of the recipes suggest using vegetable stock. The last recipe in this chapter is a recipe for homemade vegetable stock. Since not everyone has the time or resources to make their own stock, you can use vegetable bouillon in its place. You do not need to use it full strength. If the instructions suggest one bouillon cube per cup of water, then you can reduce it by half and use one bouillon per two cups of water. This will help keep the soup base from getting too strong. If you are unable to find imitation chicken seasoning, you can use vegetable bouillon in it's place.

Using Pasta in Soup

When pasta is added to a soup recipe we usually cook the pasta separately. This keeps the soup from becoming too thick from the pasta starch and gives better control over how long the pasta is cooked.

SOUPS

POTATO AND KALE SOUP
(Makes 2 quarts)

7 c. water and/or vegetable stock
2 Tbs. extra virgin olive oil
1 ¼ c. diced yellow onion
4 c. peeled and diced potatoes
1 ½ c. minced fresh kale

¼ c. chopped Italian parsley
1 vegetable bouillon cube
1 tsp. salt
dash white pepper
2 Tbs. chopped green onion

In a 2-quart saucepan, heat the water and/or vegetable stock. Use any combination of the two that you would like. Bring to a boil and reserve until needed. In a 3-quart saucepan, cook and stir the onion in the olive oil over medium heat until translucent, about 5 minutes. Add potatoes, kale, parsley, 7 cups reserved boiling water/vegetable stock, vegetable bouillon cube, salt, and white pepper. Bring to a boil and simmer gently until potatoes are tender, about 20 minutes. Serve with chopped green onion on top as garnish.

KALE AND VEGETABLE SOUP
(Makes 2 quarts)

2 Tbs. olive oil
¾ c. diced yellow onion
⅓ c. diced celery
1 clove garlic, minced
2 c. chopped kale
4 c. water
3 c. vegetable stock
2 c. peeled and diced potatoes
1 c. peeled and sliced carrots

1 c. sliced young zucchini
½ c. peeled and diced turnips
1 Tbs. onion soup mix
1 tsp. salt
¼ tsp. black pepper
⅛ tsp. garlic powder
pinch of sugar
¼ c. dry small macaroni shells

Place the olive oil in a 3-quart saucepan. Add the onion, celery, garlic and kale. Cook and stir over medium heat until onion is translucent and kale has become limp. Add the water, vegetable stock, potatoes, carrots, zucchini, and turnips. Turn up the heat and bring to a boil. Add the onion soup mix, salt, black pepper, garlic powder, and sugar. Reduce heat, cover, and boil gently for about 30 minutes or until the vegetables are tender. Prepare the macaroni shells while the soup is cooking. Cook the macaroni shells in a 1-quart saucepan according to the package instructions. Drain and add to the soup 5 minutes before the soup is finished cooking.

Note: When preparing the vegetables, they should be diced into pieces ½ to 1-inch wide. The carrots should be sliced ¼-inch thick.

SPLIT PEA SOUP
(Makes 2 quarts)

2 c. dry split peas, about 16 oz.
2 qt. cold water for soaking
2 c. additional fresh water
1 c. diced celery
½ c. diced yellow onion
½ c. diced carrot
1 Tbs. imitation chicken style
   seasoning (opt.)

1 tsp. salt
1 tsp. sugar
½ tsp. garlic powder
¼ tsp. thyme
⅛ tsp. white pepper
pinch cayenne pepper
1 bay leaf
2 Tbs. butter

Pick through the peas to remove any foreign objects. Rinse and drain two or three times to remove any chaff that may be left behind. Place the split peas in a 4-quart pot, add 2 quarts cold water, and allow to soak for at least 6 hours or overnight. When done soaking, add 2 more cups water and cook over medium heat. Be sure to watch the pot closely. Split peas have a tendency to foam up and boil over when they first begin to boil. Reduce the heat and stir the peas gently to keep them from boiling over. Allow to simmer for 30 minutes. Add the celery, yellow onion, carrot, optional imitation chicken seasoning, salt, sugar, garlic powder, thyme, white pepper, cayenne pepper, and bay leaf. Cover the pot and boil gently for 1 to 1½ hours. Remove bay leaf. Working in batches, whirl in a blender until smooth, about one minute per batch. Pour into a 3-quart saucepan and add more water if soup is too thick. Stir in butter, reheat, and serve.

Note: Soaking the split peas helps to make them easier to digest.

CANNED PEA SOUP
(Makes 7 cups)

4 c. water
½ c. diced yellow onion
⅔ c. diced celery
½ c. sliced carrots
1 yellow chili pepper, seeded and
   chopped

½ tsp. sugar
½ tsp. salt
¼ tsp. thyme
2 (15 oz.) cans sweet peas,
   drained
2 Tbs. butter

Measure the 4 cups water into a 3-quart saucepan. Add the onion, celery, carrots, chili pepper, sugar, salt, and thyme to the water. Bring to a simmer and cook for 15 minutes, or until vegetables are tender. Add the drained peas to the saucepan and return to a boil. Remove from heat and whirl in a blender for about two minutes. Return to saucepan, add the butter, and stir until melted. Reheat, if necessary, before serving.

Note: This soup is similar to the previous Split Pea Soup, but takes less time to prepare and is a little spicier. For even more kick to your soup, use a seeded and chopped Jalapeño pepper in place of the chili pepper.

CORN CHOWDER
(Makes 2 quarts)

3 Tbs. vegetable oil
1 c. diced celery
1 1/3 c. diced yellow onion
4 c. water or vegetable stock
2 c. peeled and diced red
  potatoes

1 1/2 tsp. salt
1/2 tsp. paprika
1 (15 oz.) can whole kernel corn,
  drained (1 1/2 c.)
2 Tbs. chopped parsley

In a 3-quart saucepan, cook and stir the celery and onion in vegetable oil over medium heat for 5 minutes or until tender. Add water or stock, potatoes, salt, and paprika. Bring to a boil and simmer for 5 minutes. Add corn and continue to cook until potatoes are done, about 15 to 20 minutes. Prepare the white sauce while vegetables are cooking. When the vegetables are done, beat the white sauce with a wire whisk to remove any lumps and stir into pot of vegetables. Heat, but do not boil, the chowder, and serve warm with parsley sprinkled on top.

WHITE SAUCE

1/4 c. butter (1/2 stick)
1/4 c. all-purpose flour

4 c. warm milk

In a 2-quart saucepan melt the butter over medium heat. Stir in the flour to form a paste. When the paste begins to bubble, slowly stir in the warm milk to make a white sauce. Continue to cook and stir over low heat until sauce begins to simmer. Set aside until ready to use.

Note: The vegetables should be diced into 1-inch pieces. Frozen corn or fresh corn cut from the cob can be used in place of the canned corn.

WONTON SOUP
(Makes 2 quarts with 24 stuffed wontons)

HOW TO PREPARE SHIITAKE MUSHROOMS

1 c. (about ½ oz.) dried, sliced
  Shiitake mushrooms
1 c. water

1 Tbs. soy sauce
½ tsp. sugar

In a 1-quart saucepan combine the dried Shiitake mushrooms, 1 cup water, 1 tablespoon soy sauce, and ½ teaspoon sugar. Stir together, bring to a boil, cover, and remove from heat. Allow to rest for 10 minutes. Rinse in cold water to speed up the cooling process. Squeeze the mushrooms and discard as much liquid as possible. Place on a cutting board and remove any tough pieces of stem. Finely chop the mushrooms and measure. There should be about ¼ cup for stuffing the wontons.

SOUP BROTH

8 c. water
1 Tbs. imitation chicken
  seasoning

1 tsp. peanut oil
2 tsp. salt

In a 3-quart saucepan combine 8 cups water, imitation chicken seasoning, peanut oil, and salt and bring to a boil. Simmer for 5 minutes and set aside until wontons are ready.

STUFFED WONTONS

2 scrambled eggs
½ c. finely chopped celery
¼ c. finely chopped Shiitake
  mushrooms (see above)
1 Tbs. chopped green onions (for
  filling)
1 Tbs. soy sauce

2 tsp. peanut oil
½ tsp. sugar
¼ tsp. salt
pinch white pepper
24 wonton wrappers (or wraps)
¼ c. green onion, tops only,
  sliced crosswise (for garnish)

Put the scrambled eggs in a medium size bowl and mash with a fork. Add the celery, chopped Shiitake mushrooms, 1 tablespoon chopped green onions, soy sauce, 2 teaspoons peanut oil, ½ teaspoon sugar, ¼ teaspoon salt, and white pepper; mix well. Moisten the edge of a wonton wrapper with water. Place 1 teaspoon of filling in the center of the wonton. Fold in half over the filling to form a triangle and press along the edges to seal. Twist the two opposing corners back and pinch to hold together. Set aside and repeat for the remaining wontons. Bring broth to a boil and drop filled wontons into boiling soup broth (see above). Begin counting cooking time as soon as all of the wontons have been added to the pot of broth. Let simmer gently for 3 minutes. Serve in bowl with 1 tablespoon chopped green onion tops sprinkled over soup as garnish.

(continued)

240812-16

Note: If you are unable to find wonton wrappers, you can use egg roll wrappers instead. You will need 6 egg roll wrappers. Cut each wrapper in half in both directions to make four equal size squares for stuffing. For vegan soup, use ⅓ cup mashed firm tofu in place of scrambled eggs. This recipe will make 4 to 6 servings depending on how many wontons you put in each bowl.

MATZO BALL SOUP
(Makes 2 ½ quarts with 16 matzo balls)

MATZO BALLS

4 eggs	⅛ tsp. black pepper
¼ c. vegetable oil	1 c. matzo meal
¼ c. water	1 ½ qt. water
1 tsp. salt	2 tsp. salt

Beat the eggs together in a medium size bowl. Add the vegetable oil, water, salt and pepper and mix well. Add matzo meal and stir until well blended. Refrigerate for 30 minutes. Form the chilled mixture into balls. Use 1 rounded tablespoon of the matzo mixture to make one matzo ball. The balls will be 1 ½ inches in diameter. This will make about 16 matzo balls. In a 3-quart saucepan combine 1 ½ quarts water and 2 teaspoons salt, and bring to a boil. Add the matzo balls to the pot, cover, and cook at a gentle simmer for 30 minutes. Prepare the soup stock (see below) while the matzo balls are simmering. Remove the matzo balls with a slotted spoon and set aside until ready to serve soup.

FOR THE SOUP STOCK

2 Tbs. olive oil	2 Tbs. chopped celery leaves
1 c. peeled and sliced carrots	2 Tbs. chopped parsley leaves
1 c. diced yellow onion	4 tsp. imitation chicken
⅔ c. sliced celery	seasoning
2 qt. water	1 tsp. salt

In a 3-quart pot, combine the olive oil, carrots, yellow onion, and sliced celery. Stir and cook over medium heat for five minutes. Add the two quarts water, celery leaves, parsley, imitation chicken seasoning, and salt. Cover the pot and boil gently for about 15 minutes. To serve, place two or three matzo balls in a soup bowl and pour soup over the matzo balls.

Note: Although not mandatory, a slotted spoon will make it much easier to handle the cooked matzo balls. This recipe will make 5 to 6 servings depending on how many matzo balls you put in each bowl.

JAPANESE NOODLE SOUP
(Makes 2 quarts or 4 servings)

COOK THE NOODLES

**8 to 9 oz. dried chuka soba
noodles**

In a 3-quart saucepan bring 2 quarts of water to a boil. Add the noodles and cook for 3 minutes. Drain and set aside until ready to use. Use the same 3-quart saucepan for making the broth.

SOUP BROTH

**1½ qt. water
2 tsp. imitation chicken
seasoning**

**½ tsp. peanut oil
1 tsp. salt**

In a 3-quart saucepan combine the water, imitation chicken seasoning, peanut oil, and salt. Bring to a boil and simmer covered for 5 minutes. Set aside until ready to use.

ASSEMBLE THE NOODLE SOUP

**8 oz. bok choy, about 4 lrg. stalks
8 oz. Chinese cabbage, about 6
lrg. leaves
4 green onions
1 lrg. stalk celery
1 Tbs. finely chopped fresh
ginger**

**1 Tbs. peanut oil
½ tsp. sugar
½ tsp. onion powder
¼ tsp. garlic powder
pinch white pepper
¼ c. water**

Separate the bok choy stalks from the leaves. Cut the stalks crosswise into ½-inch pieces. Cut the leaves in half lengthwise and then cut across the leaves in 1-inch pieces. Cut the Chinese cabbage leaves in half lengthwise and then cut crosswise into 1-inch pieces. Cut the green onions crosswise into 1-inch pieces. Cut the celery stalk crosswise into pieces ¼-inch thick. Place a wok over medium-high heat and add 1 tablespoon of peanut oil. Add the ginger to the heated oil and stir for 10 seconds. Add the bok choy stems and celery. Cook and stir continuously for 2 minutes. Add the bok choy leaves, Chinese cabbage, green onions, sugar, onion powder, garlic powder, and white pepper. Cook and stir continuously for 3 more minutes. Add the ¼ cup water and cook for 2 more minutes. Return the soup broth to a boil. Add the noodles and vegetables to the broth and stir until everything is mixed together.

ALTERNATE SERVING TECHNIQUE

Divide the cooked noodles evenly between 4 soup bowls. Place a serving of vegetables on top of the noodles. Reheat the soup broth to boiling and pour over everything in soup bowl to cover.

(continued)

240812-16

Note: Chuka soba are the Japanese version of Chinese egg noodles (Chuka is the Japanese word for Chinese). They are curly and made from wheat flour. They usually come in a brick wrapped in cellophane. Packages of chuka soba noodles come in a variety of sizes. Each package contains bundles of noodles that weigh either 2 or 3 ounces each.

MINESTRONE SOUP
(Makes 2 quarts or 4 large servings)

3 Tbs. olive oil
2 c. chopped savoy cabbage
1 c. finely chopped potato
1 c. finely chopped yellow onion
1 c. finely chopped carrots
1 c. fresh green beans, cut into
  ½-in. pieces
¾ c. finely chopped zucchini
½ c. finely chopped celery and
  celery leaves

¼ c. finely chopped parsley
2 cloves garlic, minced
1 (15 oz.) can diced tomatoes
6 c. water and/or vegetable stock
1 ½ c. cooked cranberry beans,
  drained
2 tsp. salt
½ tsp. crushed dried oregano
¼ tsp. black pepper
freshly grated Parmesan cheese

Heat the olive oil in a 4-quart pot. Stir in the cabbage, potatoes, onion, carrots, green beans, zucchini, celery, and parsley. Cook and stir for three minutes. Add the water and/or vegetable stock, cranberry beans, salt, oregano, and black pepper. Bring to a boil and simmer for 1 hour. Taste, adjust the seasoning, and serve with Parmesan cheese on the side.

Note: Although cranberry beans are preferred for this recipe, you can use a (15 oz.) can of drained pinto or kidney beans. Cranberry beans can be found at some health food stores or grocery stores. Italian grocers may call them borlotti. There is no set list of ingredients for minestrone because it is usually made out of whatever vegetables are in season.

LENTIL CHILI SOUP
(Makes 3 quarts)

1 ¼ c. dried lentils
7 c. water and/or vegetable stock
2 Tbs. extra virgin olive oil
2 c. chopped yellow onion
1 ½ c. diced celery
1 (28 oz.) can whole peeled
  tomatoes
1 (8 oz.) can tomato sauce
1 (7 oz.) can diced green Ortega®
  chiles

2 Tbs. soy sauce
2 Tbs. chili powder
2 tsp. salt
2 tsp. dried sweet basil, crushed
1 ½ tsp. ground cumin
1 tsp. sugar
½ tsp. garlic powder
½ tsp. onion powder
¼ tsp. cayenne pepper (opt.)

Rinse and drain lentils in a colander. In a 4-quart pot, combine the water and/or vegetable stock, lentils, olive oil, onion, and celery. Cover and simmer for 45 minutes. In a large bowl mash the canned tomatoes with a potato masher. Add the mashed tomatoes, tomato sauce, diced green chilies, soy sauce, chili powder, salt, basil, cumin, sugar, garlic powder, and onion powder to the lentils. Continue to simmer and stir for 30 more minutes. Taste and adjust seasoning, adding more salt if necessary. Add the optional cayenne pepper if you prefer a hotter chili soup. Add more water if soup becomes too thick.

LENTIL VEGETABLE SOUP
(Makes 2 ½ quarts)

½ c. lentils
2 Tbs. brown rice
7 c. water and/or vegetable stock
2 Tbs. olive oil
1 (14.5 oz.) can diced tomatoes
1 clove garlic, minced
1 ½ c. diced potatoes
1 c. chopped cabbage
1 c. diced carrots

½ c. diced yellow onion
½ c. diced celery
¼ c. chopped celery leaves
½ c. diced turnips
2 Tbs. chopped parsley
1 tsp. curry powder
1 tsp. salt
⅛ tsp. black pepper
2 c. water

Rinse and drain the lentils and brown rice in a large fine mesh strainer. Combine the lentils, brown rice, and 7 cups water and/or vegetable stock in a 3-quart pot. Add the olive oil, diced tomatoes, garlic, potatoes, cabbage, carrots, onion, diced celery, celery leaves, turnips, and parsley to the pot. Stir in the curry powder, salt, and black pepper. Bring to a boil and simmer gently for 30 minutes. The soup will have cooked down and you will need more water at this point. Add 2 cups water and continue to gently boil for another 30 minutes.

Note: When preparing the vegetables, they should be peeled and cut into ½-inch pieces.

240812-16

ONION SOUP
(Makes 4 cups)

THE SOUP

2 large onions (1 lb.)
1 large leek, white part only
2 Tbs. butter
2 Tbs. olive oil, divided (1 Tbs. +
   1 Tbs.)
½ tsp. sugar
½ tsp. salt

2 Tbs. all-purpose flour
1 qt. water
1 Tbs. onion soup mix
¼ tsp. Kitchen Bouquet®
   browning sauce
Freshly grated Parmesan cheese

Peel onions and cut in half from top to bottom. Place the flat side of the onion on the cutting board and thinly slice crosswise, from side to side, into half-moons about ¼-inch thick. Do not cut the slices of the onion from top to bottom. This is an important step that most recipes leave out. Thinly slice the white part of one leek in the same manner and measure. The onions and leeks together should measure 4 cups. Melt the butter in a 3-quart saucepan. Add the onions, leeks, and 1 tablespoon of the olive oil. Stir to coat the onions and cover the pot. Cook over a medium-low heat, while stirring occasionally, for 15 minutes. Remove the lid and add the sugar and salt. The sugar will help to caramelize the onions. Increase the heat to medium-high and continue to cook while stirring frequently. Cook until the onions turn a deep golden brown, about 10 minutes. Add flour and olive oil and stir for 1 minute. Slowly add water while stirring to keep any lumps from forming. Add the onion soup base and browning sauce. Simmer, uncovered, for 15 minutes. To serve, put a 1½-inch slice of toasted baguette (see below) in each ramekin. Pour the prepared soup over the baguette and sprinkle Parmesan cheese over top. Put the bowls on a sturdy cookie sheet and place under a broiler. Watch carefully and leave under broiler until cheese begins to brown and bubble. When serving, the ramekin should be on a plate. The remaining slices of baguette or French roll should be served on the side.

THE TOASTED BREAD

½ baguette or 2 French rolls; see
   recipes in Chapter: Breads;
   Yeast Breads

Cut the baguette or rolls into 1½-inch thick slices. Toast both sides under broiler.

Note: You will need two individual 2-cup or larger ramekins (soufflé dishes) to serve this soup according to the above directions. If you do not have any, just use oven-proof soup bowls. It may seem redundant, but adding the onion soup mix replaces the seasoning and flavor that you would normally get from beef stock.

BEAN AND RICE SOUP
(Makes 2 quarts)

1 ½ c. cooked rice
2 qt. water and/or vegetable stock
1 ½ c. cooked cranberry, pinto or
   Anasazi beans
2 Tbs. olive oil
1 ½ c. peeled and diced potato
1 c. diced yellow onion
1 c. diced carrots
¾ c. diced celery

¼ c. chopped parsley
2 Tbs. onion soup mix
1 tsp. hickory salt (opt.)
½ tsp. salt
⅛ tsp. black pepper
Cornbread or Johnny Cakes (see
   Chapter: Breads; Baking
   Powder Breads)

If you are making fresh rice, start cooking the rice before you begin preparing the soup. Combine in a 4-quart pot the water or vegetable stock, the cooked beans of your choice, olive oil, potato, yellow onion, carrots, celery, parsley, onion soup mix, optional hickory salt, salt, and black pepper. Bring to a boil and simmer for 30 minutes. Add the rice and cook for an additional 10 minutes. Serve with cornbread or Johnny Cakes (see Chapter: Breads; Baking Powder Breads).

Note: Dice vegetables into ½-inch to 1-inch pieces. This recipe is ideal for using any leftover rice. If preparing fresh rice, start with ½ cup uncooked rice and follow the directions on the package.

DILL PICKLE SOUP
(Makes 2 ½ quarts or 5 large servings)

2 lrg. fresh tomatoes, about 1 lb.
7 c. vegetable stock or water
1 (15 oz.) can tomato sauce
2 Tbs. olive oil
1 c. diced yellow onion (4 oz.)
1 c. sliced carrots (4 oz.)
¾ c. diced green bell pepper ----
   (3 oz.)
1 clove garlic, minced
1 Tbs. crushed dried basil

1 tsp. crushed dried oregano
2 c. sliced zucchini (8 oz.)
1 c. diced fresh mushrooms ---
   (2 ½ oz.)
1 c. thinly sliced dill pickles
¼ c. chopped fresh parsley
1 tsp. salt
¼ tsp. black pepper
2 c. fresh or frozen cheese
   tortellini (8 oz.)

Peel the tomatoes, remove seeds, and dice into ½-inch pieces. You should have 1 ½ cups of diced tomatoes. In a 4-quart pot combine the tomatoes, vegetable stock, tomato sauce, olive oil, yellow onion, carrots, bell pepper, minced garlic, dried basil, and dried oregano. Bring to a boil and simmer, uncovered, for 30 minutes. Add the sliced zucchini, mushrooms, dill pickles, parsley, salt, and black pepper. Cover the soup and simmer for an additional 30 minutes. Add the tortellini and simmer, covered, for 20 more minutes or until tortellini are done.

240812-16

BORSCHT
(Makes 3 quarts)

2 Tbs. olive oil
1 ½ c. diced yellow onion (6 oz.)
3 c. chopped cabbage (½ lb.)
1 c. peeled and sliced carrots ---
   (5 oz.)
1 c. sliced celery (2 large sticks)
½ c. chopped celery leaves
2 c. peeled and diced potatoes
   (about ¾ lb.)

8 c. water and/or stock
1 (14.5 oz.) can diced tomatoes
1 ½ tsp. dill weed, divided (½ tsp.
   + 1 tsp.)
1 tsp. salt
2 Tbs. red wine vinegar
1 (15 oz.) can sliced beets,
   undrained
Sour cream

In a 6-quart pot cook and stir the onion in the olive oil over medium heat for 3 minutes. Add the cabbage, sliced carrots, sliced celery, celery leaves, diced potatoes, 8 cups water and/or stock, diced tomatoes, ½ teaspoon of the dill weed, salt, and red wine vinegar. Bring the soup to a hard boil and then reduce to a simmer. Pour the can of sliced beets into a bowl. Cut any large slices of beet in half before adding to the soup. Add the sliced beets after about 45 minutes of cooking. Cook for a total of 1 hour or until vegetables are tender. To serve, place a serving of soup in a bowl. Put a dollop of sour cream in the center and sprinkle a pinch of dill weed over the top.

Note: Two ingredients are necessary for good Borscht; beets and cabbage. Fresh dill weed is preferred, but dried will work as well. You can substitute fresh beets if you like, but they should be thoroughly cooked before adding to the soup. Vegetables should be chopped into 1-inch pieces or sliced ¼-inch thick. You will need to purchase a 1-pound head of cabbage.

VEGETABLE SOUP
(Makes 3 quarts)

¼ c. small macaroni shells
¼ c. barley
1 (26 oz.) can whole stewed
  tomatoes
4 c. water
3 c. vegetable stock
2 Tbs. olive oil
1 Tbs. onion soup mix
1 c. chopped cabbage
1 c. cubed potato
¾ c. chopped yellow onion
¾ c. chopped celery and celery
  leaves

¾ c. sliced carrots
½ c. peeled and diced turnip
  (opt.)
½ c. diced zucchini
⅓ c. whole kernel corn, frozen or
  canned
⅓ c. fresh green beans, cut into
  ½-inch pieces
¼ c. peas, fresh or frozen
¼ c. chopped parsley leaves
1 tsp. salt
½ tsp. sugar
⅛ tsp. black pepper

Cook the elbow macaroni according to the package directions. Drain and set aside until ready to use. Place the barley in a large fine mesh strainer and rinse under running water. Set side until ready to use. In a 4-quart pot, place the canned whole tomatoes, including juice, and mash into small pieces with a potato masher. Add the water, vegetable stock, olive oil, onion soup mix, cabbage, potato, yellow onion, celery, carrots, optional turnip, zucchini, corn, green beans, peas, parsley, salt, sugar, black pepper, and rinsed barley that has been set aside. Cook and stir over high heat until soup comes to a boil. Reduce heat and boil gently, uncovered, for 45 minutes to one hour or until vegetables are tender. Stir in the macaroni and let stand for another 5 minutes before serving.

ADDITIONAL VEGETABLES

Sliced fresh okra
Cauliflower florets
Parsnips, peeled and diced
Rutabagas, peeled and cut into ---
  ½-inch cubes

Kale, remove stems and chop
Brussels sprouts, quartered

Vegetable soup is a work in progress and frequently relies on leftover vegetable in the refrigerator. The recipe at the top is a basic formula for vegetable soup. However, you can replace some of the vegetables, if they are unavailable, with something from this list.

Note: When preparing the vegetables, they should be peeled and cut into ½-inch to 1-inch pieces.

240812-16

SWEET AND SOUR CABBAGE SOUP
(Makes 2½ quarts)

1 (15 oz.) can tomatoes
1 c. tomato juice
2 Tbs. olive oil
6 c. vegetable stock and/or water
3 c. chopped cabbage (8 oz.)
1 c. diced potatoes (6 oz.)
1 c. diced yellow onion (4 oz.)
1 c. sliced carrot (5 oz.)
½ c. diced celery (2 oz.)

1½ Tbs. sugar
1 Tbs. onion soup mix
1½ tsp. dried dill weed
1 tsp. salt
¼ tsp. black pepper
Dash sour salt (citric acid)
pinch cayenne pepper
¼ c. small elbow macaroni

Place tomatoes in a 4-quart pot and mash with a potato masher. Add the tomato juice, olive oil, vegetable stock and/or water, cabbage, potatoes, yellow onion, carrot, diced celery, sugar, onion soup mix, dill weed, salt, black pepper, sour salt, and cayenne pepper. Bring to a boil and cook for 45 minutes to one hour. While the soup is cooking, cook the elbow macaroni in a separate 1-quart saucepan according to the package directions. Drain and set aside until ready to use. When the soup is done cooking, stir in the cooked macaroni.

Note: You will need to purchase a head of cabbage that weighs at least one pound in order to prepare this soup.

DRIED GREAT NORTHERN BEAN SOUP
(Makes 3 quarts)

1 lb. dried Great Northern beans
3 qt. water, divided (2 qt. + 1 qt.)
2 Tbs. olive oil
1½ c. diced potato
1 c. diced carrot

1 c. diced yellow onion
¾ c. diced celery
1½ tsp. salt
½ tsp. hickory salt (opt.)
¼ tsp. coarse black pepper

Pick through the dried beans and remove any small pebbles or non-bean material. Rinse beans in a colander under running cold water and drain. Place beans in a 4-quart pot, add two quarts cold water, and soak for six hours or overnight. Cover the beans and let simmer gently over low heat for 2 hours, or until tender. Stir the beans frequently so that they cook evenly. Add more water, when necessary, to keep the beans covered and prevent them from drying out. Add olive oil, potato, carrot, onion, celery, salt, the optional hickory salt, black pepper, and the last quart of water. Continue to cook slowly for 1 to 1½ hours, or until vegetables are done. Taste and adjust seasoning. Serve with freshly baked bread or dinner rolls.

Note: Allow four hours to cook prepare the soup. This soup is frequently served on New Year's Day in place of the more traditional black-eyed peas.

VEGETABLE STOCK
(Makes 5 to 6 cups stock)

Carrots, peeled or well scrubbed
Celery, including leaves
Potatoes, peeled or well scrubbed
Tomatoes
Parsley
Water cress
Spinach
Cabbage
Zucchini or any summer squash
Green beans

Green onions
Yellow onions
Broccoli
Cauliflower
Collards
Garlic cloves
Brussels sprouts
Outer lettuce leaves
Salt

The best time to make vegetable stock is when it is time to clean out the refrigerator. The above list does not include everything that can be used or everything that must be used. Two basic ingredients that are almost always used are carrots and celery leaves. They are both loaded with nutrients, have a great subtle flavor, and good color. To start the stock preparation, go through the refrigerator and use anything that you may not be able to use in the next week. Cut everything up into pieces that are no more than one inch wide. Make sure that the cole crops (such as cabbage, broccoli, cauliflower, Brussels sprouts, etc.) do not make up more than 25 to 30 % of the vegetables. They have a very strong flavor and could end up dominating the flavor of the stock. A basic batch of vegetable stock should start with two pounds of vegetables. Include leftover vegetables that you would not use in your regular recipes but have not spoiled. You can also use parts of vegetables that you just purchased and do not plan to use: the outer leaves of lettuce, Chinese cabbage or bok choy are a good example. If you do not have a scale, then use 2 quarts of chopped vegetables. Add 6 cups of water to the vegetables in a 4-quart pot. The water should just barely cover the vegetables. Cook over medium heat until everything comes to a boil. Cover, reduce to a simmer, and cook for two to three hours. Add another cup of water if the level of the stock falls below the vegetables. Place a colander over a large pot and line with a large clean, pressing cloth, dish towel, or tea towel. Pour the contents of the stock pot into the colander so that you collect the strained stock in the pot below. Draw the corners of the cloth together, twist closed, and press with a potato masher to remove as much liquid as possible. This stock will keep for 5 to 7 days in the refrigerator. The best way to store extra stock is in the freezer.

Note: You will need a 4-quart pot for this recipe. You may want to use a larger pot if you have a lot of leafy greens that you plan to use. This makes a very strong stock that can be diluted with an equal amount of water when used in cooking. Too much to cook at one time? Then cut the recipe in half and use a 3-quart saucepan.

Main Dishes

Main Dishes

The title "Main Dishes" implies that a particular recipe is the center-piece of a meal accompanied by various side dishes, etc. Some of the dishes in this chapter can also be used as a side dish. Boiled Cabbage Wedges, Cauliflower and Cheese Sauce, Collards, Curried Cabbage, Globe Artichokes, and Macaroni and Cheese can all be used as an accompaniment to another main dish or entree. So keep this in mind when planning your meals.

The reverse is also true. Some of the recipes in Chapter: Side Dishes can also serve as a main dish.

Special Occasions

Please prepare any of these recipes at least once before planning to serve them at a special occasion like a large family get-together or holiday meal. Some of the recipes here tend to be a little complex and will probably need at least one test before being served to a large group. Timing is everything, and I'm sure you don't want to keep your hungry guests waiting.

MAIN DISHES

CURRIED CABBAGE
(Makes 8 cups or 4 to 6 large servings)

SAFFRON RICE

2 ½ c. water
2 Tbs. butter
1 ¼ tsp. salt

¼ tsp. saffron threads
1 ¼ c. long grain white rice

Begin preparing the Saffron Rice before starting on the vegetables in the next step. Combine the water, 2 tablespoons butter, 1 ¼ teaspoons salt, and saffron threads in a 2-quart saucepan. Cook over medium heat until butter is melted. Cover and simmer for five minutes so that the water can absorb some of the color and flavor of the saffron. Stir in the rice and bring to a gentle boil. Place lid on saucepan, reduce heat, and simmer for 25 minutes or until rice is done. Set aside until ready to add to vegetables.

CURRIED CABBAGE

½ c. raisins
1 lrg. cabbage (2 lb.)
1 lrg. apple (8 oz.)
1 (4 oz.) can whole button
  mushrooms, drained
¼ c. butter (½ stick)
1 ½ c. diced yellow onion

1 c. sliced celery (2 lrg. stalks)
1 ½ tsp. turmeric
1 tsp. salt
½ tsp. curry powder
½ tsp. allspice
pinch dried chile pepper
¼ c. water (opt.)

Plump the raisins by soaking in warm water for 5 minutes. Drain and set aside until ready to use. Remove any damaged outer leaves from the cabbage. Quarter and remove the core of the cabbage. Cut the quarters lengthwise once and then cut across the quarters three or four times into large pieces. There should be 8 cups of chopped cabbage. Quarter, peel, and core the apple. Slice each quarter crosswise into five or six pieces. Any mushrooms that are more than 1 inch in diameter should be cut in half from top to bottom. Melt ¼ cup butter in an electric skillet or large frying pan. Add the cabbage, apple, mushrooms, yellow onion, and celery. Cook at 275° (medium-low), while stirring occasionally, for 10 minutes. Add the plumped raisins, turmeric, 1 teaspoon salt, curry powder, allspice, and dried chile pepper. Cook and stir for an additional 5 to 10 minutes or until cabbage is tender. Add ¼ cup water if cabbage begins to stick to pan. Gently stir the Saffron Rice into the vegetables and serve.

Note: You will need to purchase a head of cabbage that weighs approximately 2 pounds. For a slight variation, cook ¼ to ½ cup wild rice and add to vegetables along with the saffron rice.

GLOBE ARTICHOKES
(Makes 4 servings)

PREPARATION

4 lrg. globe artichokes (see
"Note" below regarding size)

Wash and drain the artichokes. Cut off the stem so that it is flush with the bottom of the artichoke. This will allow it to sit flat on the plate. Cut off the top 1-inch of the artichoke. Use kitchen scissors to cut off the sharp thorns of the remaining leaves of the artichoke. Smaller leaves around the base can be pulled off.

COOKING

1 Tbs. olive oil   Salt
1 clove garlic, peeled

Fill the bottom of a pot for steaming with 3 to 4 inches of water. Add the olive oil and clove of garlic to the water. Sprinkle salt over the top of each artichoke. Put the artichokes with the cut side down (stem side up) in the basket in the top of the steamer. Bring water to a boil, reduce heat to a simmer and cook for 30 to 45 minutes. The artichokes are done when a fork can easily penetrate the stem end of the choke. When done, remove the pot from the heat and turn the artichokes right side up in the steamer.

CLEANING

Remove an artichoke from the steamer and place on a small plate. Use a set of tongs to pull off the small leaves in the center at the top. You don't have to remove many, just enough to expose the fuzzy choke in the center. Use a small teaspoon to scoop out the choke. Remove any of the smaller leaves inside that may be in the way and prevent you from getting all of the choke. Return to the steamer basket and repeat for the remaining artichokes. Keep the pot covered while cleaning the artichokes. Even though there is no heat under the pot, the remaining hot water should keep the artichokes warm until ready to serve.

SERVING

Mayonnaise, melted butter, or
Italian salad dressing

Artichokes are usually served with a dipping sauce. It can be mayonnaise, melted butter, or Italian salad dressing. If you prefer the salad dressing, fill the center of the cavity left by the choke that has been removed about half way up with the dressing. To eat, pull off one of the outside petals. Dip the white fleshy part in your dipping sauce. Tightly grip the other end and place in the mouth between the teeth with the dip side down. Pull through the teeth to remove the soft fleshy part along with the sauce.

(continued)

Discard the remainder of the petal. When all of the petals have been removed, the remaining part is called the heart of the artichoke. Remove any of the fuzzy choke that may have been left behind. Cut the heart into bite size pieces and dip into sauce before eating.

Note: Artichokes come in many sizes. The large artichokes are usually 3 to 4 inches in diameter and weigh 10 to 12 ounces each. You will need a large steamer pot for this recipe. A spaghetti cooker with a steamer insert works well. Although this recipe is for 4 artichokes, you are only limited by the number of artichokes your steamer will hold at one time.

BOILED CABBAGE WEDGES WITH MUSTARD SAUCE
(Makes 4 servings)

1 lrg. fresh head of cabbage, about 2 lbs.	2 tsp. sugar
2 c. water or vegetable stock	2 tsp. imitation chicken seasoning (opt.)
1 tsp. salt	

Remove and discard the outer leaves from the cabbage. Cut vertically from top to bottom into 4 wedges of about the same size. Remove most of the core from each wedge but leave enough to hold the cabbage wedge together so that it does not fall apart when cooking. In a 3-quart saucepan combine the 2 cups water or stock, salt, sugar, and optional chicken seasoning. Add the wedges to the pot with the cut edges facing down. Bring to a boil, cover, and simmer for 15 to 20 minutes. The cabbage is done when a fork can easily penetrate the cabbage leaves near the base of a cabbage wedge. Drain in a colander, with the cut side down, for about 3 minutes. Serve with the cut sides up.

MUSTARD SAUCE

1 Tbs. cornstarch	1 Tbs. butter
2 tsp. sugar	¼ c. cider vinegar
1 tsp. dry mustard	1 tsp. prepared horseradish
½ tsp. salt	2 egg yokes, lightly beaten
1 c. water	

Combine the cornstarch, sugar, mustard, and salt in a small saucepan. Stir in 1 cup water. Continuously stir over low heat until mixture thickens and boils. Remove from heat. Add butter, vinegar, and horseradish. Beat a little of the mixture into the egg yokes. Then add egg yokes to the pan. Cook slowly, stirring until sauce thickens. Serve over cabbage.

Note: For a larger head of cabbage that weighs 2 ½ to 3 pounds, you can cut it into 6 wedges and follow the same directions in order to make 6 servings.

STIR FRIED GREEN CABBAGE
(Makes 4 large servings)

1 lrg. head green cabbage, about
   2 to 2 ½ lbs.
½ c. slivers of red or green bell
   pepper (opt.)
2 Tbs. peanut oil

1 tsp. salt
1 tsp. sugar
½ tsp. ginger powder
¼ tsp. garlic powder
½ c. water

Remove and discard tough outer leaves from cabbage. Cut from top to bottom into quarters (wedges). Remove the solid core from the base of each cabbage quarter and rinse well. Shred cabbage by cutting across each quarter into slices ½-inch thick. You should have 2 to 3 quarts of shredded cabbage when done. Heat the peanut oil in a large wok over medium heat. Add the cabbage and optional bell pepper when the wok is warm. Cook and stir for 4 to 5 minutes. Stir in the salt, sugar, ginger powder, and garlic powder. Add ½ cup of water to steam cabbage and to keep it from sticking to the pan. Cover with lid and cook over medium heat for 5 minutes. Total cooking time will be from 10 to 12 minutes. Taste and adjust seasonings if necessary. Cabbage should be slightly limp but still crisp and the water should be cooked down so that there is none remaining.

Note: This is your basic recipe for stir fried green cabbage (not Chinese cabbage). In addition to being a main dish, it can also be used to make 6 to 8 smaller servings as a side dish.

SCALLOPED POTATOES - MICROWAVE METHOD
(Makes 4 servings)

4 c. potatoes, peeled and thinly
   sliced crosswise (about 1 ¼ lb.)
¾ c. water
3 Tbs. butter
¼ c. minced yellow onion
2 Tbs. diced green bell pepper

2 Tbs. all-purpose flour
1 c. milk
1 c. freshly grated cheddar
   cheese (4 oz.)
1 tsp. salt

Place potatoes in a greased 2 or 3 quart casserole dish. Add ¾ cup of water. Cover and cook in a microwave oven for 6 minutes at full power, stirring once while baking. Remove from microwave oven and drain excess water from potatoes. In a 2-quart saucepan, cook and stir onion and bell pepper in butter over medium heat until onion is translucent. Add flour and stir until a paste is formed. Slowly stir milk into the flour mixture until sauce is smooth and begins to boil. Add grated cheese and salt. Stir until cheese is melted. Pour over drained potatoes and mix evenly until blended. Return to microwave oven and cook at full power, uncovered, for an additional 12 to 14 minutes. Stir potatoes once after 4 minutes of baking.

240812-16

FRENCH FRIED EGGPLANT STICKS
(Makes 32 pieces or 4 servings)

BATTER

1 c. all-purpose flour
½ tsp. salt
Dash white pepper

2 eggs, lightly beaten
⅜ c. milk (¼ c. plus 2 Tbs.)

Mix together the flour, salt, and white pepper in a large bowl. Make a well in the center and add the eggs. Slowly stir in the milk until well blended. The batter will be thick. Set aside until ready to use.

EGGPLANT STICKS

1 med. eggplant, 10 to 12 oz.
peanut oil for frying

½ c. Thousand Island Dressing,
(see Chapter: Salads)

Wash, pat dry and do not peel the eggplant. Cut the eggplant lengthwise into ½ x ½ x 3-inch sticks. Prepare the batter listed above. Preheat oil for frying, about ⅛-inch deep, in a medium size frying pan over medium-high heat. If you are using an electric skillet, it should be set at 325°. Dip each eggplant stick in batter and fry in oil. Cook until golden brown, about 2 to 3 minutes on each side. Remove from pan, drain on paper towel, and keep warm. Serve 2 tablespoons Thousand Island Dressing in a small condiment dish as a side dip for each person.

Note: You can use zucchini in place of the eggplant. If you do not have peanut oil on hand, use any other vegetable oil except olive oil.

CHILI ON PASTA
(Makes 4 servings)

1 pt. Chili With Tofu (see Chapter: Tofu)
12 oz. dried spaghetti noodles OR 12 oz. dried rotini (4 c.)

2 tsp. olive oil
Fresh Chile Salsa - opt. (see Chapter: Sauces and Gravies)

Heat the chili and keep warm until ready to serve. Cook the spaghetti noodles or rotini according to the package directions. Drain, add olive oil, and toss so that the pasta does not stick together. Place one-forth of the pasta on each plate and pour ½ cup of chili over the top. Put a heaping tablespoon of the optional fresh salsa on top of each serving.

Note: If you would like a break from the usual spaghetti sauce on your pasta, here is a variation that is popular. You can make this in a hurry when you are short of time and have leftover chili in the freezer. You can also use TVP Chili (see recipe Chapter: Main Dishes; TVP) or vegetarian chili from the market in place of the Chili With Tofu.

COLLARDS
(Makes 4 servings)

PREPARATION

**2 lbs. fresh collards (3 bunches
from the market)**

Wash the collards and drain. Cut and remove the thick center vein that runs the length of each collard leaf. There should be 1 ¼ to 1 ½ pounds of prepared leaves when done. Cut the leaves in half lengthwise and again crosswise. This will make it easier to put the leaves in the pot.

COOKING

**3 c. water
1 clove garlic, peeled
About 1 ½ tsp. hickory salt or
  plain salt.**

**1 ½ tsp. sugar
4 lrg. red potatoes, about 1 ½ lbs.,
  peeled
1 Tbs. olive oil**

Pour 3 cups water into a 4-quart pot and add the garlic clove. Place the collard leaves in flat layers in the pot. After about a fourth of the leaves have been placed in the pot, sprinkle a small amount of hickory salt (or regular salt) and sugar over the leaves. Repeat until all of the collards are in the pot. Press the leaves down and place the red potatoes on top. Drizzle the olive oil over the top of everything. Place over medium-high heat and bring to a boil. Reduce heat, cover, and cook at a gentle boil for 45 minutes. Check the pot about once every 10 to 15 minutes to see if you need to add more water. Test with a fork to see if they are tender and done. This may sound like a lot of time, but collard leaves are very thick and they need the long cooking time to become tender. You may have to cook them for another 15 minutes for them to reach the right tenderness. Remove the potatoes when the 45 minutes is up and keep warm until ready to serve. When done cooking, remove the collards with a fork, making sure that any drips of stock go back in the pot. Remove the garlic and discard.

SERVING

**4 slices sweet yellow or red
  onion**

**Hot pepper vinegar or hot sauce
  (serve on side as condiment)**

Place the collards on one of the heavy plastic plates. Put the other plate on top of the collards. Hold over the pot and squeeze to remove as much collard juice as possible. Plastic plates are recommended because there is less chance of them breaking under pressure. Remove the top plate and cut the collards with a sharp knife into a diamond pattern. Stir the collards before serving. To prepare each serving, put the collards on a plate in a mound. Place one of the potatoes on the side along with whatever side dish you choose and one or two Johnny Cakes. Place a slice of onion

(continued)

34

on top of the collards and serve. The stock that is left in the pot should be saved for soup and gravies. It will keep in the refrigerator for 4 days or in the freezer for up to 6 months.

Note: A bunch (bundle) of collards at the market weighs about ¾ pound. You will need 3 bunches. You will also need 2 heavy plastic plates to help squeeze out some of the liquid from the cooked collards. Johnny Cakes or cornbread (see recipes Chapter: Bread; Baking Powder Bread) are traditionally served with collards. Hot sauce or vinegar from hot peppers is served on the side.

CAULIFLOWER AND CHEESE SAUCE
(Makes 4 large servings)

COOKING THE CAULIFLOWER

1 large head white cauliflower (about 2 lb.)	2 tsp. salt
2 qt. water	2 tsp. sugar

Remove the leaves by cutting through the stem at the base of the cauliflower. Remove each floret by cutting it where it meets the stem. Discard the remaining large stem or central part of the cauliflower. The florets should be 1½ to 2 inches wide. Larger pieces can be cut in half. There should be 8 cups (24 ounces by weight) of cauliflower florets when done. In a 4-quart pot bring 2 quarts of water, 2 teaspoons salt, and the sugar to a rolling boil. Add the cauliflower and begin counting the cooking time as soon as the cauliflower is put in the boiling water. Cook over medium-high heat for 5 minutes. Drain the cauliflower into a colander and keep warm until ready to serve.

CHEESE SAUCE

3 Tbs. butter	1½ c. milk
3 Tbs. all-purpose flour	1½ c. firmly packed, freshly
¼ tsp. salt	grated, cheddar cheese (6 oz.)

Melt the butter in a 1-quart saucepan over medium heat. Add the flour and salt. Continue to stir until the flour mixture forms a paste and begins to bubble. Slowly add the milk while stirring continuously. Beat with a whisk if any lumps form. Continue to cook until the white sauce just begins to boil. Add the cheddar cheese and stir over low heat until all of the cheese is melted. Serve over the cauliflower.

Note: Cauliflower can be cooked in a large pot or a spaghetti cooker. This is essentially the same cheese sauce that appears in Chapter: Sauces and Gravies. When serving cauliflower as a side dish, omit the cheese sauce and pour melted butter over each serving. Extra cooked cauliflower will keep in the refrigerator for 4 days and can be used in stir fry vegetables or salads.

LARGE SUMMER SALAD
(Makes 4 large salads)

BASIC SALAD

Italian Salad Dressing
2 heads butter lettuce (Bibb lettuce)
1 large potato, boiled, peeled, cubed (½-inch cubes)
12 large Spanish or black pitted olives
24 tomato wedges

4 hard boiled eggs, sliced
1 c. cooked, sliced carrots
2 avocados, peeled and sliced
⅔ c. sliced celery
Pickled beets, drained (see recipe Chapter: Side Dishes)
1 c. cucumber, peeled and sliced crosswise

Prepare the salad dressing ahead of time. Pull apart the butter lettuce, wash, and spin dry or drain. Tear into pieces and measure. There should be at least 4 cups of lettuce. Cover each plate with a mound of lettuce. Place about ¼ cup of cubed potatoes in the center of the lettuce. Place 3 olives around the potatoes. Arrange six tomato wedges on the lettuce in a circle like the spokes of a wheel. Place a sliced hard boiled egg in a space between two tomato wedges. Place ¼ cup cooked carrots in the space next to the hard boiled egg. Continue to fill the spaces between the tomato wedges with half of a sliced avocado, sliced celery, pickled beets, and ¼ cup sliced cucumber. Each item should occupy a different space between the tomato wedges. Keep refrigerated until ready to serve.

VARIATIONS AND ADDITIONAL INGREDIENTS

Potato Salad (see Chapter: Salads)
Macaroni Salad (see Chapter: Salads)
Diced bell pepper
Peeled and diced jicama

Cheese sticks
Canned asparagus, drained
Red onion slices
Cooked broccoli florets
Cooked cauliflower florets
Cooked green beans

Substitutions can be made for the ingredients in the original recipe. Potato salad or Macaroni Salad can be used used in place of the boiled potato in the center of the salad. Diced bell pepper, diced Jicama, cheese sticks, canned asparagus, onion slices, broccoli, cauliflower, or green beans may be used in place of any of the ingredients placed between the tomato wedges.

Note: This salad should be served on a chilled dinner plate. All of the ingredients should be chilled before assembling the salad. Feel free to use your own favorite dressing in place of the Italian dressing. Serve with a French roll or baguette (see recipes Chapter: Breads; Yeast Breads) to complete the meal. Feel free to use any leaf lettuce in place of the butter lettuce.

240812-16

SUMMER PLATE
(One serving)

Potato Salad (see Chapter:
  Salads)
Paprika
3 Deviled Eggs (see Chapter: This
  and That)
Tomato slices
Cucumber, peeled and sliced

Carrots, peeled, sliced, cooked,
  and chilled
Pickled Beets, chilled and drained
  (See Chapter: Side Dishes)
Sweet gherkin or dill pickles
French roll
Butter

Put a large mound of potato salad in the center of a chilled plate. Sprinkle a little paprika over the potato salad. Arrange the three deviled eggs evenly spaced (like spokes of a wheel) in a circle around the potato salad. Place sliced tomato next to each deviled egg. Fill each of the remaining three spaces with the cucumber slices, cooked carrots, and Pickled Beets. Serve the pickles on the side of the plate. Serve the French roll on its own plate with butter.

Note: This meal is usually served in the middle of summer during extremely hot weather when no one wants a hot meal in the middle of the day. Everything should be cooked ahead of time and thoroughly chilled before serving. Macaroni Salad may be used in place of the Potato Salad.

FRESH MUSHROOM BURGERS
(Makes 4 Burgers)

1 lb. fresh white or brown cap
  mushrooms
2 Tbs. butter
salt to taste
olive oil

1 clove garlic, crushed
4 whole wheat hamburger buns
Thousand Island Dressing (see
  recipe in Chapter: Salads)

Gently rinse off mushrooms and pat dry. Slice mushrooms ¼-inch thick, from top to bottom, and measure. There should be about 6 cups. Put the butter in a cold frying pan and place over medium heat. When the butter has melted, add the sliced mushrooms. Cook and stir over medium heat until tender, about 5 to 6 minutes. If using an electric skillet, cook at 275°. Lightly salt to taste. Toast the buns in a separate frying pan or skillet. Add 1 to 2 teaspoons of olive oil to the skillet. Rub a crushed clove of garlic in the oil just before toasting the buns over medium heat. You will probably have to toast the buns in two batches. To serve, spread Thousand Island Dressing on both halves of the toasted buns. Drain any liquid from the pan with the mushrooms before assembling the burgers. Place the cooked mushrooms on the buns and serve.

Note: Whole wheat buns are recommended because they complement the flavor of the fresh mushrooms.

VEGETABLE POT PIE
(Makes 4 servings)

PREPARING PASTRY DOUGH AND COOKING THE VEGETABLES

**Pastry dough for Four 4-Inch Tart
  Shells (see Chapter: Desserts;
  Pies)
1 c. peeled and diced carrot**

**2 c. peeled and diced potatoes
1 c. peeled and diced turnips
  (opt.)
1 (14½ oz.) can tomatoes**

Mix pastry dough for Four 4-Inch Tart Shells and keep in the refrigerator until ready to use. When preparing the vegetables they should all be diced into ½-inch pieces. Boil carrots, potatoes, and turnips in separate saucepans until done. Drain the vegetables and reserve the broth. Add enough water to the broth so that you have 2¼ cups for making the gravy (see below). Drain the tomatoes in a colander, saving the tomato juice, and chop into small pieces. The reserved tomato juice from the tomatoes can also be added to the broth when making the gravy.

MAKING THE GRAVY

**1 Tbs. canola or olive oil
2¼ c. vegetable broth reserved
  from cooking carrots, etc.
1 tsp. instant coffee granules
¼ tsp. salt**

**¼ tsp. pepper
pinch garlic powder
1 vegetable bouillon cube
¼ c. cornstarch dissolved in ----
  ¼ c. water**

Prepare the gravy before going on to the Final Preparation. In a 1-quart saucepan combine the canola oil, vegetable broth, instant coffee, salt, pepper, garlic powder, and vegetable bouillon cube. Bring to a boil and simmer for 5 minutes. Reduce heat so that the broth is not boiling and quickly stir in the cornstarch mixture. Increase heat to medium-high. Continue to stir until gravy is smooth, begins to bubble, and thickens. Set aside until ready to use.

FINAL PREPARATION

**3 Tbs. olive oil
1½ c. diced yellow onion
1½ c. diced celery
1 c. diced bell pepper**

**1 c. diced cabbage
¼ c. frozen peas, thawed
1 tsp. salt
¼ tsp. black pepper**

In a 4-quart pot combine the olive oil, onion, celery, bell pepper, and cabbage. Cook and stir over medium heat until the vegetables are tender, about 5 to 10 minutes. Remove from heat and add the cooked carrots, potatoes, optional turnips, diced tomatoes, and peas. Stir the gravy from above into the vegetables. Divide equally among four 16-ounce ramekin baking dishes. Divide pastry dough into four equal pieces. Roll each piece into a circle slightly larger than the top of the baking dish, about 6½ inches in diameter. Cut a hole about 2 inches in diameter in the center of each

(continued)

240812-16

pastry circle. This will allow steam to escape during the baking. Place pastry dough on top of the filled ramekin. Fold dough over edge and pinch gently to seal. Place the ramekins on a large cookie sheet and bake in a preheated 400° oven for 40 to 45 minutes, or until top is lightly browned. The cookie sheet will help to collect spills if the the pies should happen to boil over. Let cool for 5 to 10 minutes before serving.

Note: You will need 4 large (about 16 fluid ounce) ramekin baking dishes. The ramekins should be about 5½ inches in diameter at the top and 2½ inches tall. If you cannot find the right size ramekins, then use smaller dishes and adjust quantities accordingly. Example: This recipe should fill 8 small (8-ounce) ramekins.

MESS O' BEANS
(Makes 4 servings)

1 ½ lbs. fresh green beans
1 c. Lima beans (¼ lb.), fresh or
frozen
3 c. water
2 Tbs. cornmeal
2 tsp. olive oil
1 tsp. salt

1 tsp. hickory salt (opt.)
¼ tsp. black pepper
1 small dried hot chile pepper or
pinch of cayenne pepper (opt.)
1 vegetable bouillon cube
4 med. red potatoes, (about 1 lb.)

Rinse green beans under cold running water and drain. Remove any strings, snap off the ends, and cut into pieces about 2 inches long. There should be about 1 pound or 4 cups of prepared green beans when done. In a 3-quart saucepan combine the green beans, Lima beans, water, cornmeal, olive oil, salt, optional hickory salt, black pepper, optional dried chile pepper, and vegetable bouillon cube. Mix together until well blended. Peel the red potatoes, cut in half, and set on top of the beans in the saucepan. Place over medium heat and bring to a boil. Cover the saucepan, reduce heat, and boil gently for 30 minutes or until potatoes are tender. Test the potatoes by piercing with a knife. The knife should easily penetrate the potatoes all of the way to the center. Leave the lid on the pot and let rest for 5 minutes before serving. Remove the hot chile pepper and discard. Serve by placing two potato halves on each plate and spooning the beans over the potatoes. Make sure to include some of the broth from the bottom of the saucepan.

Note: This is traditionally served with Johnny Cakes, cornpone, or cornbread (see recipes Chapter: Breads; Baking Powder Breads). Variations include adding ½ cup whole kernel corn to the saucepan and/ or replacing the Lima beans with an equal amount of fresh or frozen (not dried) black-eyed peas.

SPINACH CROQUETTES
(Makes 12 - 14 croquettes or 4 to 6 servings)

CORN FLAKE CRUMBS - MAKES ABOUT 1 CUP

3 c. (4 oz.) corn flakes cereal, any
brand (see Note)

Make the corn flake crumbs before mixing the croquettes. Place the corn flakes in a 1-quart size self-sealing plastic bag. Put the bag on a counter and use a rolling pin to coarsely crush the flakes into crumbs. Continue until you have the desired consistency. Set aside until ready to use.

WHITE SAUCE

3 Tbs. butter
3 Tbs. all-purpose flour
1 ¾ c. milk

¼ tsp. salt
½ cup frozen peas, cooked and
drained

Melt the butter over medium heat in a 1-quart saucepan. Add flour to form a paste and stir until it begins to bubble. Slowly stir in milk and continue to cook over medium heat until sauce thickens and begins to boil. Add the ¼ teaspoon salt and cooked peas. Cook for another minute or two and remove from heat. Keep warm or reheat when ready to serve.

PREPARING THE CROQUETTES

1 lb. fresh spinach, cooked,
drained, squeezed, and
chopped (approx. 1 cup)
⅓ c. shredded carrot
⅓ c. all-purpose flour
⅓ c. toasted bread crumbs
¼ c. grated Parmesan cheese
2 eggs, lightly beaten
1 tsp. salt

¼ c. diced yellow onion (¼-inch
pieces)
¼ tsp. black pepper
pinch garlic powder
1 c. corn flake crumbs (see
above)
2 eggs, lightly beaten
white sauce (see above)
oil for frying

In a large bowl combine the cooked spinach, carrot, flour, bread crumbs, Parmesan cheese, 2 eggs, salt, yellow onion, black pepper, and garlic powder. Mix together until well blended. Use about ¼ cup spinach mixture for each croquette. Shape mixture into approximately 16 cone-shaped croquettes. Each cone should be 1-inch in diameter at the base and 2 inches tall. Place the lightly beaten eggs in a medium bowl. Place the corn flake crumbs in a separate medium bowl. Dip each croquette in beaten egg and roll in corn flake crumbs. Fry in oil that is at least ¼-inch deep and heated to 350° (medium-high). Start with the croquettes upright in the pan. Then lay on their side and turn while frying so that they are evenly browned. Keep warm until ready to serve. Allow 2 to 3 croquettes for each serving and cover with white sauce.

(continued)

Note: Some grocery stores carry prepared corn flake crumbs in a box. Two bunches of fresh spinach weigh about 1 pound. You can use frozen spinach in place of the fresh spinach. A single (12-oz.) package of spinach yields about 1 ¼ cup of chopped spinach. These croquettes have a unique cone shape so that they will stand upright when served.

CORN DOGS
(Makes 8 Corn Dogs)

CORN DOG DIP

¼ c. mayonnaise
2 Tbs. sour cream

1 Tbs. yellow horseradish
1 ½ tsp. prepared mustard

In a small bowl, combine the mayonnaise, sour cream, horseradish, and yellow mustard. Stir until well blended. Serve alongside the corn dogs.

CORN DOG BATTER

⅔ c. all-purpose flour
⅔ c. cornmeal
1 ½ Tbs. sugar
1 egg, lightly beaten

2 tsp. baking powder
½ tsp. salt
½ c. milk

Combine the flour, cornmeal, sugar, beaten egg, baking powder, and salt in a large bowl and mix well. Stir in milk to make a thick batter. Let rest for 5 minutes before using.

COOKING THE CORN DOGS

8 vegetarian hot dogs
Corn dog batter (see above)

Vegetable oil
8 wooden skewers

Add vegetable oil to an electric skillet to a depth of about 1 inch. If you prefer, you can use a deep fryer. Heat the oil to 350°. Pat the hot dogs dry. Most wooden skewers are too long to be practical for corn dogs. The skewer only needs to be inserted into half the length of the hot dog and have a handle that is 1 to 2 inches long. Cut your skewers down to a manageable size. A 5-inch skewer will usually work best. Insert a skewer into each hot dog and roll in batter. Use a spoon to spoon batter over bare spots of the hot dog. Place the hot dog in the hot oil, turning after 15 seconds. Long handled tongs will work best for handling the corn dogs in the hot oil. Fry the corn dog, while turning occasionally, until golden brown. This will take from 2 to 3 minutes at the most. Remove from oil and drain on paper towel. Repeat for the remaining hot dogs. Serve with a scant 1 tablespoon of dip with each corn dog.

Note: Although not mandatory, a pair of long handled tongs will make it easier to handle and fry the corn dogs. The skewers can be omitted if you do not plan to eat the corn dogs as finger food.

SAVORY EGGPLANT ON RICE
(Makes 4 cups or 4 servings)

RICE PREPARATION

1 ½ c. uncooked rice
3 c. water

2 Tbs. butter
1 tsp. salt

Begin cooking the rice before cooking the eggplant. In a 2-quart saucepan combine the rice, water, butter, and salt. Place over medium-high heat and bring to a boil. Stir once, cover, and cook over low heat until the rice is done, about 20 minutes. Let the rice rest for 5 minutes and fluff with a fork before serving.

SAVORY EGGPLANT

¼ c. olive oil
1 ½ c. chopped yellow onion ---
  (1-inch pieces)
¾ c. thinly sliced celery
1 c. diced green bell pepper ---
  (¾-inch pieces)
8 c. diced eggplant, do not peel
  (½-in. cubes)
1 (15 oz.) can whole tomatoes
  (1 ½ c.)
1 (12 fl. oz.) can tomato juice,
  divided (1 c. + ½ c.)

¼ c. small Spanish pimento-
  stuffed green olives, cut in half
2 tsp. red wine vinegar
1 tsp. salt
1 tsp. sugar
1 tsp. crushed dried basil
½ tsp. crushed dried oregano
¼ tsp. coarse ground black
  pepper

Heat an electric skillet to 250° or use a frying pan over medium-low heat. Add the olive oil, yellow onion, celery, and bell pepper. Cook and stir the vegetables for 5 minutes. Add the eggplant and reduce heat to 225° (low). Simmer, covered, for 15 minutes. Stir occasionally to keep eggplant from sticking to the pan. Place the whole tomatoes in a large bowl and mash with a potato masher. Add the tomatoes, 1 cup of the tomato juice, stuffed green olives, vinegar, 1 teaspoon salt, sugar, dried basil, dried oregano, and black pepper. Simmer, covered, until eggplant is tender and sauce is thick, about 5 more minutes. Continue to stir occasionally, and add the remaining ½ cup of tomato juice. Cook for an additional 1 to 2 minutes. Serve over the buttered white rice or Rice Medley (see recipe Chapter: Side Dishes).

Note: Eight cups diced eggplant weighs about 20 ounces. You will need to purchase one large or two small eggplants that weigh a total of 1 ½ to 2 pounds.

240812-16

MACARONI AND CHEESE
(Makes 4 large servings)

MICROWAVE INSTRUCTIONS

½ lb. large elbow macaroni ---
   (2 ½ c.)
¼ tsp. salt
1 Tbs. butter
2 Tbs. freshly grated Parmesan
   cheese

2 Tbs. milk
2 c. freshly grated, firmly packed,
   cheddar cheese, (about 8 oz.)
   divided (1 ½ c. + ½ c.)
Paprika

Cook the macaroni according to the package directions and drain. Place the cooked macaroni in a 2-quart baking dish. Add the salt and butter and stir until butter is melted. Add the Parmesan cheese, milk, and 1 ½ cups (6 ounces) of the cheddar cheese. Stir until well blended. Cook at full power in a microwave oven for about 6 minutes. Stir twice during cooking. Sprinkle the remaining ½ c. (2 ounces) cheddar cheese over top. Then sprinkle a little Paprika over top. Return to microwave and cook for 1 more minute, or until cheese on top has melted.

OVEN BAKED INSTRUCTIONS

¼ c. milk
3 Tbs. seasoned toasted bread
   crumbs (opt.)

To bake your macaroni and cheese in an oven, use the list of ingredients from above with the exception that you increase the milk to ¼ cup. Cook the macaroni, drain, and place in the 2-quart baking dish. Add the salt and butter to the still hot macaroni and stir until the butter is melted. Quickly stir in the ¼ cup milk, Parmesan cheese, and 1 ½ cups (6 ounces) of the grated cheddar cheese. Bake in a preheated 350° oven, uncovered, for 10 minutes. Stir the macaroni well to remove any lumps that may remain in the cheese. Return to the oven and bake for an additional 5 minutes. Stir once more and spread the remaining ½ cup (2 ounces) cheddar cheese evenly over the top. Sprinkle the optional bread crumbs and some paprika over the top. Bake for an additional 5 minutes (for a total baking time of 20 minutes) or until cheese on top has melted. Let cool for 5 minutes before serving.

Note: You will need a 2-quart round casserole dish for this recipe. It is best to shred your cheese from a block of fresh cheese. Preshredded varieties do not always melt very well. If you like your cheese dishes to have a "stringy" texture, replace a fourth of the cheddar cheese with mozzarella cheese.

STUFFED TOMATOES
(Makes 4 servings)

2 c. stuffing for tomatoes; Deviled
   Egg Salad, Frozen Tofu Salad
   (see recipe Chapter: Tofu),
   Imitation Chicken Salad or
   Imitation Sausage Stuffing
4 lettuce leaves

4 lrg. ripe tomatoes (10 oz. each
   and/or 3 inches in diameter),
   preferably vine ripened
Salt to taste (opt.)
½ c. grated cheddar cheese
Paprika

Make sure that the stuffing you plan to use is prepared ahead of time and thoroughly chilled. You can use the Deviled Egg Salad stuffing (see below), Frozen Tofu Salad (see Chapter: Tofu), the Imitation Chicken Salad or Imitation Sausage Stuffing. The last two recipes follow immediately after this one. To peel the tomatoes, place them in a 2-quart saucepan that is two-thirds full of boiling water for exactly 1 minute. Remove from the water with a slotted spoon and then blanch in cold water for one minute. Remove the tomato peel; it should come off very easily, and remove any white part of the stem end. Place each tomato on a lettuce leaf on the plate that it will be served on. The stem end should be facing up. Cut each tomato into 6 or 8 wedges, depending on the size of the tomato. When cutting the wedges DO NOT cut all of the way through. Leave about ¼-inch of the tomato uncut so that it remains in one piece. Spread the wedges open like the petals of a flower, creating a large space inside to hold the filling. If you would like your tomato seasoned with some salt, now is the time to do it. Fill each tomato with about ½ cup of the desired filling. Spread about 2 tablespoons of the grated cheddar cheese over the filling and top with a pinch paprika. Serve immediately or keep in refrigerator until ready to serve.

DEVILED EGG SALAD

4 hard boiled eggs, chilled
2 tsp. sweet relish
2 Tbs. mayonnaise
½ tsp. yellow mustard

¼ tsp. salt
pinch black pepper
pinch cayenne pepper (opt.)

Peel and finely dice the hard boiled egg and place in a large bowl. Drain the sweet relish by placing it in wire mesh strainer and pressing out the juice. Add the sweet relish, mayonnaise, yellow mustard, salt, and pepper. If you would like a little zip in your egg salad, then add a pinch of cayenne pepper. Stir together and store in refrigerator until ready to serve.

Note: This main dish is served most frequently during the hottest days of summer, when a hot meal does not seem very appealing. Homegrown tomatoes or fresh tomatoes from the farmer's market are preferred. Supposedly the cayenne pepper is what puts the devil in the deviled egg salad.

240812-16

IMITATION CHICKEN SALAD
(Makes 2 ½ cups)

8 oz. (half of a 1 lb. roll)
  Worthington® Chic-ketts™,
  thawed
½ c. sweet relish
1 hard boiled egg, finely diced
½ c. mayonnaise
⅔ c. finely chopped celery

⅓ c. finely chopped red or green
  bell pepper
¼ c. minced sweet red onion
  (opt.)
1 tsp. celery seed, crushed
1 tsp. summery savory, crushed
⅛ tsp. black pepper

Tear or chop Chic-ketts™ into small pieces about a ½-inch wide and put in a large bowl. Place the sweet relish in a large strainer over the sink and press out as much liquid as possible with the back of a spoon. Add the sweet relish, hard boiled egg, mayonnaise, celery, bell pepper, optional red onion, celery seed, summer savory, and black pepper to the Chic-ketts™ in the bowl. Mix well, chill, and serve. Use ½ cup of chicken salad to stuff each tomato. It will stuff about 5 tomatoes. It can also be used to make sandwiches.

Note: This is a vegetarian version of the ubiquitous chicken salad. Please refer to the previous recipe for Stuffed Tomatoes. It can also be used to make sandwiches and served on crackers, etc. Chic-ketts™ can be found in the frozen food section of most health food stores.

IMITATION SAUSAGE STUFFING AND SANDWICH SPREAD
(Makes 2 cups)

1 (8 oz.) pkg. MorningStar
  Farms® Original Sausage
  Patties (6 patties)
½ c. sweet relish

⅔ c. mayonnaise
1 hard boiled egg, chopped
⅓ c. finely chopped celery

Cook the 6 frozen sausage patties in a microwave oven at full power for 1 ½ minutes. Allow to cool and chop into very small pieces. There should be about 1 ½ cups of chopped sausage patties. Measure the sweet relish, place in a fine mesh strainer, and squeeze out as much liquid as possible with the back of a spoon. In a large bowl combine the chopped sausage, sweet relish, mayonnaise, hard boiled egg, and celery. Stir together until well blended. To serve, use in the earlier recipe for stuffed tomatoes.

Note: Worthington® Prosage is the preferred main ingredient for this recipe. Since it is difficult to find (it is only sold in some health food stores), we recommend that you use MorningStar Farms® Sausage Patties in its place. The sausage patties can be found in the freezer section of most large markets. This recipe makes enough filling for 4 stuffed tomatoes or 6 sandwiches.

POTATO PANCAKES
(Makes 6 large pancakes)

4 c. peeled, coarsely grated,
  russet potatoes
1 ½ tsp. salt
2 eggs, lightly beaten
½ c. finely diced yellow onion
½ c. finely diced bell pepper

¼ c. matzo meal
3 Tbs. Bisquick® or pancake mix
2 tsp. dill weed
¼ tsp. black pepper
vegetable oil for frying
sour cream

Place grated potatoes in a large bowl. Stir in salt and let stand 5 to 10 minutes. Place a colander lined with a clean towel in the sink. Stir the potatoes one more time. Place potatoes in the lined colander, roll up towel, and squeeze out as much water as possible. Place potatoes in a large clean bowl. Add the beaten eggs, diced onion, bell pepper, matzo meal, Bisquick®, dill weed, and black pepper. Mix all of this together until well blended. Using ½ cup of the mix for each pancake, fry pancakes in a generous amount of vegetable oil in an electric skillet set at 350°, or in a frying pan over medium-high heat. Fry for 7 to 8 minutes on each side for a total of about 15 minutes. They should be a dark golden brown when done. Serve warm topped with a heaping tablespoon of sour cream.

LIGHT FETTUCCINE ALFREDO
(Makes 4 large servings.)

1 lb. dried fettuccine noodles
½ c. (1 stick) butter, divided -----
  (2 Tbs. + 6 Tbs.)
1 Tbs. all-purpose flour
1 ½ c. whole milk
¼ tsp. salt

¼ tsp. black pepper
pinch dried oregano (opt.)
1 c. freshly grated Parmesan
  cheese, divided (½ c. + ½ c.)
2 Tbs. chopped fresh Italian
  parsley for garnish

Cook fettuccine noodles in a large pot according to package directions. Reserve ¼ cup of the noodle water. Drain and return noodles to pot. If you work quickly, you should be able to make this sauce while the noodles are cooking. Melt 2 tablespoons (¼ stick) of butter in a 1-quart saucepan. Add flour and stir until all of the lumps are gone and the butter begins to bubble. Add the remaining 6 tablespoons (¾ stick) of butter and stir until melted. Slowly add the milk and stir until sauce begins to boil. Add the salt, black pepper, optional oregano, and ½ cup Parmesan cheese. Stir until mixed well. If the sauce becomes too thick, slowly stir in some of the reserved noodle water. Pour sauce over cooked fettuccine noodles and toss until coated. Sprinkle some of remaining Parmesan cheese on top of each serving. Garnish with Italian parsley.

Note: We call this "Light" because it uses milk in place of the more traditional cream. Freshly grated Parmesan cheese works best.

240812-16

SPAGHETTI WITH FRESH SAUCE
(Makes 2 to 3 servings)

PREPARING THE TOMATOES

**4 lrg. fresh slicing tomatoes
(about 1 ½ lb.)**

2 Roma tomatoes (about ½ lb.)

Place a 2-quart saucepan that is half full of water over high heat and bring the water to a boil. Place the large fresh tomatoes and Roma tomatoes in the saucepan of boiling water for 1 minute. Remove with a slotted spoon and place in a bowl under running cold water in the sink. Allow to cool for 1 to 2 minutes. Drain the tomatoes, remove skins with a knife, and dice into large chunks. Keep in a bowl until ready to use. There should be 3 ½ cups of diced tomatoes.

COOKING THE SAUCE

2 Tbs. olive oil
¾ c. diced yellow onion
1 clove garlic, minced
**2 Tbs. chopped fresh Italian
  parsley**
2 Tbs. chopped fresh sweet basil
2 tsp. chopped fresh oregano
1 bay leaf

¼ c. white wine
2 tsp. pesto sauce
½ tsp. sugar
½ tsp. salt
¼ tsp. coarse black pepper
½ lb. dried spaghetti
**1 c. noodle water from cooked
  spaghetti**

Heat olive oil in a large frying pan over medium heat. If you are using an electric skillet it should be set at 275°. Add the diced onions and cook until translucent and tender, about 5 minutes. Add the minced garlic, Italian parsley, sweet basil, oregano, and bay leaf. Stir the herbs in the pan for one minute. This allows the oil to absorb the flavors of the herbs. Add all of the chopped tomatoes and stir well. Mash the tomatoes in the pan with a potato masher. Add the white wine, pesto sauce, sugar, salt, and black pepper. Reduce the heat and simmer gently for 20 to 25 minutes. Cook the spaghetti, while the sauce is simmering, following the directions on the package. Add ½ cup of the spaghetti water to the tomato sauce after 10 minutes of cooking and again after another 5 minutes of cooking. Drain the spaghetti and return to the empty pot until ready to use. The spaghetti sauce should be fairly thin because the pasta will absorb some of the moisture when it is added. When the 20 to 25 minutes is up and the sauce is done cooking, remove the bay leaf and stir in the cooked spaghetti. Warm over low heat for 1 to 2 minutes and serve.

Note: This spaghetti sauce uses fresh, peeled tomatoes. Homegrown tomatoes are preferred. Use commercial Pesto Sauce or make your own using the recipe in Chapter: Sauces and Gravies. During the winter, when fresh tomatoes are at a premium, you can use frozen Roma tomatoes in place of fresh Romas, and 2 cups tomato juice in place of the fresh slicing tomatoes.

LASAGNA
(Makes 8 Servings)

EARLY PREPARATION

5 c. Spaghetti Sauce, (see Chapter: Sauces and Gravies)

1 (8 oz.) pkg. MorningStar Farms® Sausage Patties

Prepare the Spaghetti Sauce and sausage patties ahead of time. It can be done a day ahead if you like. Cook the 6 frozen sausage patties in a microwave oven at full power for 1½ minutes. Allow to cool and chop into small pieces. There should be 1½ cups of finely chopped sausage patties. If you like, you can substitute 1½ cups of Beef-Like Tofu (see Chapter: Tofu) for the sausage patties.

MAIN PREPARATION

12 oz. Lasagna Noodles
1 c. low fat cottage cheese (4 oz.)
1 lb. (4 c.) grated mozzarella cheese, divided (½ lb. + ½ lb.)
⅓ c. seasoned bread crumbs
2 eggs, lightly beaten, separately
3 Tbs. olive oil
¾ c. diced yellow onion

1 clove garlic, minced
¼ c. water
¼ c. chopped fresh Italian parsley
1 tsp. crushed dried oregano
½ tsp. crushed anise
¼ tsp. coarse ground black pepper

Cook the lasagna noodles according to the package directions. Drain and set aside on a flat surface until ready to use. Rinse the cottage cheese in a colander to remove the cream and drain thoroughly. This helps to keep the lasagna from falling apart. If you can find dry cottage cheese, then use it instead. In a large bowl mix together the drained cottage cheese with ½ pound (2 cups) of the grated mozzarella cheese. Stir in the bread crumbs and one of the beaten eggs. In a small frying pan cook and stir the onions and garlic in the olive oil. Cook until the onion is translucent, about 5 minutes. Stir in the finely chopped sausage patties, 1 cup of the spaghetti sauce, ¼ cup water, Italian parsley, oregano, anise, and black pepper. Cook together for an additional 1 to 2 minutes. Allow to cool for 10 minutes and then stir in the remaining beaten egg.

ASSEMBLING AND BAKING

½ c. grated Parmesan cheese

To assemble the lasagna, spread ½ cup spaghetti sauce in the bottom of a 13 x 9 x 2-inch baking dish. Place a layer of cooked noodles in the bottom of the dish. Four lasagna noodles should be able to cover the bottom of the dish. Spread 1 cup of sauce over the layer of noodles in the dish. Evenly spread the mozzarella and cottage cheese mixture over the noodles. Place another layer of noodles over the cheese mixture and spread 1 cup sauce over these noodles. Spread all of the chopped sausage

(continued)

240812-16

mixture evenly over this layer of noodles. Place the final layer of noodles on top of the sausage mixture. Spread 1 cup sauce over top and sprinkle the remaining ½ pound mozzarella cheese (2 cups) over the sauce. Sprinkle the ½ cup Parmesan cheese over the top. Cover with a sheet of aluminum foil that has been coated with non-stick spray. Bake in a preheated 350° oven for 1 hour and 15 minutes. Remove the aluminum foil for the last 30 minutes of baking. Let the lasagna rest for 15 minutes before serving.

Note: You will need a 13 x 9 x 2-inch baking dish for this recipe. This is a labor intensive and time consuming dish that is usually reserved for special occasions. For a smaller crowd (4 servings) cut the recipe in half and use an 8-inch square baking dish.

BAKED ZITI
(Makes 6 Servings)

2 c. Spaghetti Sauce (see
    Chapter: Sauces and Gravies)
8 oz. ziti, cooked
4 Morning Star Farms® sausage
    links (opt.)
1 clove garlic, minced
1 c. diced yellow onion (½-inch
    pieces)
2 sm. zucchini, sliced crosswise,
    ¼-inch thick (about 1 c.)
½ green bell pepper, sliced into -
    ¼ x 1½-inch strips (½ c.)

2 Tbs. olive oil
½ c. seasoned bread crumbs
½ tsp. dried oregano, crushed
½ tsp. dried sweet basil, crushed
½ tsp. salt
¼ tsp. anise seed, crushed
¼ tsp. black pepper
½ c. grated Parmesan cheese
1 c. mozzarella cheese, cubed ---
    (½-inch cubes)
½ c. grated mozzarella cheese

Prepare Spaghetti Sauce ahead of time. Cook ziti according to package directions and set aside to cool. Cut the sausage links into ½-inch pieces. In a large frying pan, cook and stir the minced garlic, yellow onion, zucchini, bell pepper and sausage in 2 tablespoons of olive oil, until tender. In a large bowl, combine the cooked ziti, bread crumbs, oregano, sweet basil, salt, crushed anise seed, black pepper, and grated Parmesan cheese. Mix together thoroughly. Stir in the cooked vegetables, cubed mozzarella cheese, and 1 cup of the Spaghetti Sauce. Spread this mixture evenly in a lightly oiled 2-quart casserole dish. Spread the remaining 1 cup of Spaghetti Sauce over the top. Sprinkle the grated mozzarella cheese on top. Bake in a preheated 350° oven uncovered for 25 to 30 minutes. Remove from oven and let rest for 5 minutes before serving.

Note: You will need a 2-quart casserole dish for this recipe. Mostaccioli or penne rigate may be used in place of the ziti.

EGGPLANT PARMESAN
(Makes 6 servings)

PREPARING THE EGGPLANT

1 lrg. eggplant, about 1 lb.
1 ⅓ c. Spaghetti Sauce,
    commercial or homemade (see
    Chapter: Sauces and Gravies)
1 egg

¼ c. milk
¾ c. all-purpose flour
¾ tsp. salt
⅛ tsp. black pepper
peanut oil for frying

If you plan to cook your own spaghetti sauce, cook the sauce ahead of time. Slice the eggplant crosswise into six pieces ⅜ to ½-inch thick. Save leftover eggplant in the refrigerator for use in other recipes. In a medium bowl beat together the egg and milk. In a separate bowl, about the same size, mix together the flour, ¾ teaspoon salt, and ⅛ teaspoon black pepper. Dip a slice of eggplant in the egg mixture and then in the flour. Repeat the process (double dip). Cook in a frying pan coated with a thin layer of peanut oil over medium heat. If you use an electric skillet it should be set at 325°. Cook until lightly browned on one side then turn to cook on the second side. This should take about 2 minutes on each side. Drain the eggplant on paper towels.

BROILING THE EGGPLANT PARMESAN

1 ½ tsp. dried oregano
1 tsp. dried sweet basil
½ tsp. whole anise seed
8 oz. mozzarella cheese, cut into
    ⅛-in. thick slices

¼ c. freshly grated Parmesan
    cheese

Crush the oregano, sweet basil, and anise together with a mortar and pestle or by hand. Reserve this herb blend until ready to use. Place the fried eggplant slices on a large cookie sheet. Spread Spaghetti Sauce over the top of each slice. Cover with sliced mozzarella cheese. Spread a small amount of the Spaghetti Sauce, about ½ tablespoon, over the cheese on the eggplant. Sprinkle a small amount of Parmesan over each slice of eggplant. And finally, sprinkle some of the reserved herb blend over the top of each eggplant. Place under a broiler and broil until cheese has melted and started to brown. This is frequently served with buttered spaghetti noodles and Parmesan cheese on the side.

Note: Peanut oil is recommended for cooking eggplant because supposedly eggplant does not absorb as much oil when fried in peanut oil. If you do not have peanut oil, feel free to use any other good vegetable oil in it's place. Fresh Parmesan cheese is recommended because it melts better than processed cheese. A good substitute would be fresh Italian Pecorino Romano.

 240812-16

FARMER'S SPAGHETTI
(Makes 4 to 6 servings)

¼ c. olive oil
2 c. yellow onion, sliced thinly, top to bottom in strips ¼-inch wide (1 lrg. onion)
2 cloves garlic, minced (2 tsp.)
1 c. celery, sliced julienne (about 2 stalks)
1 c. red or green bell pepper, sliced julienne
1 c. peeled and thinly sliced carrot (1 lrg. carrot)
2 ½ c. thinly sliced cauliflower florets (about ½ lb.)
1 c. zucchini, sliced julienne ---- (1 sm. zucchini)

1 tsp. salt
½ tsp. sugar
½ tsp. dried oregano, crushed
½ tsp. dried sweet basil, crushed
¼ tsp. anise seed, crushed
¼ tsp. black pepper
pinch crushed red chile peppers
1 (15 oz.) can whole tomatoes (1 ½ c.)
¼ c. white wine
1 c. tomato juice, divided (½ c. + ½ c.)
1 Tbs. butter
1 lb. dried spaghetti noodles

Heat olive oil in a large frying pan. Add onion, garlic, celery, bell pepper, carrots, cauliflower, and zucchini. Cook over medium heat for 1 to 2 minutes. If you are using an electric skillet, it should be set at 275°. Add salt, sugar, oregano, sweet basil, anise, black pepper, and chile pepper. Continue to cook for 5 to 10 minutes, or until onions are translucent. Drain tomatoes, reserving the liquid. Dice tomatoes and add to vegetables in frying pan along with the reserved liquid, white wine, ½ cup tomato juice, and butter. Continue to cook for another 10 to 15 minutes, or until remaining vegetables are tender. Add remaining ½ cup tomato juice if needed. Keep vegetables warm while cooking spaghetti noodles. Cook spaghetti noodles according to the package directions and drain. Return them to the pot they were cooked in and add cooked vegetables from frying pan. Stir until well blended and serve at once.

Note: This could just as easily be called Summer Spaghetti. It is usually made in the early summer when fresh young vegetables are abundant. "Sliced julienne" (sometimes called shoestring) means to cut vegetables so that they are about ¼ x ¼ x 2-inches long.

LARGE PIZZA
(Makes one 17 x 12-inch pizza)

PIZZA DOUGH

2 ¼ c. all-purpose flour, divided ---   1 c. warm water
   (1 c. + 1 ¼ c.)   ¾ tsp. salt
1 ½ tsp. sugar   2 tsp. olive oil
1 ½ tsp. instant active dry yeast

In a large bowl combine 1 cup flour, the yeast, and sugar. Stir in 1 cup of warm water and let stand for a minute while the yeast becomes active. Add the salt, 2 teaspoons olive oil, and remaining 1 ¾ cups of flour. Mix together to form a ball of dough. Turn out onto a lightly floured surface and knead for 3 minutes, or until it is smooth and elastic. Place in a lightly greased bowl and let rise for 30 minutes. Turn out onto a dry surface and knead for 1 minute. Add more flour if the dough becomes sticky. Roll out into a rectangle the approximate size of the baking sheet. Spread the dough out on the lightly greased 17 x 12 x 1-inch baking sheet. Use your fingers to spread the dough until it covers the entire pan and goes up the sides. Bake in a preheated 400° oven for 10 to 12 minutes. Carefully watch the dough during baking. Use a long knife to burst any bubbles that may appear in the dough. The pizza dough should be lightly browned when done. Remove from oven and set aside.

PIZZA SAUCE

1 tsp. olive oil   1 ⅓ c. Spaghetti Sauce (see
2 Tbs. tomato paste   Chapter: Sauces and Gravies)

Prepare the sauce while the dough is rising. Heat 2 teaspoons olive oil in a 1-quart saucepan over medium heat for about 15 seconds. Add the tomato paste and stir until it begins to bubble. Add the spaghetti sauce and simmer over low heat for about 10 minutes so that the sauce thickens. Stir frequently. Set aside until ready to assemble the pizza.

ASSEMBLING AND BAKING THE PIZZA

6 Morning Star Farms® Sausage   1 bell pepper, washed, seeded
   Links   and cut into thin strips (¾ c.)
2 tsp. olive oil   1 (4 oz.) can sliced mushrooms,
1 lb. mozzarella Cheese, grated (4   drained
   c. packed)   2 tsp. dried basil
1 yellow onion, sliced vertically in   1 tsp. dried oregano
   ¼-inch wide pieces (1 c.)   ½ tsp. whole anise seed

Thaw or defrost Morning Star Farms® sausage links. Fry in 1 tablespoon olive oil in a small frying pan over medium heat until lightly browned. Remove from pan and drain on paper towel. Tear the sausage links into pieces with a fork. Spread all of the pizza sauce evenly over the baked

(continued)

pizza dough. Spread the grated cheese over the sauce. Now spread the onion, bell pepper, mushrooms, and cooked sausage links over the top of the cheese. In a mortar and pestle crush together the basil, oregano, and anise (or crush by hand) and sprinkle evenly over the top. Place under a broiler until cheese is melted, lightly browned, and bubbly, 3 to 4 minutes.

Note: You will need a 17 x 12 x 1-inch baking sheet (half-sheet pan).

SMALL CHEESE PIZZA
(Makes one 9 to 10-inch diameter pizza)

PIZZA DOUGH

¾ c. all-purpose flour, divided ---
  (¼ c. + ½ c.)
½ tsp. sugar
½ tsp. instant active dry yeast

⅓ c. warm water
1 tsp. olive oil
¼ tsp. salt

In a medium bowl combine ¼ cup of the flour, the sugar, and active dry yeast. Stir in the warm water and olive oil until well blended. Add the salt and remaining ½ cup of flour and stir until dough is formed. Turn out onto a lightly floured surface and knead for about one minute. Place in a lightly oiled bowl and let rise until double in bulk, about 25 minutes.

CHEESE PIZZA

½ c. Spaghetti Sauce (see
  Chapter: Sauces and Gravies)
1 tsp. olive oil
dash salt
dash pepper

6 oz. grated fresh mozzarella
  cheese (1 ½ c. packed)
1 tsp. dried basil
½ tsp. dried oregano
¼ tsp. whole anise seed

While the dough is rising, place the spaghetti sauce in a small saucepan and simmer over low heat for about 5 minutes or until sauce has thickened. The sauce should be almost as thick as canned tomato paste. Remove the dough from the bowl when it is done rising and gently knead for about 1 minute. Roll into a circle large enough to cover the pizza pan. Lightly spray your pizza pan with a thin layer of non-stick spray. Place the circle of dough on the pizza pan and press gently to spread the dough to the edge of the pan. Rub 1 teaspoon of olive oil over the top and sprinkle a small amount of salt and pepper over the dough. Spread the thickened spaghetti sauce over the dough and sprinkle the grated mozzarella cheese evenly over top. Crush together the basil, oregano, and anise in a mortar and pestle (or crush by hand) and sprinkle over the cheese. Bake the pizza in a preheated 500° oven for 18 to 20 minutes.

Note: You will need a 9 to 10-inch diameter pizza pan. You can use homemade Spaghetti Sauce from Chapter: Sauces and Gravies or canned sauce from the market. This recipe makes 2 servings or 6 small pieces.

PICKLED GARDEN RELISH
(Makes 6 large servings)

PREPARING THE VEGETABLES

2 c. cauliflower florets (6 oz.) cut into 1½-inch pieces
2 c. fresh green beans (8 oz.) cut into 2-inch pieces
2 c. sliced carrots (8 oz.) sliced ¼-inch thick

1 tsp. salt, divided ----- (½ tsp. + ½ tsp.)
2 qt. water, divided (2 c. + 6 c.)

In a 1-quart saucepan combine the carrots, ½ teaspoon salt, and 2 cups water over high heat. When the water comes to a boil, reduce the heat and gently cook the carrots until tender, about 10 minutes. Drain the carrots, reserving the carrot stock, and set aside until ready to use. In a 2-quart saucepan combine 6 cups water and the remaining ½ teaspoon salt. Place over medium-high heat and bring to a boil. Add the cauliflower, reduce the heat when the water boils, and simmer for exactly 5 minutes. Begin counting the cooking time as soon as the cauliflower is added to the pot. Remove the cauliflower with a slotted spoon and set aside until ready to use. Heat the cauliflower water until it returns to a boil and add the green beans. Cook for 8 minutes. Drain the green beans, reserving the stock, and set aside until ready to use. Put the carrot stock in a 2-cup measuring cup and add enough green bean stock to make a total of 2 cups of stock. Use this carrot stock in the following section. Discard the remainder of the bean stock.

COOKING THE RELISH

¼ c. olive oil
2 c. sliced fresh mushrooms ---- (4 oz.)
2 c. diced yellow onion (8 oz.)
1½ c. sliced celery
1 c. diced green bell pepper
½ c. diced red bell pepper
¾ c. small pimiento stuffed Spanish olives
2 Tbs. sugar

2 tsp. dried oregano leaves, crushed
1 tsp. salt
¼ tsp. black pepper
1½ c. Spaghetti Sauce (see Chapter: Sauces and Gravies)
2 c. carrot stock (from above)
⅓ c. cider vinegar
2 Tbs. cornstarch dissolved in --- 2 Tbs. water

Add the olive oil to an electric skillet set at 275° or a large frying pan over medium-low heat. Add the sliced mushrooms, onion, celery, green bell pepper, and red bell pepper. Cook and stir for 5 to 8 minutes or until onion is tender. Add the cooked cauliflower, green beans, carrots, Spanish olives, sugar, oregano, 1 teaspoon salt, and black pepper. Cook and stir the vegetables for 1 to 2 minutes to allow the flavors to blend. Add the spaghetti sauce, reserved carrot stock, and vinegar. Cook and stir until it begins to

(continued)

simmer. Stir in the cornstarch mixture and cook until sauce thickens and begins to bubble. Remove from heat and cover until ready to serve.

SERVING

12 oz. pkg. dried wide egg noodles
Parmesan cheese

French bread (see Chapter: Breads; Yeast Breads)

Cook the egg noodles according to the package directions and drain. To serve, put a mound of the cooked egg noodles on a plate and spoon cooked vegetable relish over the top. Serve with Parmesan cheese and French bread.

Note: A slotted spoon will be very helpful in removing the cauliflower from the saucepan.

THIN PASTA SAUCE AND RIGATONI
(Makes 1 quart sauce)

2 Tbs. olive oil
⅔ c. finely minced white onion
1 clove garlic, finely minced
2 Tbs. chopped flat Italian parsley leaves
1 tsp. dried oregano, crushed
¼ tsp. anise seed, crushed
¼ tsp. black pepper
¼ tsp. onion powder
⅛ tsp. garlic powder

pinch cayenne pepper
2 (15 oz.) cans tomato sauce
1 (12 oz.) can tomato juice
1 c. water
½ c. vegetable stock
⅓ c. white wine
1½ tsp. sugar
½ tsp. salt
1 lb. dried rigatoni

In a 3-quart saucepan combine the olive oil and minced white onion. Cook and stir over medium heat until the onion is translucent, about 5 minutes. Add the finely minced garlic, parsley, oregano, anise, black pepper, onion powder, garlic powder, and cayenne. Stir and cook in oil for about 1 minute. Add tomato sauce, tomato juice, 1 cup water, ½ cup vegetable stock, white wine, sugar, and salt. Cook over low heat, while stirring occasionally, for 1½ to 2 hours. Shortly before the sauce is done, cook the rigatoni according to package directions. Drain thoroughly and return to pot. Add about 3 cups of the sauce and stir so that all of the pasta is coated and serve. The extra sauce can be kept in the refrigerator for up to one week or in the freezer for several months.

Note: This is a special thin sauce that is used with hollow pasta like rigatoni and mostaccioli. Unlike thick sauce, it is easier for the thin sauce to get into the hollow parts of the pasta.

VEGETABLE FRITTATA
(Makes 4 to 6 servings)

2 oz. dried spaghetti
2 imitation sausage patties
　(Morning Star Farms® or
　something similar)
Vegetable oil
1 Tbs. olive oil
1 c. diced yellow onion (4 oz.)
½ c. diced bell pepper (2 oz.)

⅔ c. thinly sliced celery (2 oz.)
1 c. sliced zucchini (4 oz.)
Salt
Pepper
4 oz. mozzarella cheese, thinly
　sliced
6 eggs
¼ c. whole or canned milk

Cook the spaghetti following the directions on the package, drain, and set aside until ready to use. In a small frying pan cook the imitation sausages in a small amount of oil. Remove from pan and chop into small pieces. There should be about ⅔ cup of chopped sausage. Add the 1 tablespoon olive oil to a 9-inch oven-safe frying pan. Place over medium heat and add the onions, bell pepper, celery, and zucchini. Season the vegetables with salt and pepper. Cook and stir for 10 to 15 minutes until the vegetables are fully cooked. Remove from heat, stir in the chopped sausage, and spread everything evenly over the bottom of the pan. Spread the spaghetti noodles evenly over the top. In a medium bowl beat together the eggs and milk. Pour over the vegetables in the pan (do not stir). Cover and cook over low heat until eggs just begin to set, 2 to 3 minutes. Remove lid and bake in a preheated 350° oven for 15 to 20 minutes. Remove from oven, place lid on pan, and let stand for 5 minutes before serving. The steam from the hot frittata will soften the bottom so that it is easy to remove from the pan. Cut into 4 to 6 pieces and serve.

VARIATIONS

Sliced carrots, cooked
Cauliflower florets, cooked
Broccoli florets, cooked
Asparagus, cut into 2-inch pieces
　and cooked

Whole kernel corn, cooked
Peas, cooked
Boiled potatoes in ½-inch cubes
Cheddar, Jack or Swiss cheese

Frittatas can be filled with just about any leftover vegetables that you may have in the refrigerator. This is a list of more ingredients that can be used as filler. All vegetables should be fully cooked before adding them to the frittata. The boiled potato can be used in place of the spaghetti noodles. Any one of the three cheeses listed can be used in place of the mozzarella.

Note: Frittata, which is basically a fancy omelet, can be served at breakfast, lunch or dinner. You will need a 9-inch oven-safe frying pan for this recipe. A pan with a heavy bottom such as stainless steel or cast iron works best.

240812-16

BEAN BURRITO
(Makes 4 Burritos)

4 lrg. (8 in. diameter) flour
  tortillas, preferably homemade
  (see Chapter: Bread; Baking
  Powder Bread)
1 pt. refried beans
1 c. grated Jack cheese (4 oz.)
¼ c. chopped yellow onion

2 Jalapeño peppers, stemmed
  and seeded (opt.)
1 ½ Guacamole Sauce (see
  Chapter: Sauces and Gravies)
⅓ c. Fresh Chile Salsa (see
  Chapter: Sauces and Gravies)

Warm the tortillas so that they are pliable and will roll up easily. The easiest
way to do this is to heat a tortilla in a microwave for about 10 seconds.
Spread ½ cup of the refried beans down the center of a tortilla. Sprinkle
¼ cup of the Jack cheese over the beans. Spread 1 tablespoon of the
chopped onion over the beans. If you would like to use the Jalapeño
peppers, cut each pepper in half lengthwise and cut each half into three
strips. Place 3 strips of Jalapeño along the edge of the refried beans and
roll up the tortilla. You can heat the burrito in a microwave oven on high
power for about 20 seconds if necessary. Place the burrito on a plate with
the seam side down. Spoon about ⅓ cup Guacamole Sauce over the
burrito and top with 1 heaping tablespoon of Fresh Chili Salsa. Repeat for
remaining burritos.

MEXICAN BEANS AND RICE
(Makes 4 servings)

Mexican Red Rice (see Chapter:
  Side Dishes) about 1 qt.
2 c. cooked whole pinto beans
½ tsp. hickory salt (opt.)
Chile Colorado Sauce (see
  Chapter: Sauces and Gravies)

1 c. freshly grated cheddar
  cheese (4 oz.)
Fresh Chile Salsa (see Chapter:
  Sauces and Gravies)

Make the Mexican Red Rice first. Place the pinto beans in a 1-quart
saucepan and stir in the (optional) hickory salt. Place over medium heat
and cook until beans come to a gentle simmer. Keep warm until ready to
serve. To serve, place 1 cup of rice in a mound on a plate. Make a small
well in the center and add ½ cup of whole pinto beans. Pour a generous
amount of Chili Colorado Sauce over everything. Sprinkle about ¼ cup
grated cheddar cheese over the top and serve. If you like, you can use
Fresh Chili Salsa (see Chapter: Sauces and Gravies) in place of the Chili
Colorado Sauce. This is usually served with a salad and tortillas on the side.

Note: One variation of this meal is to serve Pinto Beans With Jalapeño
Peppers (see Chapter: Side Dishes) in place of the whole pinto beans.
You can also use Chili With Tofu (see Chapter: Tofu) in place of the pinto
beans and omit the Chile Colorado Sauce.

CHEESE ENCHILADAS
(Makes 6 Enchiladas)

ENCHILADA SAUCE

2 Tbs. olive oil
¼ c. minced yellow onion
1½ Tbs. all-purpose flour
2 tsp. chili powder

¾ tsp. salt
¼ tsp. cumin
¼ tsp. garlic powder
1½ c. water

In a 1-quart saucepan, cook and stir the onion in the olive oil until translucent. Stir in the flour, chili powder, salt, cumin, and garlic powder. Continue to stir until the mixture begins to bubble. Slowly add the water. Beat with a whisk as sauce thickens and simmer for about 10 minutes, stirring occasionally. Set aside until ready to use.

PREPARING THE ENCHILADAS

Enchilada Sauce (see above)
6 corn tortillas
Vegetable oil
8 oz. grated jack cheese (2 c.
  lightly packed)
4 oz. grated mozzarella cheese --
  (1 c. lightly packed)

6 Tbs. (¼ c. + 2 Tbs.) minced
  yellow onion
2 oz. grated cheddar cheese ---
  (½ c. lightly packed)
⅓ c. sour cream
2 Tbs. chopped green onion tops

Prepare the enchilada sauce. Heat a small amount of oil in a medium frying pan over medium heat. Using tongs, cook corn tortillas just long enough to make them pliable, about 5 seconds on each side. Drain on paper towel. Spread ½-cup of the enchilada sauce evenly over the bottom of an 8-inch square baking dish. Mix the jack and mozzarella cheeses together. To assemble, place a tortilla on a flat surface or a plate. Spread 2 ounces (½ cup) of the jack cheese mix and 1 tablespoon minced yellow onion down the center of the tortilla and roll up. Place the enchilada in the 8-inch square baking dish with the seam side down. Continue until all of the ingredients have been used. Arrange the enchiladas so that 5 of them are parallel to each other and the sixth is perpendicular to the others at the end. Place the enchiladas in a preheated 350° oven for 10 minutes. Spread all of the enchilada sauce evenly over the enchiladas. Sprinkle the grated cheddar cheese over the sauce. Return to the oven for an additional 10 minutes. Place a dollop of sour cream and some chopped green onion on top of each enchilada when serving.

Note: You will need an 8-inch square baking dish for this recipe. To make 12 enchiladas, double this recipe and use a 13 x 9 x 2-inch baking dish.

240812-16

LARGE GUACAMOLE TOSTADO
(Makes 4 servings)

TOSTADO SAUCE

1 (8 oz.) can tomato sauce
¼ cup taco sauce

1 tsp. cornstarch dissolved in ---
1 tsp. water

Prepare the Tostado Sauce ahead of time so that it can be chilled before serving. In a 1-quart saucepan combine the tomato sauce, taco sauce, and cornstarch mixture. Stir over medium heat until sauce begins to simmer. Remove from heat and chill before making tostado.

GUACAMOLE

3 lrg. avocados, about 8 oz. each
2 tsp. lime juice
⅓ c. sour cream

¼ tsp. garlic salt
⅛ tsp. salt

Pit, peel, and mash the avocados in a medium bowl. Stir in the lime juice, sour cream, garlic salt, and salt. Taste and add more salt if necessary. Cover with plastic wrap and store in refrigerator until ready to use.

DIRECTIONS FOR ASSEMBLING TOSTADO

4 corn tortillas, fried until crisp
1 (15 oz.) can refried beans or ---
   1 ½ c. New Mexico Refried
   Beans (see Chapter: Side
   Dishes)
Tostado Sauce (see above)

Guacamole from 3 avocados, (see
   above)
2 sm. heads lettuce (about 2 lb.)
¼ lb. grated cheddar cheese ----
   (1 c. lightly packed)
4 lrg. pitted black olives

Prepare the Tostado Sauce, Guacamole, and crisp tortillas in advance. The refried beans should be heated until they are warm but not hot. Wash the lettuce and drain. Slice with a sharp knife into ⅛ to ¼-inch thick shreds. There should be 6 to 8 cups of shredded lettuce. The lettuce works best when it is from a solid head. To assemble a tostado, place a tortilla on a dinner plate. Spread ⅓ cup refried beans evenly over the tortilla. Spread about 1 tablespoon of Tostado Sauce over beans. Now put 1 ½ cups of shredded lettuce (about ¼ pound) on top. Distribute the lettuce evenly over the tortilla. Carefully spread about ⅓ cup of Guacamole over the lettuce. Pour 2 more tablespoons of Tostado Sauce over the Guacamole. Sprinkle ¼ cup grated cheddar cheese over the guacamole and finish by putting a pitted black olive on top in the center.

Note: Please notice that this recipe is for LARGE guacamole tostados. This tostado will take up a whole plate when completed. A side dish of Mexican rice (see Chapter: Side dishes) is all you need to make this a complete meal. For a truly decadent and diet blasting tostado, a bed of Fritos Scoops™ (large Fritos™) may be used in place of the crisp corn tortillas.

TAQUITOS WITH GUACAMOLE SAUCE
(Makes 24 taquitos or 4 to 6 servings)

TAQUITO FILLING

1 (8 oz.) pkg. MorningStar
  Farms® Original Sausage
  Patties (6 patties)
½ tsp. cumin
½ tsp. garlic powder

2 tsp. chili powder
2 tsp. paprika
1 egg, lightly beaten
2 tsp. vital wheat gluten flour

To make the filling, thaw or defrost the Morning Star Farms® Sausage Patties. Crumble in a large bowl with a fork or pastry blender. There should be about 1 ½ cups of crumbled sausage when done. Add the cumin, garlic powder, chili powder, and paprika. Mix well until the spices are blended into the crumbled sausage. Stir in the beaten egg and vital wheat gluten flour.

FRYING TAQUITOS

1 ½ c. Guacamole Sauce (see
  Chapter: Sauces and Gravies)

24 corn tortillas
Oil for frying

Prepare the Guacamole Sauce before you start to cook the taquitos. Use a set of tongs to work with the tortillas. Trim about ½-inch off of the edge of one tortilla. Trim another ½-inch piece off of the tortilla opposite to and parallel to the first cut. Cook each tortilla in a small amount of oil in a frying pan over medium heat just long enough so that it becomes pliable and can be rolled up without breaking, about 10 seconds. Place on a plate covered with paper towel in order to absorb as much of the oil as possible. Place a small amount of filling, about 1 tablespoon, along one curved edge of the tortilla. Spread the filling out evenly along the edge. Roll the tortilla up and hold its shape with the long handled tongs. If you do not have tongs, then a toothpick can be used to hold the taquito closed while it is being cooked. Place in a small frying pan over medium-high heat that has about ¼-inch of oil in it. Hold the taquito in place in the hot oil while it cooks until you can let go of it without it coming undone. Fry until lightly browned on the bottom. Turn and cook on the other side until it too is lightly browned. Remove from pan and place on paper towel to drain. You can start to work on the next taquito while the first one is frying. With a little practice you may be able to cook three or four at a time. When the taquitos are done draining, put in an oven-proof dish and keep warm until ready to serve. To serve, put 4 to 6 taquitos on a plate and spread Guacamole Sauce on top.

Note: MorningStar Farms® products can be found in the freezer section of most large grocery stores. TVP® (textured vegetable protein) can be used in place of the sausage patties. You will need about ¾ cup of dried TVP®. See recipe in the TVP section of this chapter for instructions on how to reconstitute TVP®. Long handled tongs will be very helpful when frying the taquitos.

240812-16

CHILES RELLENOS
(Makes 4 servings)

CHILES RELLENOS SAUCE

1 Tbs. olive oil
¼ c. minced yellow onion
1 clove garlic, minced
¾ c. tomato sauce

¼ c. tomato juice
¼ c. red taco sauce
¼ tsp. sugar
⅛ tsp. salt

In a 1-quart saucepan over medium heat, cook and stir the olive oil, onion, and garlic together until onion is translucent, about 5 minutes. Add the tomato sauce, tomato juice, red taco sauce, sugar, and salt. Simmer gently for about 10 minutes. Keep warm until ready to serve.

BATTER

⅔ c. all-purpose flour
1 egg, lightly beaten
¼ tsp. salt

¼ tsp. garlic powder
⅜ c. water (¼ c. + 2 Tbs.)

In a large bowl combine flour, egg, salt, and garlic powder. Slowly stir in water to make a thick batter.

PREPARING STUFFED CHILES

4 oz. freshly grated jack cheese
(1 c. lightly packed)
2 oz. freshly grated mozzarella
cheese (½ c. lightly packed)
4 lrg. whole green Ortega® chiles
(4 to 5 inches long)

Oil about ¼ in. deep in frying pan
Chiles Rellenos Sauce from
above

In a large bowl combine the jack and mozzarella cheese and mix well. Stuff the chiles with the grated cheese. A chopstick may be helpful here to get the cheese all of the way to the end of the chiles. Heat oil over medium-high heat to 350° for frying. Place a stuffed green chili in the bowl of batter and cover thoroughly. Lift out gently with a flat wire whisk, fork, or spatula and place in the hot oil. Fry until golden brown on the first side and then turn. Long handled tongs are helpful in handling the chiles in hot oil. Remove from oil when the second side is lightly brown. This usually takes 4 to 5 minutes on each side. Drain on paper towel and keep warm until ready to serve. Repeat process for remaining 3 chiles. Serve each chile relleno covered in a generous amount of Chiles Rellenos Sauce from above.

AMERICAN GRUEL
(Makes 3 to 4 servings)

COOKING THE BARLEY

1 c. pearl barley (½ lb.)   ½ tsp. salt
2 ½ c. water

Rinse and drain the barley. Place in a 3-quart saucepan with 2½ cups water and ½ teaspoon salt. Bring to a hard boil, reduce heat, and simmer for 45 minutes. Add more water if necessary. Set aside until ready to use.

PREPARING THE VEGETABLES

1 ½ c. broccoli or cauliflower
  florets, cooked
1 c. sliced carrots, cooked
½ c. frozen whole kernel corn,
  cooked
2 Tbs. peanut oil
1 ½ c. yellow onion, sliced top to
  bottom into strips ½-inch wide

1 c. zucchini sliced crosswise, ---
  ¼-inch thick
⅔ c. sliced celery
½ c. diced bell pepper, any color
  (½-inch dice)
1 (10¾ oz.) can cream of celery
  soup
½ c. water

Cook and stir the onion, zucchini, celery, and bell pepper in a wok or a 2-quart saucepan with the 2 tablespoons of oil. Cook until onions are translucent and vegetables are tender, 5 to 6 minutes. Stir the cream of celery soup and ½ cup water into the barley in the 3-quart saucepan. Add all of the cooked vegetables and mix together until well blended. Reheat over medium heat until the gruel is heated through. Serve.

VARIATIONS

½ c. brown rice
½ c. snow peas
1 c. Brussels sprouts, cooked
  and cut in half
1 c. fresh asparagus, cut into ---
  2-in. pieces, cooked

1 c. green beans cut into 1-in.
  pieces, cooked
½ c. frozen green peas, cooked
½ c. peeled and diced turnips,
  cooked (½-inch dice)

The brown rice can be used in place of ½ cup of the barley. Rinse and cook the two grains together. The snow peas can be cooked in the oil with the onions. The remaining vegetables should be cooked separately and drained before adding to the gruel. This is just a partial list. As noted below, you can use whatever vegetables you have on hand. Some people even add (gasp!) cooked okra.

Note: This recipe was inspired by the gruel that is served in Eastern Buddhist monasteries. It is a one dish meal which may be a very, very, distant cousin to the Asian gruel which obviously does not use Cream of Celery Soup. In Asia, gruel is frequently a thin barley soup that has whatever vegetables happen to be available added to the soup.

SAUTÉED VEGETABLES ON RICE
(Makes 4 servings)

PREPARING THE RICE AND SOME OF THE VEGETABLES

1 ½ c. uncooked long grain rice
5 ½ c. water, divided (4 c. + 1 ½ c.)
1 ½ c. green beans cut into 2-in.
  pieces

2 c. broccoli florets
1 ½ c. sliced carrots

Cook the rice according to the package directions and keep warm until ready to serve. In a 2-quart saucepan bring 4 cups water to a boil. Add the green beans and return to a low boil. Cook beans for a total of 8 minutes. Remove beans with a slotted spoon and set aside. Return the water to a boil and add the broccoli. Cook for exactly 3 minutes. Remove the broccoli with a slotted spoon and set aside. Place the sliced carrots in a 1-quart saucepan and add 1 ½ cups water. Bring to a boil and simmer for 10 minutes or until tender. Drain the carrots and reserve the carrot stock. Add enough of the bean water to the carrot stock to make a total of 1 ⅓ cups of carrot stock that will be used below.

BRINGING EVERYTHING TOGETHER

2 Tbs. peanut oil
2 c. sliced yellow onion, cut from
  top to bottom
1 c. sliced celery
2 c. sliced zucchini
1 ½ c. asparagus spears cut into
  2-inch pieces (opt.)

1 tsp. onion powder
½ tsp. salt
½ tsp. garlic powder
¼ tsp. sugar
2 Tbs. cornstarch dissolved in ---
  2 Tbs. water.

Add the peanut oil to a wok over medium heat. Add the onion, celery, zucchini, and asparagus. Cook and stir over medium-high heat for about 5 minutes. Add the onion powder, salt, garlic powder, and ⅔ cup of the carrot stock that has been set aside. Continue to cook for about 4 more minutes. Add the cooked green beans, carrots, and another ⅔ cup of the carrot stock. Cook and stir for about 1 minute. Add the cornstarch solution and stir until liquid thickens and begins to boil. Quickly stir in the cooked broccoli and serve. To serve place 1 cup of cooked rice on a plate and spoon vegetables over the rice. For a variation, the vegetables can be served over pan fried noodles (see Chapter: Side Dishes) in place of the rice.

Note: You will need a wok for this recipe. A large frying pan will do in a pinch. Some of the vegetables are precooked so that everything is tender when served. The amounts of the vegetables are approximate, depending on what is available. You can use cauliflower florets boiled for 5 minutes in place of the broccoli. You can also add some snow peas when you cook the onions, etc.

JAPANESE VEGETABLE TEMPURA
(Makes 4 to 6 servings)

TEMPURA DIPPING SAUCE

1⅓ c. water
⅓ c. soy sauce
½ sheet roasted seaweed
  (Sushinori) torn into pieces
1 tsp. olive oil

2 green onions cut into 2-inch
  pieces
1 tsp. sugar
3 shakes Shichimi powder (opt.)
  or pinch hot pepper flakes

Prepare this dipping sauce ahead of time so that the flavors have a chance to blend together. In a 1-quart saucepan combine 1 ⅓ cups water, the soy sauce, onion soup mix, roasted seaweed, olive oil, green onion stems, sugar, optional Shichimi powder, and dried pepper flakes. Simmer for about 5 minutes. Strain the sauce through a tea strainer. Keep warm until serving time. This sauce is used for dipping the vegetables when eating. NOTE: Shichimi is a red pepper seasoning that comes in a small bottle with a hole in the top that is used as a shaker. This is why the directions specify "3 shakes". Since it is generally found at Japanese grocery stores, it may be difficult to find at your local market.

BATTER FOR FRYING

1 c. cake flour
2 Tbs. cornstarch
1 tsp. baking powder

1 egg white
¾ c. water

In a large bowl mix together the cake flour, cornstarch, baking powder, and egg white. Quickly stir in the water to make a medium batter. Be careful not to overmix the batter. The batter will be lumpy.

RICE AND VEGETABLE PREPARATION

2 c. uncooked medium grain rice
¼ lb. cauliflower florets cut into --
  2 in. pieces, about 1 c.
¼ lb. green beans, in 3-inch
  pieces
1 small sweet potato
12 fresh button mushrooms,
  about 1-inch in diameter

1 small bundle curled parsley
Green onion, cut into 3-inch
  pieces
Bell pepper, diced into 1 ½-inch
  pieces
Yellow onion, sliced into rings ---
  ½-inch thick
Oil for frying

Cook the rice according to the package directions and keep warm until ready to serve. Fill a 2-quart saucepan with 1 quart of water and bring to a boil. Add the cauliflower florets and boil for 3 minutes. Remove the florets with a slotted spoon and drain. Return the water to a boil and add the green beans. Cook the green beans for 5 minutes. Remove from the water and drain. Peel the sweet potato and slice into rounds ¼-inch thick that are no more than 2-inches across. Cut the parsley into small bundles that

(continued)

are 1 ½ to 2-inches across. To fry the vegetables, dip each piece into the batter and then fry in 350° oil for 1 to 2 minutes or until very lightly browned. Drain on paper towel and keep warm. Cook enough pieces of vegetables so that each person can have 2 to 3 pieces of each different vegetable.

HOW TO SERVE

To serve, place the tempura vegetables on a small plate for each person along with a bowl of rice and a small dish with dipping sauce. To eat, dip a piece of vegetable in the dipping sauce and hold it over the rice to catch any dripping sauce before you eat the fried vegetable.

Note: A deep fryer makes preparation easier. If you do not have a deep fryer, use a frying pan over medium-high heat or an electric skillet set at 350° with oil ½ to ¾-inch deep.

VEGETABLE CHOW MEIN
(Makes 4 servings)

NOODLE AND VEGETABLE PREPARATION

2 (6 oz.) pkg. dried chow mein
  noodles (chuka soba)
¼ lb. broccoli florets (2 c.) cut
  into 2-inch pieces
¼ lb. snow peas (1 ½ c.)

1 (8 oz.) bag fresh mung bean
  sprouts (3 c.)
1 lrg. yellow onion (8 oz.)
½ c. thinly sliced celery (1 stalk)

Cook the noodles according to package directions, drain, and set aside. Precook broccoli florets 2 minutes in boiling, salted, water. Drain and set aside. Remove tips and strings from snow peas. Rinse and drain mung bean sprouts. Peel yellow onion and cut in half from top to bottom. Lay each onion-half flat on a cutting board and slice from top to bottom into slices ¼-inch thick. There should be 1 ½ cups of prepared onion.

COOKING THE CHOW MEIN

1 Tbs. finely minced fresh ginger
2 Tbs. peanut oil
½ tsp. garlic salt
½ tsp. sugar
¼ tsp. onion powder

dash white pepper
¾ c. water
1 Tbs. cornstarch dissolved in --
  1 Tbs. water.
1 Tbs. soy sauce

Heat the peanut oil in a warm wok over medium-high heat and add the minced ginger. Cook and stir for 10 seconds, just long enough to season the oil. Add the snow peas, sliced yellow onion, and sliced celery. Cook and stir the vegetables for 3 minutes. Add the bean sprouts, garlic salt, sugar, onion powder, and white pepper. Add the ¾ cup water to steam the vegetables slightly. Continue cooking for 2 minutes. Add the cornstarch mixture and stir until water in pan is thickened. Stir in the cooked broccoli, noodles, and soy sauce. Cook for 1 more minute to heat through and serve.

STIR FRIED BOK CHOY
(Makes about 4 servings)

PREPARATIONS

1 ½ c. uncooked white rice
2 bundles saifun bean threads
1 lrg. head bok choy, about 2 lb.

1 lrg. yellow onion, about ¾ lb.
½ lrg. red bell pepper
2 lrg. stalks celery

Prepare the white rice according to the package directions. Keep warm until ready to serve. You should have about 4 cups cooked rice when done. Place the two bundles of saifun bean threads in a large bowl. Cover with a generous amount of warm water. Cover bowl with a plate and let stand for 15 to 20 minutes. Drain the noodles and place on a cutting board. Cut through the noodles once or twice and reserve. Don't overdo it. You just want to shorten them slightly so that they are not too long. Wash and drain the bok choy. Cut the green leaves from the white stems and set aside. Cut the stems crosswise into 1-inch pieces. Cut the green leaves in half lengthwise. Fold over and cut crosswise into strips about 2 inches wide. Keep the stems and leaves separate. There should be 10 cups (or 1 ½ lb.) of prepared bok choy when done. Peel the onion and cut from top to bottom into pieces ½ inch wide. Wash the bell pepper, drain, and remove the stem and seeds. Cut into strips 2 ½ inches long and ½ inch wide. Wash the stalks of celery and drain. Lay flat on a cutting board and cut across the stems at an angle, Chinese style.

BRINGING EVERYTHING TOGETHER

1 Tbs. peanut oil
1 tsp. freshly grated ginger
2 tsp. imitation chicken
   seasoning (opt.)

1 tsp. sugar
½ tsp. salt
½ tsp. garlic powder
⅔ c. water or vegetable stock

Heat the wok over medium-high heat for 15 to 20 seconds. Drizzle the peanut oil around the edge of the wok so that it runs down the sides of the pan. Add the grated ginger and cook for about 10 seconds, just long enough to flavor the oil. Add the bok choy stems, onion, and celery. Cook for 3 minutes while stirring constantly. Add the bok choy greens, optional imitation chicken seasoning, sugar, salt, and garlic powder. Cook for another minute or two. Add about ⅔ cup water or stock and the reserved bean threads. Continue cooking for an additional 3 to 4 minutes or until the bok choy is tender and the liquid has cooked down. Serve over white rice.

Note: Dynasty® brand saifun bean threads (sometimes called cellophane noodles) are usually sold in 5.29 oz. (150 gr.) packages. Each package has three bundles of noodles. You will need two bundles for this recipe. If you omit the bean threads, you can serve the bok choy over pan fried noodles. Bok choy can also be spelled pak choy, pak choi, or bok choi. It's all the same.

240812-16

VEGETABLE CORNISH PASTY
(Makes 4 pasties)

PASTRY FOR PASTIES

1 ½ c. all-purpose flour
⅔ c. vegetable shortening

½ tsp. salt
¼ c. cold water

In a large bowl combine the flour, vegetable shortening, and salt. Cut the shortening into the flour with a pastry blender until mixture resembles fine crumbs. Stir in the cold water with a fork. Turn out onto a lightly floured surface and knead a few times until the dough is soft and forms a smooth ball of dough. Cut into 4 equal size pieces.

FILLING AND BAKING PASTIES

4 MorningStar® Sausage Patties
1 Tbs. vegetable oil
¾ c. diced potato
¾ c. diced yellow onion
¾ c. diced carrot

½ c. diced turnip
1 tsp. salt
¼ tsp. black pepper
1 egg, lightly beaten

In a small frying pan cook the sausage patties in the vegetable oil until lightly browned on each side. Chop into ½-inch pieces and set aside. When preparing the vegetables, dice into ¼-inch pieces. In a large bowl combine the cooked sausage patties, diced potato, yellow onion, carrot, turnip, salt, and pepper. Mix the filling together until well blended and set aside. Roll each piece of pastry dough into a circle about 8 inches in diameter. Place ¾ cup of the filling on half of a circle of pastry dough. Wet the edge of the pastry dough with water. Fold the dough over the filling to form a "D" shape. Press the edge with a fork to seal. Repeat for remaining circles of dough. Place the pasties on a lightly greased large cookie sheet or a cookie sheet lined with parchment paper. Brush the tops of the pasties with beaten egg. Poke the top of each pasty 3 or 4 times with a fork to allow steam to escape while baking. Bake in a preheated 400° oven for 40 minutes.

Note: Pasties are essentially a large turnover stuffed with meat and vegetables instead of fruit. Originally from Cornwall, they can now be found all over Great Britain. They are pronounced pasties as in "fast". These are strictly intended to be finger food.

Textured Vegetable Protein

HOW TO RECONSTITUTE TEXTURED VEGETABLE PROTEIN
(Makes about 1 ½ cups)

1 c. TVP® granules, Textured
  Vegetable Protein (about 3 oz.)
1 c. hot water

1 tsp. Kitchen Bouquet®
  Seasoning Sauce

Place the TVP® in a medium bowl. Add the Kitchen Bouquet® Seasoning Sauce to the hot water and stir into the TVP® until well blended. Let stand for 10 minutes. Line the colander with the pressing cloth and place in a sink or a very large bowl. Pour the TVP® into the cloth lined colander. Join the four corners of the cloth together over the colander and twist to close. Twist and mash the TVP® to remove as much of the extra liquid as possible. Discard any water that is pressed from the TVP®. Place the TVP® in a bowl and fluff with a fork. The TVP® is now ready to use.

Note: You will need a metal colander, a sturdy pressing cloth, and a potato masher. TVP® is a soybean product that is used as a meat substitute in vegetarian recipes. The most common form, which we use exclusively in this book, is plain, granular, unflavored, and uncolored. Bob's Red Mill® brand can be found online and at most markets.

BURGERS WITH TEXTURED VEGETABLE PROTEIN
(Makes 5 patties)

1 c. TVP® granules, reconstituted
  (see previous recipe)
2 Tbs. all-purpose flour
2 Tbs. soy flour
1 Tbs. Vital Wheat Gluten Flour
1 Tbs. seasoned bread crumbs
½ tsp. powdered cumin

¼ tsp. salt
¼ tsp. onion powder
⅛ tsp. black pepper
pinch garlic powder
1 egg beaten with ¼ c. water
olive oil

Reconstitute the TVP® by following the instructions in the previous recipe. Empty the reconstituted TVP® back into the bowl. Add the all-purpose flour, soy flour, vital wheat gluten flour, bread crumbs, cumin, salt, onion powder, black pepper, and garlic powder. Mix together until well blended. Stir in the beaten egg and water. Place a scant ⅓ cup of mix on a small plate or saucer. Flatten into a patty about 3 ½ inches in diameter. Gently lift off of the plate with a spatula and fry in an electric skillet, lightly coated with olive oil, set at 350°. If using a frying pan, cook over medium-high heat. Fry until dark brown in color, about 4 to 5 minutes on each side.

240812-16

MEATLOAF WITH TEXTURED VEGETABLE PROTEIN
(Makes one small meatloaf)

1 c. TVP® granules, reconstituted
  (see earlier recipe)
¼ c. minced yellow onion
½ c. finely crushed saltine
  crackers or matzo meal
½ c. grated carrot
2 Tbs. all-purpose flour

1 tsp. salt
½ tsp. rubbed sage
¼ tsp. black pepper
¼ tsp. onion powder
1 Tbs. ketchup
2 eggs beaten with 1 Tbs. water
olive oil

Reconstitute the TVP® according to the directions in the earlier recipe "How To Reconstitute TVP®." Return the TVP to the bowl and add the yellow onion, crushed saltine crackers, grated carrot, flour, salt, rubbed sage, black pepper, and onion powder. Mix together until well blended. Stir in the 1 tablespoon ketchup, beaten eggs and water and mix well. Coat the 5½ x 3 x 2-inch loaf pan with olive oil. Firmly pack the TVP® mixture into the loaf pan. Coat the bottom of the 11 x 7 x 1½-inch baking pan with olive oil. Turn the the small pan with the TVP upside down in the larger pan. Tap the small pan to release the loaf if needed. You can adjust the shape of the loaf with your hands if necessary. Place the TVP® loaf in a preheated 350° oven and bake for 40 minutes. Begin to prepare the barbecue sauce as soon as the meatloaf is in the oven. Gently pour the barbecue sauce over the loaf after the 40 minutes of baking. After 10 more minutes of baking, take a spoon and ladle some of the barbecue sauce from the bottom of the pan over the top of the meatloaf. Bake for an additional 10 minutes for a total baking time of 1 hour. Remove the pan from the oven after the 1 hour and let stand for about 5 minutes before serving. This allows the loaf to set up slightly before you cut into it. Serve the meatloaf cut into slices. Pour extra sauce from the bottom of the pan over each serving of the TVP® loaf. Makes 6 to 8 servings.

BARBECUE SAUCE

¼ c. finely chopped yellow onion
1 Tbs. olive oil
1½ Tbs. brown sugar
½ c. tomato sauce
¼ c. ketchup

¾ c. water
½ tsp. dry mustard
¼ tsp. chili powder
¼ tsp. hickory salt (opt.)

In a 1-quart saucepan cook the onion in the olive oil over medium heat until translucent, about 5 minutes. Add the brown sugar, tomato sauce, ketchup, water, dry mustard, chili powder, and optional hickory salt. Heat to boiling and simmer for 3 minutes. Set aside until ready to use.

Note: You will need an 11 x 7 x 1½-inch baking pan for this recipe. You will also need a 5½ x 3 x 2-inch loaf pan to use as a mold for the meatloaf. It will take about 16 saltine crackers to make ½ cup of finely crushed crackers.

TAMALES WITH TEXTURED VEGETABLE PROTEIN
(Makes 16 to 18 Tamales)

CORN HUSKS

Chili Colorado Sauce (see
Chapter: Sauces and Gravies)

2 to 3 oz. dried corn husks, ---
about 36

In a large bowl cover the corn husks with cold water and place a plate on top to keep them submerged. Soak the husks in water for 1 hour. Drain husks just before you begin to assemble tamales. Leftover husks can be dried and used later. Prepare the Chili Colorado Sauce ahead of time and set aside until ready to serve. Reheat the sauce just before serving,

FILLING

1 c. TVP® granules, reconstituted
(see earlier recipe)
1 Tbs. olive oil
½ c. finely chopped yellow onion
1 clove garlic, minced
1 (4 oz. can) diced green chiles

1 ½ tsp. chili powder
½ tsp. cumin
¼ tsp. garlic salt
⅓ c. tomato sauce
½ tsp. sugar

Reconstitute the TVP® according to the directions in the earlier recipe "How To Reconstitute TVP®." Place the TVP® in a 2-quart saucepan. In a small frying pan, cook and stir the yellow onion, minced garlic, and diced green chiles in the olive oil until the onion is translucent, about 5 minutes. When done, stir into the 2-quart saucepan with the TVP®. Add the chili powder, cumin, garlic salt, tomato sauce, and sugar to the TVP®. Stir and cook over medium heat for 2 to 3 minutes to let the flavors blend. Set aside until ready to make tamales.

MASA DOUGH

2 c. masa harina
1 tsp. baking powder
½ tsp. salt

½ c. shortening
1 ⅓ c. water.

In a large bowl combine the masa, baking powder, salt, and shortening. Using a pastry blender cut the shortening into the masa until the mixture resembles fine crumbs. Slowly stir in the water to make a moist dough.

HOW TO ASSEMBLE, COOK, AND SERVE THE TAMALES

Sour cream

Place a corn husk that is 6 inches wide on a plate. If a corn husk is too narrow, then overlap with another 1 or 2 husks to make it the right width. Place 2 heaping tablespoons of masa dough in the center of the corn

(continued)

husk. Spread the masa dough out until it is about 4 inches square. Spread a level tablespoon of TVP® filling down the center of the masa dough. Roll the dough over to cover the filling in masa. Wrap the corn husk around the masa and fold over the ends to seal closed. Place the tamale upright in the steamer basket. Continue until the basket is full. Place 1 quart of water in the bottom of the steamer. Place the basket in the steamer and cover. Steam the tamales over gently boiling water for 1 hour. Check the water level once or twice and add more water if necessary. To serve, remove the corn husks from around the tamales. Place 2 to 3 tamales on a plate. Spoon Chili Colorado Sauce over tamales and put a dollop of sour cream on top of each serving.

Note: You will need a steamer to cook the tamales. This is a time consuming recipe that is easier to handle when you have extra help. In spite of this, after you have eaten a few tamales, you may wish that you had made more. Extra tamales can be stored in the freezer for 1 to 2 months. To save time you can use enchilada sauce in place of the Chili Colorado Sauce.

CHILI WITHOUT BEANS
(Makes 6 cups)

1 ½ c. TVP® granules
3 Tbs. olive oil
1 c. diced yellow onion (¼-inch
   pieces)
1 clove garlic, minced
2 (15 oz.) cans tomato sauce ---
   (3 ½ c.)
3 c. water or vegetable stock
2 Tbs. chili powder

1 ½ tsp. salt
1 ½ tsp. sugar
1 tsp. paprika
½ tsp. cumin
½ tsp. dried oregano leaves,
   crushed
¼ tsp. garlic powder
¼ tsp. black pepper

In a 3-quart saucepan, cook and stir over medium heat the diced onion in the olive oil until translucent, about 5 to 10 minutes. Add the minced garlic and cook for another minute or two. Stir in the tomato sauce and water or vegetable stock. Add the 1 ½ cups TVP® granules and mix well. Stir in the chili powder, salt, sugar, paprika, cumin, dried oregano, garlic powder, and black pepper. Cook and stir over medium-high heat until chili comes to a simmer. Reduce heat so that chili will continue to simmer for an additional 10 to 15 minutes. Keep warm until ready to serve.

Note: Unlike the other TVP® recipes in this section, you will not need to reconstitute the TVP® before adding to the chili. It will absorb moisture and flavor when it is added to the saucepan. Leftover chili freezes well.

SWEDISH MEATBALLS WITH TEXTURED VEGETABLE PROTEIN
(Makes 12 meatballs or 4 servings)

MEATBALLS

1 c. TVP® granules, reconstituted
 (see earlier recipe)
2 slices bread
2 eggs, lightly beaten
2 Tbs. milk
4 Tbs. butter, divided --- (1 Tbs. +
 3 Tbs.)

1 c. finely chopped yellow onion
2 Tbs. all-purpose flour
½ tsp. salt
¼ tsp. ground black pepper
¼ tsp. nutmeg
¼ tsp. allspice

Reconstitute the TVP® according to the directions in the earlier recipe "How To Reconstitute TVP®." Place the TVP® in a large bowl. Chop the bread into small pieces and add it to the TVP®. In a small bowl beat together the eggs and milk. Stir the eggs into the TVP® and let stand while cooking the onion. The bread should absorb some moisture before adding the next ingredients. In a small frying pan melt 1 tablespoon of the butter and add the onion. Cook and stir the onion until lightly browned, about 5 minutes. Add the cooked onion to the TVP® in the bowl. Stir in the flour, salt, black pepper, nutmeg, and allspice. Shape a heaping tablespoon of TVP® mixture into a ball. Repeat for all of the mixture and set aside. There should be about 12 meatballs. In a medium frying pan cook the meatballs in the remaining 3 tablespoons butter until lightly browned. Remove from pan and use the pan to prepare the following gravy.

GRAVY

2 Tbs. butter
3 Tbs. all-purpose flour
½ tsp. salt
¼ tsp. ground black pepper

1 vegetable bouillon cube
 dissolved in 2 c. hot water
½ c. sour cream

Place a frying pan over medium heat and add 2 tablespoons butter. Stir in the flour, salt, and pepper and cook until it forms a paste. Slowly stir in the bouillon with a wire whisk. Cook until gravy thickens and begins to boil. Stir in the sour cream and add the meatballs to the gravy. Keep warm while cooking the noodles.

FINAL PREPARATION AND HOW TO SERVE

12 oz. egg noodles

Raspberry jelly (opt.)

Prepare the egg noodles according to the package directions. Place a mound of cooked noodles on a plate for each serving. Put 3 meatballs and a generous amount of gravy over each serving of noodles. Serve with a small amount of optional raspberry jelly on the side.

 240812-16

MEXICAN MEATBALL SOUP ----
ALBONDIGAS SOUP
(Makes 4 large servings)

12 TVP® meatballs (see below)
3 Tbs. olive oil
½ c. chopped yellow onion
1 clove garlic, minced
1 tsp. dried oregano, crushed
2 Tbs. all-purpose flour
1 (15 oz.) can diced tomatoes
6 c. vegetable stock or water
1 ½ c. shredded cabbage

¾ c. diced potato
½ c. diced carrots
½ c. diced turnip
½ c. diced zucchini
½ c. green beans cut into 1-inch pieces
½ c. diced celery
⅓ c. whole kernel corn
1 tsp. salt

In a 4-quart pot combine the 3 tablespoons olive oil, onion, and garlic. Cook and stir over medium heat until onion is translucent, about 5 minutes. Stir in the oregano and flour. Cook for 1 minute and then add the diced tomatoes and vegetable stock. Add the cabbage, potato, carrots, turnip, zucchini, green beans, celery, corn, and salt. Bring to a boil and simmer for 1 to 1½ hours, or until vegetables are tender. Taste and adjust seasoning. Add the meatballs and cook until heated through before serving.

TVP® MEXICAN MEATBALLS (Makes 12 meatballs)

1 c. TVP® granules, reconstituted (see earlier recipe)
2 eggs
1 Tbs. milk
½ c. toasted bread crumbs
¼ c. finely chopped yellow onion
1 (4 oz.) can diced green chiles (½ c.)

2 Tbs. minced Jalapeño pepper
2 tsp. dried oregano, crushed
1 tsp. salt
¼ tsp. black pepper
1 clove garlic, minced
olive oil

Reconstitute the TVP® according to the directions in the earlier recipe "How To Reconstitute TVP®." In a small bowl beat together the eggs and milk. Place the reconstituted TVP® in a large bowl. Add the bread crumbs, beaten eggs, onion, green chiles, Jalapeño pepper, oregano, salt, black pepper, and minced garlic. Stir together until well blended. Use one heaping tablespoon of mix for each meatball. Shape mixture into meatballs. Fry in olive oil in a medium pan over medium heat until evenly browned. Set aside until ready to add to soup.

Note: Start the soup first and prepare the meatballs while the soup is cooking. Vegetables should be cut into 1-inch chunks.

Gluten

FRESH RAW GLUTEN MADE THE OLD FASHIONED WAY
(Makes 12 oz. or 1 ½ cups)

MIXING THE DOUGH

6⅔ c. all-purpose flour (2 lb.)
2 tsp. salt
2 ½ c. water

2 tsp. Kitchen Bouquet®
Browning Sauce

Combine the flour and 2 teaspoons salt in a large bowl. Mix the Kitchen Bouquet® into the water. Make a well in the center of the flour and stir in the water until a stiff dough is formed. Place on a lightly floured surface and knead a few times until the ball of dough sticks together. Wrap in a damp towel and place in a clean bowl to help keep the dough from drying out. Let stand for 20 to 30 minutes. If you can't get to the washing right away, the gluten can rest in the refrigerator for several hours or overnight.

WASHING THE GLUTEN

Place the bowl in a sink. Add enough water to cover the dough. Gently knead and squeeze the dough in the water. Squeeze until you have a long piece of dough. Fold the dough over on itself and squeeze together. Knead the dough by continuing this process of squeezing and folding and squeezing again. The starch will begin to separate from the gluten and cause the water to become milky. When the water becomes thick with starch, drain the water and carefully add fresh. Be careful not to lose any pieces of dough when draining the water. Continue to knead, drain, and add fresh water until you have a solid elastic mass of gluten. If the dough falls apart into small pieces, don't panic! Drain the contents of the bowl through a large fine-mesh strainer. Return the dough from the strainer to the bowl with some fresh water and continue to knead the small pieces of dough together. You may have to repeat this 2 or 3 times before the mass of gluten will stick together in one large lump. Continue to knead, drain and add fresh water until you have a solid mass of gluten. The water should be almost clear. This will take about 20 minutes and cannot be rushed. Place the finished gluten in a bowl and let stand for 10 minutes. Some of the water in the gluten will drain into the bowl. Pour this water off. This fresh gluten can be stored in the refrigerator for up to 48 hours.

Note: Fresh gluten made from all-purpose flour takes longer to make but is more economical than using Vital Wheat Gluten flour (see recipe later in this chapter). Many feel that it has a better texture. Two pounds of all-purpose flour makes enough for about 4 steaks in the recipes later in this chapter.

FRESH RAW GLUTEN MADE FROM WHOLE WHEAT FLOUR
(Makes 12 oz. or 1 ½ cups)

5 ½ c. whole wheat flour (2 lb.)   2 ½ c. water
2 tsp. salt

Combine the whole wheat flour and 2 teaspoons salt in a large bowl. Make a well in the center of the flour and stir in the water. Continue to mix until a stiff dough is formed. Place on a lightly floured surface and knead a few times until all of the flour adheres to the ball of dough. Wrap in a damp dishtowel and place in a clean bowl to help keep the dough from drying out. Let stand for 20 to 30 minutes. If you can't get to the washing right away, the gluten can rest in the refrigerator for several hours or overnight.

WASHING THE GLUTEN

Remove the damp cloth and place the bowl in a sink. Add enough water to cover the dough. Squeeze until you have a long piece of dough. Fold the dough over on itself and squeeze together. Knead the dough by continuing this process of squeezing and folding and squeezing again. The bran, wheat germ, and starch will begin to separate from the gluten and cause the water to become milky. Most of the bran and germ will sink to the bottom of the bowl. When the water becomes thick with starch, pour the water into a large 6 to 8-quart pot. Add about 3 to 4 cups of fresh water to the bowl. Be careful not to lose any pieces of dough when draining the water. Continue to knead, drain, and add fresh water at least two more times until you have a solid elastic mass of gluten. Make sure that you recover all of the rinse water and collect it in the large pot. If the dough falls apart into small pieces, don't panic! Drain the contents of the bowl through a large mesh strainer. Return the contents of the strainer to the bowl with some fresh water and knead the small pieces of dough together. You may have to repeat this 2 or 3 times. The rinse water should eventually be almost clear. This washing of the gluten will take 15 to 20 minutes and cannot be rushed. Some of the bran and germ will remain in the gluten. This fresh gluten can be stored in the refrigerator for up to 48 hours.

COLLECTING AND USING THE BRAN-WATER

The water that was collected in the large pot will contain wheat bran, germ, and starch. Let the water rest for at least 1 hour. This will allow the bran to settle to the bottom of the pot. Pour off as much of the starchy water as possible, through a large wire mesh strainer, without losing any of the bran. Any bran collected in the strainer should be returned to the pot. There should be about 2 cups of bran-water when finished. Use the bran-water to make Special Bran Bread. See the last recipe in Chapter: Breads.

Note: You will need a large bowl for washing the gluten and a 6 to 8-quart pot for saving the rinse water.

FRESH RAW GLUTEN MADE FROM VITAL WHEAT GLUTEN FLOUR
(Makes 12 oz. or 1 ½ cups)

1 c. Vital Wheat Gluten Flour
1 ½ tsp. (½ pkt.) Instant dry yeast
½ tsp salt
½ tsp. onion powder
¼ tsp. garlic powder

¼ tsp. ginger powder
½ tsp. Kitchen Bouquet®
   Browning Sauce
1 c. water

In a large bowl combine the Vital Wheat Gluten Flour, instant dry yeast, salt, onion powder, garlic powder, and ginger powder. Mix together thoroughly, because when you add the water to the gluten later, it will become a solid mass almost immediately. Stir the Kitchen Bouquet® into the water in a measuring cup. Pour the water mixture into the Vital Wheat Gluten and mix well to form a dough. Knead for about one minute to make the dough more elastic. Let the dough rest for 15 to 20 minutes before using.

Note: This is by far the most trouble-free way of preparing fresh gluten. Fresh gluten can be cut into slices to make Fried Gluten Steaks. The active dry yeast adds small air bubbles to the gluten which keeps it from becoming too elastic.

FRIED GLUTEN STEAKS
(Makes 4 steaks)

12 oz. Fresh Raw Gluten ---- (see
  3 previous recipes)
3 Tbs. olive oil, divided (2 Tbs. +
  1 Tbs.)

Salt
Onion powder

Cut the gluten into 4 equal pieces. Place one piece on a large cutting board. Turn the small cutting board upside down and place on top of the gluten. Now press down on the small cutting board to help flatten the gluten into the shape of a steak. The gluten should be ¼ to ⅜-inch thick when done. Repeat for remaining gluten. Put 2 tablespoons olive oil in a warm skillet or frying pan and add the gluten. Fry in an electric skillet at 325° for 6 to 8 minutes or until gluten is light brown on the bottom. If you are using a frying pan, place the pan over a medium-high heat. Lightly sprinkle some salt and onion powder over the gluten in the pan. Turn and repeat for second side. Add the remaining 1 tablespoon of olive oil if pan becomes too dry. Place cooked gluten on paper towel to drain when done.

Note: You will need a large cutting board and a smaller cutting board for pressing the gluten into shape. These fried steaks are the basis for many of the other recipes that follow in this section.

 240812-16

GLUTEN STEAKS WITH BARBECUE SAUCE
(Makes 2 ½ cups sauce for 4 steaks)

4 Fried Gluten Steaks (see
previous recipe)
2 Tbs. olive oil
½ yellow onion, sliced into rings
1 clove garlic, crushed
½ c. brown sugar
1 Tbs. water

2 c. tomato sauce
⅓ c. water
3 Tbs. white wine
1 Tbs. soy sauce
1 Tbs. chili powder
½ tsp. ground cumin
¼ tsp. hickory salt (opt.)

Prepare the gluten steaks ahead of time. In a 2-quart saucepan cook and stir the onion and garlic in olive oil over medium heat until onion is lightly browned. Remove the onion and garlic with a slotted spoon and discard. Stir in the brown sugar. Add 1 tablespoon water and stir until a syrup is formed. Add the tomato sauce, ⅓ cup water, white wine, soy sauce, chili powder, cumin, and optional hickory salt. Bring to a boil and simmer for about 3 minutes. Add the gluten steaks to the saucepan and make sure that they are covered with sauce. Simmer gently for 5 minutes. This allows the gluten to absorb more flavor and moisture. If you have just fried the gluten steaks, you can return the steaks to the frying pan that they were cooked in. Pour the barbecue sauce over the gluten steaks and simmer gently for 5 minutes. Cover and keep warm until ready to serve.

HONEY BARBECUE SAUCE FOR BROILED GLUTEN
(Makes enough for 4 to 6 Fried Gluten Steaks)

4 to 6 Fried Gluten Steaks (see
earlier recipe)
1 Tbs. olive oil
¼ c. finely chopped yellow onion
1 clove garlic, minced
¼ c. honey

1 (8 oz.) can tomato sauce (1 c.)
½ tsp. chili powder
½ tsp. salt
Dash coarse black pepper
2 Tbs. white wine
¼ tsp. liquid smoke

In a 1-quart saucepan, cook and stir the chopped onion in the olive oil over medium heat until onion is translucent, about 5 minutes. Add the minced garlic and continue to cook for 1 minute. Stir in the honey, tomato sauce, chili powder, salt, black pepper, white wine, and liquid smoke. Reduce heat and simmer for 10 minutes or until sauce thickens slightly. Set aside until ready to use. Place gluten steaks in a shallow pan or cookie sheet. Brush a generous amount of Honey Barbecue Sauce on both sides of each gluten steak. Place under a broiler and cook until sauce begins to bubble and turn brown around the edges, about 2 to 3 minutes on each side. Extra sauce can be served on the side as a dipping sauce.

BREADED GLUTEN STEAKS
(Makes 4 servings)

12 oz. Fresh Raw Gluten (from
  one of earlier recipes)
2 Tbs. all-purpose flour
½ c. milk

1 egg, lightly beaten
¾ c. Seasoned Bread Crumbs
  (see Chapter: This and That)
Vegetable oil

Cut the raw gluten into 4 equal pieces. Place one piece on a large cutting board. Turn the small cutting board upside down and place on top of the gluten. Press down on the small cutting board to help flatten the gluten. It should be ¼ to ⅜-inch thick when done. Repeat for remaining gluten. Put the flour in a medium bowl. Slowly stir in the milk until mixed together and smooth. Stir in the beaten egg. Dip each steak in the milk mixture, then dredge in the bread crumbs. Preheat an electric skillet to 350°. You can also use a frying pan over medium-high heat. Fry the coated gluten in a thin layer of vegetable oil until lightly browned, about 3 to 5 minutes on each side. Drain on paper towel and keep warm until ready to serve. Serve with either mushroom gravy, brown gravy, or country gravy (see recipes in Chapter: Sauces and Gravies).

Note: You will need a large cutting board and a smaller cutting board for pressing the gluten into shape.

GLUTEN PARMESAN
(Makes 4 servings)

4 Breaded Gluten Steaks (see
  previous recipe)
1 ½ c. Spaghetti Sauce (see
  Chapter: Sauces and Gravies)
½ tsp. dried oregano

½ tsp. dried sweet basil
¼ tsp. whole anise seed
4 oz. sliced mozzarella cheese
4 Tbs. grated fresh Parmesan
  cheese

Combine the oregano, basil, and anise in a mortar. Crush the herbs with a pestle to form a fine powder. Set the herb mixture aside until ready to use. Place the 4 breaded gluten steaks on a cookie sheet about 1 inch apart. Spread ⅓ cup of Spaghetti Sauce evenly over each steak. There should be 1 to 2 tablespoons of Spaghetti Sauce left over. Place an equal amount of Mozzarella cheese on top of each gluten steak. Spread 1 teaspoon Spaghetti Sauce over the cheese. Sprinkle 1 tablespoon grated Parmesan on top of the thin layer of sauce. And finally, sprinkle a small amount of the crushed herb mixture over the top of each steak. Place the cookie sheet under a broiler and cook until the mozzarella bubbles and turns a light brown around the edges. Serve immediately, preferably with buttered noodles and freshly grated Parmesan cheese.

Note: This is the vegetarian version of veal Parmesan. Canned spaghetti sauce can be used in place of the homemade Spaghetti Sauce.

240812-16

GLUTEN STEAKS WITH ONIONS
(Makes 4 servings)

4 Breaded Gluten Steaks (see
  earlier recipe)
2 lrg. onions (about 1 lb.) peeled
  and sliced into rings
2 Tbs. vegetable oil
1 tsp. paprika

1 tsp. hickory salt (or ½ tsp. salt)
½ tsp. ground black pepper
¼ tsp. onion powder
¼ c. sour cream
¼ c. white wine
2 Tbs. water

Prepare the Breaded Gluten Steaks in oil according to directions in earlier recipe. Remove the steaks from the frying pan but do not clean the pan. Keep gluten warm while cooking onions. Add 2 tablespoons vegetable oil, the onions, and paprika to the oil that is left in the pan. Cook and stir the onions in the pan set at 275° or medium-low until onions are limp but not browned, about 10 minutes. Stir in the hickory salt (or salt), black pepper, and onion powder. Add the sour cream, white wine, and 2 tablespoons water. Simmer for 2 to 3 minutes. Serve over the Breaded Gluten Steaks.

OPEN-FACED HOT GLUTEN SANDWICHES
(Makes 4 servings)

4 Fried Gluten Steaks (see earlier
  recipe)
salt and pepper

Brown Gravy for Gluten (see
  below)
4 slices bread, any variety

Prepare Fried Gluten Steaks according to earlier recipe. Season the steaks with salt and pepper. Prepare the Brown Gravy from below and set aside. Place the gluten steaks in a medium frying pan and pour the gravy over the steaks so that they are completely covered. Heat the steaks gently over medium heat until the gravy begins to simmer. To serve, place one slice of bread on a plate. Place a gluten steak on the slice of bread. When finished, pour any gravy remaining in the pan over the steaks.

BROWN GRAVY FOR GLUTEN SANDWICHES

3 Tbs. vegetable oil
¼ c. finely chopped yellow onion
3 Tbs. all-purpose flour
½ tsp. salt

¼ tsp. crushed sage
2 c. water or vegetable stock
2 Tbs. soy sauce

In a 1-quart saucepan combine the oil and onions. Cook and stir the onions over medium heat until translucent, about 5 minutes. Stir in the flour, salt, and sage to form a paste. Cook until the flour begins to bubble. Slowly add the water or stock and stir with a whisk to remove any lumps. Bring to a gentle boil while stirring occasionally. Remove from heat and cover until ready to use.

CHINESE GREEN BEANS AND GLUTEN
(Makes 4 servings)

2 Fried Gluten Steaks (see earlier
  recipe) cut into ½-inch strips
4 c. cooked rice, approx.
4 c. fresh green beans ---- (about
  1 lb.) cut into 2 to 3-inch pieces
1 qt. water

1 Tbs. peanut oil
½ tsp. onion powder
¼ tsp. garlic powder
⅜ c. (¼ c. + 2 Tbs.) soy sauce
¼ c. cornstarch dissolved in ----
  ¼ c. water

Be sure to make the gluten strips ahead of time. Cook the rice and keep warm until ready to serve. In a 2-quart saucepan bring 1 quart of water to a boil. Add the green beans, return to a gentle boil, and cover. Cook for a total of 8 minutes from the time the beans were put in the water. Drain the beans, reserve 2 cups of the bean stock, and discard the remaining stock. Place a wok over medium heat and add the peanut oil and cooked beans. Cook and stir the beans for about 1 minute. Add the gluten strips, onion powder, and garlic powder. Continue to cook over medium heat for another 1 to 2 minutes to make sure everything is evenly heated through. Add the soy sauce, 2 cups of reserved bean stock, and cornstarch mixture to the wok. Increase heat and stir until liquid thickens and begins to boil. Remove from heat and serve over rice.

Note: You will need to purchase 1 ¼ to 1 ½ pounds green beans.

TERIYAKI GLUTEN STRIPS
(Makes 4 servings)

3 Fried Gluten Steaks (see earlier
  recipe)
½ c. soy sauce
1 c. water
¼ c. sugar
½ tsp. ginger powder

¼ tsp. garlic powder
1 Tbs. Sriracha® Hot Chili Sauce
1 Tbs. peanut oil
1 Tbs. cornstarch dissolved in ---
  1 Tbs. water

Cut the gluten steaks into ½-inch wide strips. In a medium bowl combine the soy sauce, water, sugar, ginger powder, garlic powder, and hot chili sauce. Stir together until well blended and add the gluten strips. Marinate for about 30 minutes. Remove the gluten from the bowl and reserve the marinade. Heat the oil in a medium frying pan and add the marinated gluten. Cook and stir for 5 minutes or until gluten strips start to brown. Add ¼ cup of the marinade to the gluten strips. Cook and stir until all of the liquid has been cooked down. Remove from heat, cover, and keep warm. Reserve the remaining marinade for the following recipe.

Note: In addition to the following recipe you can add teriyaki gluten strips to other Asian meals (Sautéed Vegetables on Rice, Stir Fry Bok Choy, Vegetable Chow Mein, etc.) for added variety and more protein content.

240812-16

CHINESE GREEN BEANS AND TERIYAKI GLUTEN STRIPS
(Makes 4 servings)

PREPARATIONS

Teriyaki Gluten Strips from
  previous recipe
Reserved teriyaki marinade from
  previous recipe

4 c. cooked rice
1 ½ lb. fresh green beans
1 qt. water
½ tsp. salt

Cook the rice ahead of time and keep warm until ready to serve. Wash and drain the green beans. Remove any strings and cut into pieces about 3 inches long. In a 2-quart saucepan bring the 1 quart of water and salt to a boil. Add the green beans and cook for 8 minutes. Begin counting cooking time as soon as the beans are put in the water. Drain the green beans and set aside until ready to use in the next step.

COOKING THE BEANS

1 Tbs. peanut oil
1 Tbs. finely chopped fresh
  ginger

2 Tbs. soy sauce
1 Tbs. cornstarch dissolved in ---
  1 Tbs. water

Place a wok over medium heat and add the peanut oil and fresh ginger. Cook and stir for about 30 seconds, just long enough to season the oil. Add the green beans and 2 tablespoons soy sauce. Continue to cook and stir for 1 minute. Add ¼ cup of the teriyaki marinade reserved from the previous recipe. Continue to cook until all of the liquid has been cooked down and remove from heat. In a 1-quart saucepan combine the remaining teriyaki marinade (there should be about 1 cup) and the cornstarch mixture. Cook and stir until the teriyaki gravy comes to a gentle boil and remove from heat.

HOW TO SERVE

1 Tbs. sesame seeds

To serve, place 1 cup of rice on a plate or in a large bowl. Then place one-fourth of the green beans over the rice. Neatly place some of the teriyaki gluten strips over the beans and pour ¼ cup teriyaki gravy over the gluten. Sprinkle sesame seeds over the top for garnish and serve.

Note: You will need to purchase 1 ½ pounds of fresh green beans for this recipe. There are two versions of this recipe. This version is the most complex of the two and is something that you may want to serve on special occasions. The recipe on the previous page, "Chinese Green Beans and Gluten", is quicker and easier to prepare.

GLUTEN STROGANOFF
(Makes 4 servings)

PREPARATION

3 Fried Gluten Steaks (see earlier recipe)

4 oz. fresh whole mushrooms
1 (12 oz.) pkg. wide noodles

Cut the gluten steaks into ¼-inch wide strips. None of the strips should be more than 3-inches long. Gently rinse off mushrooms and pat dry. Slice mushrooms ¼-inch thick, from top to bottom and measure. There should be 1 ½ cups. Set aside until ready to use. Cook the wide noodles according to the package directions. Keep warm until ready to serve. With careful planning you can cook the noodles while you are cooking the stroganoff.

COOKING THE STROGANOFF

4 Tbs. butter, divided --- (2 Tbs. + 2 Tbs.)
1 c. chopped yellow onion
1 clove garlic, minced
2 Tbs. all-purpose flour

1 ¼ c. vegetable stock or water
½ c. sour cream
2 Tbs. white wine
1 Tbs. ketchup

Melt 2 tablespoons butter in a medium frying pan over medium heat. Add the sliced mushrooms, yellow onion, and minced garlic. Cook and stir until the onions are translucent and the mushrooms are tender, 6 to 8 minutes. Remove the onions and mushrooms from the pan and reserve. Add the flour and remaining 2 tablespoons of butter to the pan. Stir until a paste is formed. Slowly stir in the vegetable stock with a whisk to help remove any lumps in the sauce. Add the sour cream, white wine, and ketchup. Stir together until well blended. Add the gluten strips and let simmer gently for 3 to 5 minutes. Stir in the reserved mushrooms and onions. Remove from heat and serve over the wide noodles.

Tofu

Tofu

In spite of its long history in Asia, tofu has not become readily available in this country until just recently. Tofu has gained so much popularity in recent years that it is now available in most supermarkets in 16-ounce plastic tubs and comes in a variety of styles from silken (soft) to extra firm. Most of the tofu recipes in this chapter can be prepared with tofu from the market.

Homemade Tofu

Making tofu is a little like baking your own bread. Even though it takes a little extra time and can be a bit messy, there is a certain satisfaction in making your own. In addition to that, you get a byproduct called okara that you cannot get, with very few exceptions, at your local market.

Equipment Suggestions

It is possible to make fresh tofu at home without using a lot of special equipment. You may even have a tofu press at home and not even know it. You will need the following:

Blender

Ladle

2 large 16 to 20-quart stock pots.

A 4-piece spaghetti cooker. The pot should be at least an 8-quart size. The steamer insert will be used as the mold for the tofu. The spaghetti insert for draining pasta will not be used.

2 pressing cloths; one for straining the okara and one for lining the tofu mold. A dish towel, cheese cloth, or muslin cloth will work.

8-inch cake pan that will fit inside the steamer insert of the spaghetti pot. This will be used to help press the tofu in the mold.

Heavy weight; two quart jars with lids, filled with water or similar objects.

Solidifier

There are several forms of solidifier, but epsom salts is what is used in these recipes. Epsom salts is readily available, gives consistent results, gives a very high yield of tofu from the soymilk, and is inexpensive.

Frozen Tofu

The texture of fresh tofu changes dramatically when frozen. The water in the tofu separates out leaving a porous tofu that behaves like a fine sponge. You can thaw the tofu and squeeze out most of the water and/or simmer in broth to add flavor. A 16 ounce block of tofu will weigh about 9 ounces after being frozen, thawed, and pressed.

When you are preparing a recipe that uses frozen tofu, you will need to begin your preparations at least a day ahead of time. Slice the tofu into the correct shape and then keep it in the freezer for at least 24 to 48 hours before you actually begin to cook the dish. There are no shortcuts to this step in the preparation. Frozen tofu that is not used right away can be stored in a plastic bag in the freezer. It will keep for up to six months.

TOFU

FIRM TOFU MADE WITH AUTOMATIC SOYMILK MAKER
(Makes 14 ounces firm tofu)

1 c. dried soybeans, divided ----   2 tsp. epsom salts
  (½ c. + ½ c.)   ½ c. warm water

Pick through the soybeans and soak overnight in two separate bowls. Prepare one batch of soymilk with your soymilk maker, using ½ cup soaked soybeans. Carefully follow the directions that came with your machine. Place a colander over a 4-quart pot. Line the colander with a pressing cloth. Pour the soymilk into the colander so that it is collected in the pot below. This will remove any okara (soybean fiber) that is in the soymilk. Remove the okara from the machine that was created in making the soymilk and save it in a bowl. Repeat this cooking process for the second batch of soybeans. Pour this soymilk through the pressing cloth in the colander also. Combine all of the okara from preparing the soymilk and from the pressing cloth in a 1-quart saucepan. Add one cup of water and heat until the okara begins to simmer. Gently cook for 10 minutes. Pour the okara into the lined colander again so that the soymilk from the okara is added to the rest of the soymilk. Bring the four corners of the pressing cloth together, twist closed and gently squeeze with a potato masher to collect any additional soymilk that is still in the okara. Place the okara in a storage container and refrigerate. The okara will keep for three days in the refrigerator or up to six months in the freezer. Heat and stir the soymilk until it begins to boil. Quickly remove it from the heat so that it does not boil over. Stir the epsom salts into ½ cup warm water until dissolved. Pour into the soymilk while stirring slowly. Put the lid on the soymilk and let stand for 10 minutes. Place the tofu press in a colander in the sink or over a pot. Line the tofu press with the cheesecloth. Gently ladle the curds and whey into the cheesecloth-lined tofu press. If you cannot get all of the curds into the press, then fold the cheesecloth over the top of the curds and gently press with the top of the press to make room for the remaining curds. Open the cheesecloth and pour the remaining curds into the press. Fold the cheesecloth over the curds and place the top on the press. Place a quart jar filled with water on top to press down on the curds. Allow to stand for 30 minutes. For the firmest tofu, press the curds for two hours. Remove tofu from press and store in the refrigerator submerged in water.

Note: Most automatic soymilk makers come with a tofu press, cheesecloth, and directions for making tofu. The resulting tofu is usually very soft. By using two batches of soymilk, it is possible to make firm tofu with your tofu maker. We use a SoyQuick™ soymilk maker, but there are many other models that will work just as well.

HOMEMADE FIRM TOFU
(Makes 4 pounds tofu and 4 pounds okara)

PREPARING THE SOYBEANS

2 lbs. dried soybeans (5 cups)   *2 Tbs. epsom salts (solidifier)*
Lots of fresh water   *1 c. warm water*

Make sure that you have all of the necessary equipment listed in the beginning of this chapter. Pick through the soybeans, remove any small pebbles or non-bean material, and place in the 8-quart pot. Rinse and drain the soybeans three times. The water from the third rinsing should be fairly clear. Add 14 cups of cold water and let soak for 10 hours. The most practical routine is to start in the evening, let the beans soak overnight, and then make the tofu in the morning.

COOKING THE Gô

Place the colander in the sink and pour the soaked beans into the colander. Heat three quarts of water in one of the large stock pots, over high heat, until it comes to a boil. In a blender combine 2 cups of drained soybeans with 2 cups of water. Whirl at a high speed for 2 to 3 minutes. Stir into the boiling water in the stock pot. Repeat with the remaining soybeans until all have been added to the pot. This puréed soybean mixture is called gô. Continue to cook and stir the gô over high heat. The gô will foam up when it begins to boil. Watch the pot very carefully, and turn down the heat when it starts to boil to prevent it from boiling over. Reduce the heat and simmer slowly, while stirring frequently, for about 10 to 15 minutes. This is the ideal amount of time to cook the gô which makes it easy to digest and does not break down any of the desirable nutrients.

MAKING SOYMILK AND OKARA

2 qts. cold water

Place the colander in the top of the other large stock pot. Line the colander with a pressing cloth. Pour the gô into the colander so that the soymilk is collected in the pot below and the soybean pulp stays in the pressing cloth. This pulp left in the pressing cloth is called okara. You will not be able to put all of the gô in the colander at once. Add more gô to the colander as soymilk fills the bottom pot and room becomes available. Stir the gô occasionally to help the soymilk drain into the pot. Once all of the go has been placed in the colander, raise the four corners of the cloth lining the colander and twist together over the gô. Twist so that all of the gô remains in the cloth. Press the cloth with a potato masher to remove as much soymilk as possible. Now open the cloth. The soybean pulp left in the cloth is called okara. Make an indentation or "well" in the okara. Pour one quart of cold water into this indentation and stir to mix with the okara. This rinsing will allow you to remove even more of the milk from

(continued)

the okara and cools the okara so that it can be twisted by hand. Repeat this procedure with one more quart of cold water. Twist the pressing cloth closed one final time and squeeze and twist by hand to expel as much soymilk as possible. Refrigerate the okara until ready to use. See the following section on okara for ways to store your okara. Okara does not keep well in the refrigerator so it should be used within about three days.

FINALLY - - - - - THE TOFU

Put the pot of soymilk over medium-high heat, while stirring frequently, and bring to a gentle simmer. Watch carefully, because if the soymilk begins to boil it could easily boil over and create a terrible mess. Stir the soymilk frequently to help keep it from sticking to the bottom of the pan. If you use a thermometer, you need the soymilk to reach 190° before adding the solidifier. Stir the two tablespoons epsom salts into one cup of warm water in a measuring cup. This is the solidifier which will cause the tofu curds to form. Once the soymilk has reached a gentle simmer, turn off the heat and slowly stir the soymilk while gently adding the solidifier. Continue to slowly stir for about 30 seconds so that the solidifier is evenly distributed in the soymilk. Cover the soymilk and allow to rest for 10 minutes. Remove the lid and you will see fluffy white curds of tofu floating in light amber colored whey. Put the steamer insert in the spaghetti pot and line the bottom and sides of the insert with a clean dish towel, cheesecloth, or muslin cloth. This will be the mold for your tofu. It will create a round wheel of tofu about eight inches in diameter and two inches thick. This is an unconventional shape but will keep you from having to spend additional money for a mold. Gently ladle the curds and whey in the pot into the mold until it is full. Allow to settle before adding more tofu curds. The whey will be collected in the pot below the tofu. Watch the pot so that you can discard the whey when the pot becomes too full. Continue until all of the curds and whey have been poured into the mold. Fold the cloth liner over the top of the tofu and cover with a flat object such as a round 8-inch cake pan. Put two quart jars filled with water, or another heavy object, in the pan to press down on the tofu. Press the tofu for about 15 minutes, then remove the weight and check the top of the tofu. Spread any tofu that has been pushed up around the edge of the mold onto the top of the tofu so that it has a smooth top. Return the cake pan and weights and continue to press for a total of one to two hours. The longer you press the tofu, the more firm it will be. Remove the weight, leave the tofu in the mold, and chill for about 12 hours. This will make it easier to cut the tofu for storage. Cut the tofu into the desired size pieces and cover with water. The tofu will keep this way for at least five days.

Note: Most recipes for homemade tofu start with one pound or less of dried soybeans. Making tofu is very time consuming, and quite frankly, messy. Cleaning up can be quite a chore. By starting with two pounds of soybeans you get twice as much tofu and okara with the same equipment and only a modest increase in time. In short, it is more efficient to start with more soybeans.

CRUMBLED TOFU
(Makes 1 ½ to 1 ¾ cups)

1 (16 oz.) tub firm tofu or 1 lb. of
    homemade tofu
1 ¼ c. water

1 ½ tsp. Kitchen Bouquet®
    Browning Sauce

Drain tofu and place in a 2-quart saucepan. Mash with a potato masher until the tofu is the consistency of mashed potatoes. You should have about 2 cups of mashed tofu. Add the browning sauce to the 1 ¼ cups water and stir into the tofu. Cook over medium heat, while stirring frequently, until tofu begins to bubble. Simmer gently for 5 minutes. Place a colander lined with a pressing cloth or dish towel in the sink. Pour the tofu into the lined colander. Join the four corners of the cloth together above the tofu and twist closed. Squeeze and press with a potato masher to remove as much liquid as possible. Remove the tofu from the pressing cloth and return it to the saucepan. Mash again with the potato masher until it resembles cottage cheese. What you have now is about 1 ¾ cups of crumbled tofu. This is a major ingredient in the next four recipes.

Note: One (16 oz.) tub of tofu is equal to two cups of firmly packed, mashed tofu.

TOFU BURGER
(Makes 6 patties)

1 ¾ c. Crumbled Tofu (see
    previous recipe)
¼ c. all-purpose flour
2 Tbs. seasoned bread crumbs
1 Tbs. Vital Wheat Gluten Flour
2 Tbs. minced yellow onion
2 Tbs. minced green bell pepper
½ tsp. salt

¼ tsp. ground cumin
⅛ tsp. garlic powder
dash black pepper
1 egg
⅓ c. water
¼ tsp. Kitchen Bouquet®
    Browning Sauce
vegetable oil

Prepare the Crumbled Tofu. In a large bowl stir together the crumbled tofu with the all-purpose flour, bread crumbs, vital wheat gluten flour, yellow onion, bell pepper, salt, cumin, garlic powder, and black pepper. In a small bowl beat together the egg, ⅓ cup water, and ¼ teaspoon browning sauce. Stir the egg mixture into the tofu until well blended. Let stand for 5 minutes. Shape ⅓ cup of the tofu mix into a patty on a small plate. The patty should be 3 to 3½-inches in diameter and ½-inch thick. Gently lift the patty off of the plate with a spatula. Fry in a 325° electric skillet or frying pan over medium heat, coated with a thin layer of vegetable oil. Cook both sides of patties until browned, about 4 to 5 minutes on each side.

240812-16

TOFU MEATLOAF
(Makes 1 small loaf)

TOFU MEATLOAF

1 ¾ c. Crumbled Tofu (see recipe
   earlier in this chapter)
⅓ c. minced yellow onion
1 Tbs. chopped parsley
½ tsp. dried oregano, crushed
1 tsp. salt
¼ tsp. black pepper
¼ c. all-purpose flour

⅓ c. seasoned bread crumbs
2 Tbs. Vital Wheat Gluten Flour
2 eggs, lightly beaten
½ c. water
½ tsp. Kitchen Bouquet®
   Browning Sauce
Olive oil
Barbecue Sauce (see below)

Combine Crumbled Tofu, ⅓ cup onion, parsley, oregano, salt, and black pepper in a large bowl. In a small bowl stir together the all-purpose flour, bread crumbs, and vital wheat gluten flour. Add to the tofu and mix well. In a small bowl beat together the eggs, ½ cup water, and browning sauce. Stir egg mixture into tofu until evenly moistened. Press the tofu firmly into an oiled 7 x 3½ x 2-inch loaf pan. Rub the bottom of a 12 x 7½ x 2-inch baking pan with olive oil. Flip the loaf pan over into the the center of the baking pan. Gently lift the loaf pan up to leave the molded meatloaf in the center of the baking pan. If you do not have the necessary bread pan to use as a mold, you can pour the tofu into the baking pan and shape by hand. Bake in preheated 350° oven for 30 minutes. Start to prepare the Barbecue Sauce as soon as the meatloaf goes into the oven. Remove loaf from oven after 30 minutes and gently pour the barbecue sauce over top. Return meatloaf to oven and continue baking for another 30 minutes. Spoon some of the extra barbecue sauce from the baking pan over the meatloaf after 15 minutes (total cooking time: one hour). Remove from oven and let rest for five minutes before serving.

BARBECUE SAUCE

¼ c. finely chopped yellow onion
1 Tbs. olive oil
2 Tbs. brown sugar
1 c. water
⅓ c. ketchup

1 (8 oz.) can tomato sauce ------
   (¾ cup)
½ tsp. dry mustard
¼ tsp. chili powder
¼ tsp. hickory salt (opt.)

In a 1-quart saucepan cook and stir ¼ cup finely chopped onion in olive oil until translucent, about 5 minutes. Add sugar and stir until thickened. Add 1 cup water, ketchup, tomato sauce, dry mustard, chili powder, and optional hickory salt. Stir together and simmer for 3 minutes. Set aside until ready to use. The thin barbecue sauce will thicken when in the oven.

Note: You will need a 7 x 3½ x 2-inch loaf pan which will be used as a mold to shape the tofu loaf. The loaf will be baked in a 12 x 7½ x 2-inch rectangular baking pan. While this recipe is similar to the TVP Meatloaf in the previous chapter, it has a very different texture and flavor.

TOFU ITALIAN MEATBALLS
(Makes 14 to 16 meatballs)

4 to 5 c. Spaghetti Sauce (See
  Chapter: Sauces and Gravies)
1 ¾ c. Crumbled Tofu (See recipe
  earlier in this chapter)
⅓ c. seasoned toasted bread
  crumbs
⅓ c. uncooked oats
¼ c. Parmesan cheese
¼ c. chopped flat Italian parsley
½ tsp. dried chile peppers,
  crushed

½ tsp. salt
½ tsp. whole anise, crushed
½ tsp. crushed dried oregano
½ tsp. crushed dried basil
¼ tsp. garlic powder
¼ tsp. black pepper
2 eggs, lightly beaten
2 Tbs. milk
olive oil

Begin preparing the Spaghetti Sauce first. Prepare the meatballs while
the Spaghetti Sauce is simmering. In a large bowl combine the Crumbled
Tofu, bread crumbs, oats, Parmesan cheese, chopped parsley, dried chile
peppers, salt, anise, oregano, basil, garlic powder, and black pepper. Stir
with a fork until well blended. In a separate small bowl, beat together eggs
and milk. Pour over tofu and mix well. Let stand for about 5 minutes.
Shape rounded tablespoonfuls of mixture into meatballs. Fry the meatballs
in a 325° electric skillet coated with olive oil. You can also use a regular
frying pan over medium-high heat. Turn meatballs occasionally until crisp
and browned on the outside. This will take 12 to 15 minutes. Remove from
pan and drain on paper towels. Add the meatballs to the Spaghetti Sauce
shortly before the sauce is done cooking. Simmer slowly for about 15
minutes. The sauce can be refrigerated overnight so that the meatballs
absorb more of the flavor of the sauce. Slowly reheat sauce with meatballs
before serving. Meatballs will swell when left in Spaghetti Sauce overnight.

Note: Any form of spaghetti sauce that you have will work with this recipe.

240812-16

BEEF-LIKE TOFU
(Makes 2 ⅓ cups)

3 c. Crumbled Tofu (double the
    recipe earlier in this chapter)
3 Tbs. olive oil

1 tsp. salt
¼ c. water

Preheat a skillet to medium-low or 275°. Add the olive oil and Crumbled Tofu. Spread the tofu out to an even thickness in the pan and sprinkle the salt over the top. Cover the pan, increase heat to 325°, and cook undisturbed for five minutes. Use a spatula to scrape loose any tofu that has stuck to the bottom of the pan. Using the spatula, stir the tofu and break up the large curds. Cover and continue to cook for another five minutes. Stir and break up any large curds again. Continue the process of stirring, breaking up curds, and covered cooking for a total of 40 minutes. Stir in ¼ cup water when done. Cover and set aside to cool for 10 minutes before using. This last step helps to keep the tofu from getting too dry.

Note: Start with Crumbled Tofu made from 2 tubs of tofu. This recipe can be used as a substitute for fried crumbled ground beef in many recipes that call for crumbled beef including products like Hamburger Helper®. Beef-Like Tofu can be stored in the freezer for up to 6 months.

CHILI WITH TOFU
(Makes 3 ½ quarts)

1 ½ c. Beef-Like Tofu (see
    previous recipe)
2 c. diced yellow onion (½-inch
    pieces)
¼ c. olive oil
2 cloves garlic, minced
2 qt. cooked pinto beans (do not
    drain)
2 qt. tomato juice

4 Tbs. chili powder
2 tsp. salt
2 tsp. paprika
2 tsp. cumin
½ tsp. crushed dried oregano
½ tsp. garlic powder
¼ tsp. cayenne pepper (opt.)
¼ c. cornstarch dissolved in ----
    ¼ c. water

Prepare the Beef-like Tofu ahead of time and set aside. In a 6-quart pot, cook and stir the onion in the olive oil over medium heat for 5 minutes. Add the minced garlic and continue to cook for 2 to 3 more minutes, or until onion is translucent. Add the pinto beans, tomato juice, Beef-Like Tofu, chili powder, salt, paprika, cumin, oregano, garlic powder, and the optional cayenne pepper. Bring to a boil and simmer slowly for 15 to 20 minutes. Stir in cornstarch mixture and cook until chili thickens and returns to a simmer. The chili is now ready to serve.

Note: Home cooked pinto beans work best in this recipe. If you plan to use canned beans, you will need five (15-ounce) cans of whole pintos. Extra chili will keep in the freezer for up to 6 months.

CINCINNATI FIVE-WAY CHILI
(Makes 6 to 8 large servings)

BASIC CINCINNATI CHILI WITH TOFU

2 c. Beef-Like Tofu (See recipe
   earlier in this chapter)
¼ c. olive oil
2 c. diced yellow onion
4 cloves garlic, peeled and
   minced, about 2 tsp.
1 (6 oz.) can tomato paste
1 (7 oz.) can diced green Ortega®
   chile peppers
2 (8 oz.) cans tomato sauce
4 c. water

2 bay leaves
2 Tbs. chili powder
1 Tbs. brown sugar
1 Tbs. unsweetened cocoa
2 Tbs. cider vinegar
1 ½ tsp. allspice
1 ½ tsp. cumin
1 tsp. salt
¼ tsp. ground cloves
¼ tsp. nutmeg
¼ tsp. black pepper

Prepare the Beef-Like Tofu in advance. Then place ¼ cup of olive oil in a 3-quart saucepan. Add the 2 cups of diced yellow onion. Cook and stir over medium heat for 5 minutes. Add the minced garlic and cook for an additional 2 minutes or until onion is translucent. Add the tomato paste and stir for 2 minutes. Add and stir together the diced green chilies, tomato sauce, and 4 cups water. Add the bay leaves, chili powder, brown sugar, unsweetened cocoa, cider vinegar, allspice, cumin, salt, ground cloves, nutmeg, and black pepper. Stir together until well blended. Cook over medium heat until chili begins to boil. Reduce heat and simmer gently for about 20 minutes. Leftover chili can be kept in the freezer for several months.

HOW TO SERVE

Basic Cincinnati Chili from above
1 ½ lb. dried spaghetti noodles,
   cooked and drained
additional olive oil

1 qt. cooked pinto beans, drained
1 c. diced yellow onion
Shredded fresh cheddar cheese
oyster crackers

Cook the spaghetti according to the directions on the package. Drain and return to pot. Stir in about one tablespoon of olive oil to keep the spaghetti from sticking together. To serve, place a serving of spaghetti on a plate, topped with ½ to ⅔ cup of pinto beans, a heaping cup of chili, diced onion, and top with shredded cheese. You can adjust the quantity of each ingredient to suit your own taste. You can also vary the assembly sequence to: spaghetti, beans, onions, chili, and cheese OR spaghetti, chili, beans, onions, and cheese. Serve the oyster crackers on the side.

Note: The "Five-Way" refers to the number of separate ingredients that make up this meal: spaghetti, chili, beans, onions, and cheese. Red beans may be used in place of the pinto beans. This chili is spicier than traditional Texas chili and has a unique flavor.

240812-16

GOULASH WITH TOFU
(Makes 9 cups or 6 servings)

1 c. Beef-Like Tofu (see recipe
  earlier in this chapter)
3 c. dry medium macaroni shells
  (about 8 oz.)
3 Tbs. olive oil
2 c. diced yellow onion
1 ½ c. diced celery
1 c. diced red or green bell
  pepper

2 c. tomato juice
1 ½ tsp. salt
1 tsp. sugar
1 tsp. dried oregano, crushed
¼ tsp. garlic powder
¼ tsp. black pepper
1 (28 oz.) can whole peeled
  tomatoes

Prepare Beef-Like Tofu ahead of time. Cook the macaroni shells according to the package directions. Drain and set aside until ready to use. Add the olive oil to an electric skillet that has been preheated to 275° or a frying pan over medium heat. Add the celery, bell peppers, and onion. Cook and stir for 12 to 15 minutes or until onion is translucent. Add the beef-like tofu, cooked macaroni shells, tomato juice, salt, sugar, oregano, garlic powder, and black pepper. Place a colander over a large bowl. Drain the canned whole tomatoes into the colander, making sure to collect the tomato juice in the bowl. Take the drained tomatoes from the colander and chop into small pieces. Add the chopped tomatoes to the frying pan along with the collected tomato juice in the bowl. Continue to cook at 250° or over low heat for about 5 minutes. Stir once or twice while cooking. Turn off heat, place lid on pan, and allow to stand for 5 minutes before serving. Makes about six 1 ½-cup servings. Leftover goulash can be stored in the refrigerator for up to 5 days. If Goulash becomes too thick, add a little more tomato juice to thin it down.

Note: When preparing the celery, bell pepper and onion, they should be diced into approximately 1-inch pieces. Sliced zucchini and/or small cauliflowerets may be added along with the diced yellow onion.

TOFU MAYONNAISE
(Makes ½ cup)

½ (16 oz.) tub firm tofu
¼ c. canola oil
1 Tbs. white vinegar

2 tsp. lemon juice
½ tsp. sugar
¼ tsp. salt

Drain the tofu, cut into small pieces, and place in a blender. Add the canola oil, white vinegar, lemon juice, sugar and salt. Whirl in blender until smooth, about 1 minute. Store in the refrigerator. Will keep for about 1 week.

Note: For added flavor you can use olive oil in place of the canola oil and add two teaspoons Dijon mustard.

GANMO BALLS OR PATTIES
(Makes 2 dozen balls or 8 patties)

PREPARING GANMO DOUGH

1 (16 oz.) tub firm tofu
⅓ c. finely diced yellow onion
¼ c. grated carrot
3 Tbs. finely chopped walnuts
1 Tbs. chopped green onion tops

1 Tbs. soy sauce
¾ tsp. salt
2 Tbs. Vital Wheat Gluten flour
2 eggs, lightly beaten

Drain the tofu and wrap in a clean dish cloth. Squeeze the tofu over the sink to remove as much water as possible. Place tofu in a large bowl and mash with a fork. Add the diced yellow onion, carrots, walnuts, green onion tops, soy sauce, salt, vital wheat gluten flour, and eggs. Mix together until well blended.

GANMO BALLS

Sweet and Sour Sauce (see
   Chapter: Sauces and Gravies)

Oil for deep frying

Take a slightly rounded tablespoonful of ganmo dough and drop into hot oil (350°) for deep frying. Fry until golden brown, turning once, for a total of 2 to 3 minutes. Remove from oil and drain. Keep warm while preparing Sweet and Sour Sauce. Serve the Sweet and Sour Sauce on the side.

GANMO PATTIES

Prepared ganmo dough from
   above.
2 Tbs. frozen peas, thawed

2 Tbs. finely chopped celery
Thousand Island Dressing - opt.
   (see Chapter: Salads)

Prepare the ganmo dough from above. Fold in the peas and chopped celery. Shape ⅓-cup of ganmo mixture into a patty 3½-inches in diameter and ¼-inch thick. Cook in a frying pan, coated with a small amount of vegetable oil, over medium-high heat. If using an electric skillet fry at 325°. Cook for 5 to 7 minutes on each side. May be served topped with the optional Thousand Island Dressing or on a hamburger bun for a unique vegetarian burger.

Note: These are essentially tofu fritters. Most traditional ganmo recipes do not include egg. The Japanese usually add Japanese yam (yamaimo) to help hold the ganmo together. This recipe calls for eggs and vital wheat gluten flour in place of the yam as a binding agent.

240812-16

TOFU DIP
(Makes 1 cup)

½ (16 oz.) tub firm tofu
⅔ c. Italian salad dressing
2 Tbs. vegetable oil

1 Tbs. cider vinegar
⅛ tsp. salt

Drain the tofu, cut into small pieces, and put in a blender. Add the Italian salad dressing, vegetable oil, cider vinegar, and salt. Whirl at low speed for 1 minute or until smooth. This dip is very thick so you may have to whirl and scrape the sides of the blender several times before your dip is smooth. Taste and adjust seasoning if necessary. Chill before serving.

Note: Other varieties of vinegar and oil salad dressing can be used in place of Italian salad dressing.

TOFU IMITATION FISH STICKS
(Makes 16 pieces or 4 servings.)

FREEZING THE TOFU

1 (16 oz.) tub firm tofu

Drain tofu and place on a cutting board. Cut across the width of the tofu into eight equal size pieces about a ½-inch wide. Place tofu pieces on a cookie sheet and keep in the freezer for at least 24 hours.

PREPARING THE TOFU FISH STICKS

Frozen tofu from above
⅔ c. Toasted Bread Crumbs, (see
   Chapter: This and That)
¼ tsp. salt
¼ tsp. garlic salt
¼ tsp. paprika
dash black pepper

1 Tbs. flour
2 Tbs. milk
1 egg, lightly beaten
Vegetable oil
Tartar Sauce, (see Chapter:
   Sauces and Gravies)

Thaw tofu or defrost in a microwave oven. Press each piece of tofu between your hands over the sink to remove as much water as possible. Cut each slice of tofu in half lengthwise. In a medium bowl stir together the flour and milk until free of lumps. Stir in the beaten egg. In a separate medium bowl combine the Toasted Bread Crumbs, salt, garlic salt, paprika, and black pepper. Dip each tofu strip in beaten egg mixture and roll in toasted bread crumbs. Fry in an electric skillet at 350° or a frying pan over medium-high heat that is coated with a thin layer of vegetable oil. Cook for 2 to 3 minutes on each side or until lightly browned. Serve warm with tartar sauce.

93

FROZEN TOFU NUGGETS
(Makes 16 pieces or about 4 servings)

FREEZING THE TOFU

1 (16 oz.) tub firm tofu

Drain tofu and place on cutting board. Cut in half lengthwise from top to bottom. Cut in half again perpendicular to your first cut. You should now have four small blocks of tofu about the same size. Trim the corners of the pieces so that they are rounded. Save the tofu that has been trimmed from the corners, which can be used in any recipe that calls for mashed tofu. Lay each piece of tofu on its side on the cutting board and cut into four equal pieces, from top to bottom, about ⅜-inch thick. Place the tofu on a cookie sheet and put in the freezer for 24 to 48 hours.

CRUSHED CORN FLAKE CEREAL COATING - MAKES ¾ CUP

2 c. (about 2½ oz.) corn flakes
   cereal, any brand
2 tsp. dried parsley flakes
1 tsp. rubbed sage

½ tsp. salt
½ tsp. paprika
¼ tsp. garlic salt
⅛ tsp. black pepper

Place the corn flakes in a 1-quart size self-sealing plastic bag. Put the bag on a counter and use a rolling pin to roll over the bag and crush the corn flakes. Continue until you have reached the desired consistency. Place in a bowl and stir in the parsley flakes, sage, salt, paprika, garlic salt, and pepper. Mix until well blended.

PREPARING THE TOFU NUGGETS

¾ c. Crushed Corn Flake Cereal
   Coating (see above)
Frozen tofu pieces from above
1 Tbs. all-purpose flour
1 Tbs. milk

1 egg, lightly beaten
Oil for frying, about ¾ c.
Tartar Sauce, (see Chapter:
   Sauces and Gravies)

Prepare the corn flake coating and set aside until ready to use. Remove tofu nuggets from freezer and thaw or defrost in the microwave oven. Place a piece of tofu between the palms of your hands over the sink and squeeze out as much water as possible. Repeat for the remaining tofu. Put the flour in a medium bowl and slowly stir in the milk until you have a smooth paste. Stir in the beaten egg. Place the Corn Flake Coating in a medium bowl. Heat a thin layer of oil, about ¼-inch deep, in a frying pan or electric skillet to 350°. Dip a piece of tofu in the beaten egg and then in the corn flake coating. Repeat for remaining tofu. Cook each nugget, while turning once, for 2 to 3 minutes on each side or until golden brown. Keep warm until ready to serve. Serve with Tartar Sauce on the side. You can also bake the tofu after it has been dipped in the corn flake coating. Place on a baking sheet that has been coated with non-stick spray. Bake in a 375° oven for 25 minutes. Turn once after baking for 15 minutes.

 240812-16

SPICY FROZEN TOFU PATTIES
(Makes 4 patties)

FREEZING THE TOFU PATTIES

1 (16 oz.) tub firm tofu

Drain the tofu and place on a cutting board. Take the empty fruit or vegetable can and press down on the tofu to make a round cylinder of tofu. Remove all of the trimmings from around the cylinder and set aside. Place the cylinder of tofu on its side and cut from top to bottom into four round patties of the same thickness, about ⅜-inch. Lay the patties on a cookie sheet and put in the freezer for 24 to 48 hours. The trimmings, which will weigh about 7 ounces, can be used in any tofu recipe that calls for mashed tofu. They can also be frozen and used to make half of the recipe of Frozen Tofu Salad (see following recipe).

SPICY SEASONED FLOUR FOR COATING - MAKES ½ CUP

½ c. all-purpose flour
1 tsp. paprika
½ tsp. salt

½ tsp. onion powder
¼ tsp. ground black pepper
¼ tsp. cayenne pepper

In a medium bowl combine the flour, paprika, salt, onion powder, black pepper, and cayenne pepper. Mix together until well blended and set aside until ready to use.

PREPARING THE SPICY TOFU PATTIES

½ c. Spicy Seasoned Flour from above
Frozen Tofu Patties from above
3 Tbs. water

1 Tbs. Sriracha® Hot Chili Sauce
1 egg, lightly beaten
Oil for frying, about ½ to ¾-cup

Remove tofu patties from freezer and thaw or defrost in the microwave oven. Place a piece of tofu between the palms of your hands over the sink and squeeze out as much water as possible. Repeat for the remaining tofu. In a medium bowl mix together the 3 tablespoons water, Sriracha® Sauce, and lightly beaten egg. Heat a thin layer of oil, about ¼-inch deep in a frying pan or electric skillet to 350°. Dip a tofu patty in the egg mixture and then dredge in the seasoned flour until completely coated. Repeat the process for the same patty (double dip) and place in the hot oil in the frying pan or skillet. Continue with the remaining tofu patties. Cook each patty until golden brown, about 6 to 7 minutes on each side. Drain on paper towel before serving.

Note: This recipe was inspired by the currently popular chicken patties. You will need an empty fruit or vegetable can that is about 3¼ inches in diameter. You will have leftover tofu "trimmings" that can be used in other tofu recipes.

FROZEN TOFU SALAD
(Makes 3 cups)

FREEZING THE TOFU

1 (16 oz.) tub firm tofu

Drain the tub of tofu and place on a cutting board. Slice across the width of the tofu into six slices. Each slice should be about ⅜ inch thick. Place the tofu slices on a cookie sheet and put in the freezer for at least 24 hours.

PREPARING THE TOFU SALAD

Frozen tofu slices from above
1 hard boiled egg, chilled
⅓ c. sweet pickle relish
¾ c. mayonnaise
½ c. finely chopped celery
1 ½ tsp. salt

½ c. finely chopped red bell pepper
½ tsp. dried summer savory leaves, crushed
½ tsp. celery salt
dash black pepper

Thaw the tofu or defrost in the microwave oven. Place a slice of thawed tofu between your hands over the sink and squeeze out as much water as possible. Repeat for all six slices. Chop the tofu into small pieces and place in a large bowl. Peel and finely chop the hard boiled egg. Add to the tofu in the bowl. Place the sweet relish in a large strainer over the sink and squeeze out as much liquid as possible with the back of a spoon. Add the relish, mayonnaise, chopped celery, salt, chopped bell pepper, summer savory, celery salt, and pepper to the bowl of tofu. Gently mix together. Taste and adjust seasonings. Refrigerate until ready to serve.

Note: This is essentially a vegetarian version of chicken salad. This recipe will make 6 to 8 sandwiches or stuff 4 to 6 tomatoes.

FRIED FROZEN TOFU STRIPS
(Makes about 4 servings)

1 (16 oz. tub) firm tofu   **Vegetable oil**

Cut the tofu into 6 slices and freeze according to the directions in the previous recipe. Thaw the tofu or defrost in a microwave oven. Place a slice of thawed tofu between your hands over the sink and squeeze out as much water as possible. Repeat for all six slices. Cut each piece lengthwise into two pieces. Fry the tofu in a small amount of oil in a medium frying pan. Fry for 3 to 5 minutes on each side or until lightly browned.

Note: Frozen tofu is more porous than fresh tofu. Frying the frozen tofu makes it more firm and ideally suited for adding to stir fried vegetables. Being more porous means that these strips can also be added to salads where they will easily absorb the flavors of the dressing.

NOODLE SOUP WITH FROZEN TOFU
(Makes 2 quarts or 4 servings)

PREPARING THE FROZEN TOFU

8 oz. (½ tub) tofu

Drain the tofu and wrap in plastic wrap. Place on a saucer and keep in the freezer for 24 to 48 hours. Remove tofu from freezer, remove plastic wrap, and allow it to thaw or defrost in a microwave oven. Press the thawed tofu over a sink between the palms of your hands. Press out as much liquid as possible. Place the tofu on a cutting board and tear into small bite-size pieces with a fork. Set aside until ready to use.

PREPARING THE SOUP BROTH

8 c. water
1 Tbs. imitation chicken
*   seasoning*
1 Tbs. butter

1 tsp. olive oil
1 tsp. salt
1 tsp. celery salt
Dash black pepper

In a 3-quart saucepan combine the 8 cups water, imitation chicken seasoning, butter, olive oil, salt, celery salt, and black pepper. Bring to a boil and simmer gently for 5 minutes. Remove from heat, set aside, and keep warm until ready to serve.

COOKING THE NOODLES AND ASSEMBLING THE SOUP

6 oz. dried egg noodles (half of a   *2 Tbs. chopped fresh parsley*
*   12-oz. pkg.)*

Cook the noodles according to the package directions. This should be done just before you plan to serve the soup. Drain the noodles when done cooking and place an equal amount in each bowl. Divide the frozen tofu evenly between the four bowls and place on top of the noodles. Pour enough soup broth in each bowl to cover the noodles and tofu. Sprinkle parsley over each bowl and serve.

Note: You will need 4 soup bowls that hold at least 2 cups of soup each.

Okara · Soybean Pulp

FREEZING FRESH OKARA

*Fresh okara from making
  homemade tofu*

Firmly pack the fresh okara in a ½-cup dry measuring cup. Turn it upside down on the cookie sheet and tap it so that the the mound of okara lands on the cookie sheet. If the okara is stubborn and will not release from the cup, run a paring knife around the inside edge to loosen it and try again. Repeat until all of the okara has been used. You can also freeze smaller portions by using a ¼-cup measuring cup. Place the cookie sheet in the freezer until the okara is frozen solid, about 24 hours. Remove it from the cookie sheet and store in a plastic bag in the freezer. When you want to use the okara, remove it from the bag and let it thaw in the refrigerator or defrost in the microwave. Use the okara in any recipe that calls for fresh okara.

Note: You will need a large cookie sheet and a ½-cup dry measuring cup. Freezing is the best way to store fresh okara. Decide what you plan to do with your okara fairly soon after making tofu or soymilk because okara does not keep well in the refrigerator. Make sure that you do not leave it in the refrigerator for more than 3 days.

DRIED OKARA POWDER
(Makes 1 cup + 2 tablespoons)

1 qt. fresh okara (2 lbs.)

Spread the okara out evenly on a large cookie sheet. Break up as many of the large lumps as possible. Place in a 275° oven and dry for 4 to 5 hours. Stir the okara about once every hour with a spatula. Continue to break up as many lumps as possible when stirring. To test the okara for dryness, take a large lump from the cookie sheet and press it between your thumb and forefinger. The okara should be dry all of the way through. When thoroughly dry, whirl the okara in a blender until it is a fine powder, about 2 minutes. Sift through a fine mesh strainer and return any large pieces to the blender. Repeat the process with the blender and discard any large pieces that remain in the strainer. Store in an airtight container. Dried okara should keep for up to six months.

Note: You will need a large cookie sheet, blender, and large fine mesh strainer for this recipe. The tofu from one pound of soybeans will yield about four cups of the fresh okara that is used in this recipe. If you have a grain mill, it can be used to grind the DRY (not the fresh) okara into an even finer powder.

240812-16

DRIED OKARA USING A JUICE EXTRACTOR
(Makes 1 cup + 2 tablespoons)

1 qt. fresh okara (2 lbs.)

Run the fresh okara through an extraction juicer. Spread evenly over a large cookie sheet. Place in a 275° oven and dry for 2 to 3 hours. The liquid soymilk from the extractor will be almost as thick as yogurt and contain some very fine okara. Place a colander lined with a pressing cloth over a large pot. Pour the thick soymilk into the lined colander. Join the four corners of the cloth together above the soymilk and twist closed. Press with a potato masher to remove as much soymilk as possible. The soymilk in the pot can be added to your soymilk for making tofu or it can be refrigerated for use later. The fine okara left in the pressing cloth can be used in any recipe calling for fresh okara, or it can be frozen. To test the okara in the oven for dryness, take a large lump from the cookie sheet and press it between your thumb and forefinger. The okara should be dry all of the way through. When thoroughly dry, whirl in a blender until it is a fine powder, about two minutes. Sift the okara through a large fine-mesh strainer. Return any large lumps to the blender, whirl again for 30 seconds, and sift. Discard any large pieces. Store in an airtight container.

Note: You will need an extraction juicer, large cookie sheet, colander, pressing cloth, large pot, potato masher, blender, and large fine-mesh strainer. This takes longer to prepare the okara than the previous method, but allows you to recover more of the soymilk. It also does not take the okara as long to dry in the oven.

OKARA PEANUT BUTTER CHOCOLATE CHIP COOKIES
(Makes 3 dozen cookies)

½ c. butter, softened
½ c. brown sugar
½ c. white sugar
1 egg, lightly beaten
¾ c. peanut butter

1 tsp. vanilla extract
¾ c. firmly packed fresh okara
¾ c. all-purpose flour
½ tsp. baking soda
1 ½ c. chocolate morsels

Combine the butter, brown sugar, and white sugar in a large bowl. Beat together until smooth. Add the egg, peanut butter, and vanilla extract. Mix together until well blended. In another large bowl, combine the okara, flour, and baking soda. Mash together with a fork or pastry blender. Stir the peanut butter mixture into the bowl with the flour. Mix together until well blended. Fold in the chocolate morsels. Drop batter by heaping teaspoonfuls onto a lightly greased cookie sheet and flatten slightly with a fork. Bake at 350° for 20 minutes or until lightly browned around the edges.

OKARA TORTILLAS
(Makes 4 large tortillas)

1 c. fresh okara   ½ tsp. salt
⅓ c. all-purpose flour

Combine fresh okara, flour, and salt in a large bowl. Mash flour into okara with a fork or pastry blender, and then stir until well blended. Divide dough into four equal pieces, about ¼-cup each. Shape each one into a ball. Place one piece of dough between two square sheets of wax paper. Flatten and roll into a circle approximately 8 inches in diameter. Remove the top piece of wax paper and set aside. (If you are careful, one square of wax paper may be used twice before discarding.) Cut a circle 7½ inches in diameter in the dough. You can use an inverted bowl as a guide. Remove excess dough and add it to the next ball of dough that will be used. Place "tortilla" face down on a dry, hot electric skillet set at 350° or a regular frying pan on medium-high heat. Quickly but gently remove remaining piece of wax paper. If the wax paper sticks to the tortilla, you can coax it loose with the back of a spatula. Place the spatula at the far edge of the tortilla. Gently pull the wax paper towards you over the spatula as it is drawn along the back of the tortilla. Cook tortilla on first side until the edges begin to curl and it begins to turn a light beige, about 3 minutes. Turn and cook on the second side for an additional 2 minutes. Remove from skillet and place on a plate covered with a clean dish towel. Fold the dishtowel over the top of the tortilla and cover with a large bowl. This helps to keep the tortillas from drying out. Repeat process for remaining dough. To reheat before serving, heat each side of a tortilla for 5 to 10 seconds on a preheated skillet set at 350°. You can also place 4 tortillas wrapped in a clean dish towel in a microwave oven for 20 seconds.

MEDIUM OKARA TORTILLAS (Makes 6 medium tortillas)

Okara tortilla dough from above

To make medium size tortillas, divide the dough into 6 equal pieces. Roll each piece into a circle approximately 7 inches in diameter. Trim to make a tortilla with a diameter of 6½ inches. Follow the instructions from above for cooking the tortillas

Note: You will need wax paper for this recipe. A wheel-type pizza cutter works best for trimming the tortillas. Dried okara powder does not work very well with this recipe. While the recipe recommends using a frying pan, if you you use a griddle you can work with two tortillas at once.

OKARA CHIPS
(Makes 48 chips)

6 Medium Okara Tortillas from
  the previous recipe

Vegetable oil for deep frying
Salt (popcorn salt works best)

Cut each Medium Okara Tortilla into 8 pie-shaped pieces. Preheat oil for frying at least ½-inch deep in an electric skillet set at 350°. You can also use a deep fryer. Cook tortilla wedges in hot oil for about 1 minute, or until they begin to turn light brown. Quickly turn okara chips with a slotted spoon. Continue frying until chips are light brown on both sides, for a total of about 2 to 2½ minutes. Remove from oil and place on a paper towel to drain. Sprinkle salt on chips immediately before they cool.

Note: Having a large slotted spoon will be very helpful when frying these chips. These chips can also be used in the recipe Homemade Cheese Nachos (see Chapter: Side Dishes). Variation: Onion chips --- Sprinkle onion powder on the chips along with the salt.

OKARA BREAD
(Makes 1 loaf)

½ c. Dried Okara Powder (See
  recipe this chapter)
2 c. bread flour, divided ---- (1 c.
  + 1 c.)
1 ½ Tbs. sugar

1 Tbs. instant active dry yeast
1 ½ c. warm water
2 Tbs. melted butter
½ c. all-purpose flour
1 ½ tsp. salt

In a large bowl combine the dried okara, 1 cup of the bread flour, sugar, and active yeast. Stir in the warm water and let stand for at least 5 minutes and preferably 10 minutes. This will give the okara time to absorb enough moisture. Stir in the melted butter. Add the remaining 1 cup of bread flour, the all-purpose flour, and salt. Mix well and turn out onto a lightly floured counter top. Knead for about 5 minutes or until smooth and elastic. Place in a greased bowl and allow to rise until double in bulk, about 30 minutes. Turn out onto a dry counter top. Knead for about 1 minute and roll out into a 10 x 15-inch rectangle. Roll up from the narrow end and pinch seams to seal. Place in a greased 9 x 5 x 3-inch bread pan. Allow to rise for 45 minutes or until double in bulk. The top of the dough should be about ½ inch above the edge of the pan. Place in a preheated 425° oven and bake for 25 to 30 minutes. Remove from pan and allow to cool on a rack.

Note: If you have never made yeast bread before, you may want to bake one of the basic white breads (see Chapter Breads: Yeast Breads) before you try this recipe. Okara bread is a little heavier and more moist than regular white bread.

SIMPLE OKARA PANCAKES
(Makes eight 5-inch pancakes)

PANCAKES MADE WITH FRESH OKARA

1 ½ c. Basic Pancake Mix (See
   recipe in Chapter: Breads;
   Baking Soda Breads)
½ c. fresh okara

2 eggs
3 Tbs. vegetable oil
3 Tbs. water

Put the Basic Pancake Mix in a large bowl. Add the okara and mix into the pancake mix with a pastry blender. Continue to blend until okara is evenly distributed in the pancake mix, about 1 to 2 minutes. This is the best method to use to make sure that the okara does not form lumps in the pancakes. Add the eggs, vegetable oil, 3 tablespoons water, and mix well. You can add an additional 1 to 2 tablespoons of water for thinner pancakes. Pour a scant ½-cup of batter onto the griddle for each pancake. They should be 5 to 5 ½ inches in diameter. Cook the pancakes on a dry griddle set at 350° until lightly browned, about 3 to 4 minutes on each side. If the pancakes tend to stick, then try using a little nonstick spray on the griddle. Serve warm with syrup or your favorite topping.

PANCAKES MADE WITH DRIED OKARA

1 ½ c. Basic Pancake Mix
3 Tbs. dried okara
2 eggs

3 Tbs. vegetable oil
1 c. water

Put the Basic Pancake Mix in a bowl and stir in the dried okara. Add the eggs, vegetable oil, and water. Beat until well blended. Let stand for at least 10 minutes to give the dried okara a chance to absorb some moisture. Cook the pancakes using the same technique as above. Add 2 more tablespoons of water if you would like thinner pancakes. These pancakes will not be quite as moist as the ones made with fresh okara.

Note: A pastry blender, Teflon® coated griddle, and 4-ounce ladle will be very helpful. This simple recipe for okara pancakes uses the Basic Pancake Mix recipe. Bisquick® or some other commercial brand of mix can be used instead of the pancake mix. If so, omit the oil and use milk in place of the water. These pancakes have a slightly chewy texture similar to buttermilk pancakes.

240812-16

Side Dishes

Side Dishes

The title "Side Dishes" implies that a particular recipe is intended to play second fiddle to another, larger main course. As mentioned in the previous chapter, some of the dishes in this chapter can also be used as a main dish. Broccoli becomes a great main dish when you smother it in cheese sauce. Corn Fritters and Okra Fritters both qualify as possible main dishes. Who would not be willing to have Sweet and Sour Pineapple Walnuts served over rice as a main course? So try to be a little flexible when planning your meals.

SIDE DISHES

FRIED APPLES
(Makes 8 slices or 4 servings)

2 apples (about ¾ lbs.)
½ c. all-purpose flour
1 egg, lightly beaten
⅛ tsp. salt

¼ c. of water
oil for frying
sour cream
ground nutmeg

Peel and core apples. Slice each apple into four rounds about ½-inch thick. Steam the apples over gently simmering water for exactly 3 minutes and drain on paper towel. The apples should be tender but not mushy when done. In a large bowl, stir together the flour, egg, salt, and ¼ cup water to make a thick batter. Heat about a ⅛-inch layer of oil in a medium frying pan over medium-high heat to about to 350°. Dip apples in batter and fry in oil for 2 to 3 minutes on each side until golden brown. Serve warm topped with sour cream and a pinch of nutmeg.

Note: You will need a vegetable steamer for this recipe. These apple slices go well with steamed cabbage and boiled potatoes.

BAKED ACORN SQUASH
(Makes 2 to 4 servings)

PREPARATION

1 large acorn squash

First remove the stem of the squash. Any acorn squash that weighs up to 1½ pounds should be cut in half from top to bottom. Any squash over 1½ pounds should be cut into quarters. Remove the seeds and soak squash in cold water for 15 to 20 minutes.

BAKING

2 - 4 tsp. butter
White wine

brown sugar
cinnamon sugar (opt.)

Remove from water, pat dry, and place in a large baking dish with the cut side up. Place a teaspoon of butter in the bottom of each piece. Season each section with 1 teaspoon white wine and ½ teaspoon brown sugar. You may also sprinkle a small amount of the optional cinnamon sugar over top for additional seasoning. Pour ¾ cup water in the pan to help keep the squash from drying out. Bake in a preheated 375° oven for 1½ hours. Every 30 minutes during baking, brush the butter in the bottom of each section around the inside of the squash. Test with a fork for doneness.

IMITATION BAKED BEANS
(Makes 3 cups)

2 (15 oz.) cans vegetarian beans
  in tomato sauce
2 Tbs. ketchup
2 Tbs. brown sugar
1 tsp. hickory salt (opt.)

½ tsp. ground mustard
½ tsp. paprika
½ tsp. onion powder
⅛ tsp. garlic powder
⅛ tsp. chili powder

Place the vegetarian beans in a 2-quart saucepan. Add the ketchup, brown sugar, optional hickory salt, ground mustard, paprika, onion powder, garlic powder, and chili powder. Stir together and cook over medium heat until the beans begin to simmer. Reduce heat, simmer gently for 5 minutes, and serve.

BEETS WITH PINEAPPLE
(Makes 4 servings)

2 Tbs. brown sugar
1 Tbs. cornstarch
¼ tsp. salt
1 small (8 oz.) can crushed
  pineapple, do not drain

1 Tbs. white vinegar
1 Tbs. butter
1 (15 oz.) can sliced beets,
  drained

Combine the brown sugar, cornstarch, and salt in a saucepan. Add crushed pineapple, white vinegar, and butter. Cook over medium heat, while stirring constantly, until sauce thickens. Add beets, stir, and bring to a simmer. Cook for 1 to 2 minutes to heat through and serve.

Note: You can use two cups of fresh beets that have been cooked until tender, peeled, and sliced in place of the canned beets.

PICKLED BEETS
(Makes 3 to 4 servings)

1 (15 oz.) can plain sliced beets
½ c. sugar

⅓ c. white vinegar

Drain the beets, reserving the juice. Combine sugar, vinegar, and ½ cup of the reserved beet juice in a small saucepan. Discard the remaining beet juice. Cook and stir pickling juice until mixture begins to boil. Add beets and simmer over medium heat for five minutes. Serve warm or chilled.

Note: These taste much better than the prepared beets at the market. When using whole beets, simmer in the pickling juice for about 10 minutes.

BROCCOLI
(Makes 4 servings)

PREPARATION

1 lb. broccoli crowns

Rinse the broccoli under cold running water and drain. Cut the head from top to bottom into florets with a small knife so that the stems are no wider than ½ inch. The florets should be 2 to 3 inches long. Remove any tough outer skin with a small knife or potato peeler. There should be 6 cups (about 10 to 12 ounces) of florets when done.

COOKING

2 tsp. salt   **1 tsp. sugar**

Fill a 3-quart saucepan three-quarters full with water. Place the pot over high heat and bring the water to a full boil. Slowly stir in the salt and sugar. Allow to return to a boil and add all of the broccoli florets at once. Begin counting the cooking time as soon as they enter the water. Stir and cook the broccoli for exactly 3 minutes. Pour the contents of the pot into a colander that is over the sink so that all of the broccoli ends up in the colander. See the notes below if you are using a spaghetti cooker. If you cannot serve the broccoli immediately, then return it to the pot and cover with the lid. You can keep it warm this way for 10 to 15 minutes, but not much longer. If you leave it in the pot longer than this, you run the risk of having it turn from a bright green color to a drab olive green. You can reheat the broccoli by stirring over medium heat for 1 to 2 minutes.

SERVING

2 to 4 Tbs. melted butter

Drizzle some of the melted butter over each serving of broccoli. To serve as a main dish, pour cheese sauce over each serving (See recipe Chapter: Sauces and Gravies) in place of the melted butter. This recipe will make 2 to 3 servings if you plan to us the broccoli as a main dish. If you want to use the broccoli in a stir fry or other vegetable medley, then do not return it to the pot but place it in an uncovered bowl until ready to use. If you would like to use some of the broccoli in a salad, then it should be chilled before serving.

Note: This is a basic broccoli recipe. Even when preparing stir fry, precook the broccoli this way and then add it at the last minute. The broccoli will be tender and have good color. You can use a spaghetti cooker with a removable insert in place of the 3-quart saucepan. When the cooking time is done, just remove the insert with all of the broccoli and let it drain in the sink.

CARROT MEDLEY
(Makes 6 servings)

1 lb. carrots
2 lrg. stalks celery (4 oz.)
1 med. bell pepper (6 oz.)
1 med. onion (8 oz.)

1 Tbs. peanut oil
¾ tsp. salt
½ tsp. powdered ginger

Wash and peel carrots. Cut into sticks ⅜-inch wide and 2 to 2½ inches long. Place in a saucepan and cover with water. Cook for 8 to 10 minutes or until tender. Drain, reserving the stock, and set aside. The carrot stock can be used in other recipes that require vegetable stock. Wash and cut the celery and bell pepper into sticks about the same size as the carrots. There should be 1 cup of celery sticks and 1½ cups of bell pepper sticks when done. Peel the onion and cut in half from top to bottom. Lay each onion half flat on the cutting board and cut from top to bottom into slices about ⅜-inch wide. There should be 2 cups of sliced onion when done. Add the peanut oil to an electric skillet and heat to 250°. If using a frying pan, place over medium heat. Add the celery, bell pepper, and onion to the heated pan. Cook and stir for 10 to 15 minutes, or until onion is translucent and tender. Add the cooked carrots, salt, and powdered ginger. Cook together for about 1 minute to let the seasonings blend with the vegetables. Keep warm until ready to serve.

CORN FRITTERS
(Makes 5 to 6 large fritters)

1 (15 oz.) can whole kernel corn,
    drained (about 1⅔ c.)
2 Tbs. minced yellow onion
⅓ c. all-purpose flour
1 Tbs. cornmeal
1 egg, lightly beaten

¼ c. milk
¼ tsp. salt
⅛ tsp. black pepper
vegetable oil
sour cream or Brown Gravy (see
    Chapter: Sauces and Gravies)

In a large bowl combine the corn, yellow onion, flour, cornmeal, beaten egg, milk, salt, and pepper. Stir together until well blended. Cover the bottom of an electric skillet with a thin layer of vegetable oil and heat to 350°. If using a frying pan, place over medium-high heat. Spoon a scant ⅓-cup of batter onto the pan and flatten like a pancake to an even thickness. The fritter should be 4 inches in diameter. Cook until the bottom is golden brown, about 5 to 6 minutes. Turn and repeat for second side. Remove from pan and drain on paper towel. Serve warm with a heaping teaspoon of sour cream on top. As an alternative, you can spoon brown gravy over each fritter (see Chapter: Sauces and Gravies).

240812-16

EGGPLANT MEATBALLS
(Makes 12 to 14 meatballs)

2 c. Spaghetti Sauce (see
   Chapter: Sauces and Gravies)
1 lrg. eggplant, about 16 oz.
3 Tbs. olive oil
2 cloves garlic, minced
½ tsp. salt
4 Tbs. water, divided (2 Tbs. plus
   2 Tbs.)
¼ c. fresh Italian parsley, minced

¾ c. Seasoned Toasted Bread
   Crumbs (see Chapter: This and
   That)
1½ tsp. dried oregano
2 lrg. eggs, lightly beaten
¼ c. freshly grated Parmesan
   cheese
¼ c. vegetable oil
1 lb. dried spaghetti, uncooked

Prepare the Spaghetti Sauce ahead of time and keep warm until ready to serve. Peel the eggplant and dice into ½ to 1-inch pieces. You should have 6 cups of diced eggplant when done. Heat the olive oil in an electric skillet set at 275°. If using a frying pan it should be placed over medium heat. Add the garlic and cook for 1 minute. Do not let the garlic turn brown. Add the eggplant, salt, and 2 tablespoons of water. Stir, cover, and steam the eggplant over low heat or 250° for 20 to 25 minutes. Stir occasionally while cooking. If the eggplant starts to stick to the pan, then add an additional 2 tablespoons of water. The eggplant should be very soft when done. Set aside and let cool slightly. The eggplant will have cooked down considerably. You will have about 1 heaping cup of cooked eggplant when done. Place the cooled eggplant in a large bowl. Add the Italian parsley, bread crumbs, oregano, eggs, and grated Parmesan cheese. Mix well and let stand for about 10 minutes. This allows the bread crumbs time to absorb some of the moisture. Shape a heaping tablespoon of this mixture into a ball. There should be enough to make 12 to 14 meatballs. Wash and dry the skillet that the eggplant was cooked in. Add the vegetable oil, and cook the meatballs in the vegetable oil at 325°, turning them occasionally so that they are evenly browned. If using a frying pan it should be placed over medium-high heat. This will take 15 to 20 minutes. Prepare the spaghetti noodles, according to the package directions, while the meatballs are cooking. To serve, place a portion of noodles on a plate, along with 3 or 4 meatballs and cover with spaghetti sauce.

BAKED MEATBALLS

Meatball mixture from above

Shape the meatballs as directed above. Place on a lightly oiled baking dish or cookie sheet with a raised edge. Bake in a preheated 375° oven for 25 to 30 minutes. Meatballs will be lightly browned when done.

Note: Peeling the eggplant is optional. If you prefer not to peel the eggplant, then you should dice it into ½-inch pieces or smaller. Italian Pecorino Romano cheese can be used in place of the Parmesan cheese. Store bought seasoned bread crumbs can be used in place of the Seasoned Toasted Bread Crumbs.

GREEN BEANS AND SHIITAKE MUSHROOMS
(Makes 3 servings)

HOW TO PREPARE SHIITAKE MUSHROOMS

1 c. dried sliced shiitake
*   mushrooms (about ½ oz.)*
1 c. water

1 Tbs. soy sauce
¼ tsp. sugar

In a 1-quart saucepan combine the dried Shiitake mushrooms, 1 cup water, 1 tablespoon soy sauce, and ¼ teaspoon sugar. Stir together, bring to a boil, cover, and remove from heat. Let rest for 15 minutes. When the mushrooms are cool enough to handle, squeeze out and discard as much liquid as possible. Place on a cutting board and remove any tough pieces of stem. Cut in half any mushroom slices that are longer than 1½ inches.

MADE WITH CANNED GREEN BEANS

2 tsp. vegetable oil
1 (14.5 oz.) can green beans,
*   drained*

1 Tbs. soy sauce
¼ tsp. onion powder
2 Tbs. water

In a 2-quart saucepan cook and stir the prepared Shiitake mushrooms in the vegetable oil for 1 minute. Add the green beans, 1 tablespoon soy sauce, onion powder, and 2 tablespoons water. Cook gently over low heat until all of the water has cooked away, about 2 to 3 minutes. Serve while still warm.

MADE WITH FRESH GREEN BEANS

12 oz. fresh green beans
3 c. water

½ tsp. salt

Rinse the fresh green beans and drain. Remove stems and cut the beans into pieces 1½ to 2 inches long. You should have 2 cups (½ pound) of green beans when done. In a 1-quart saucepan bring the 3 cups water to a boil. Add the salt and beans to the water and boil for 8 minutes. Begin counting the cooking time as soon as the beans are added to the boiling water. Quickly drain the beans and use in place of the canned beans in the above recipe.

240812-16

FRIED GREEN TOMATOES
(Makes 4 servings)

3 lrg. green tomatoes, about 3
   inches in diameter (1 ½ lb.)
½ c. all-purpose flour
1 egg
1 Tbs. milk
1 c. toasted bread crumbs

¼ tsp. salt
⅛ tsp. black pepper
Pinch garlic powder
Vegetable oil for frying
Thousand Island Dressing (see
   Chapter: Salads)

Slice each green tomato into 4 slices about ¼ inch to ½ inch in thick. Put the flour on a small plate. In a small bowl, beat together the egg and milk. Combine the bread crumbs, salt, pepper, and garlic powder in a medium bowl. Heat a medium frying pan with a thin layer of oil on the bottom. Dip each tomato slice in the flour, then dip in the egg, and then dip in the bread crumbs. Make sure that the bread crumbs cover the complete surface of the tomato. Heat the frying pan to 350° or medium high heat. Fry in the oil, turning once, until golden brown on both sides. This should take 2 to 3 minutes on each side. Drain on paper towel and keep warm until ready to serve. Allow three tomato slices for each serving. Serve with Thousand Island Dressing on the side as a dip.

Note: For the home gardener, this is usually prepared in the summer before the tomatoes have started to ripen, and in the fall when the first frost is about to threaten the tomato plants.

TURNIPS AND GREENS
(Makes 4 servings)

2 bunches young Spring turnips
   with tops
1 Tbs. peanut oil

1 tsp. garlic salt
Dash black pepper

Remove the tops from the turnips and set aside. Peel the turnips, cut in half from top to bottom, then slice crosswise into half-moon pieces ¼-inch thick. You should have 4 cups turnips. Place in a 2-quart saucepan and cover with water. Bring to a gentle boil and cook until turnips are tender, about 5 to 6 minutes. Drain, reserving 1 cup stock, and set aside until ready to use. Remove the tough center stem from the greens and discard. Chop the remaining greens, crosswise, into large pieces. You should have 6 to 8 cups of greens. Heat the oil in a wok. Add the greens and 1 cup reserved stock. Stir and cook over medium-high heat for 6 to 10 minutes, or until just tender. Add the cooked turnips, garlic salt, and pepper. Cook for 1 more minute to heat through and let flavors blend.

Note: If you are unable to find turnips with the tops intact, then purchase 2 pounds purple top turnips and one bunch of turnip or mustard greens. A bunch of greens usually weighs about 10 ounces.

ITALIAN STYLE ONIONS AND BELL PEPPERS
(Makes 4 servings)

2 lrg. yellow onions, about 1 lb.
1 med. red bell pepper
1 med. green bell pepper
1 med. yellow bell pepper
2 Tbs. olive oil
½ tsp. dried oregano
¼ tsp. whole anise

¼ tsp. coarse black pepper
½ tsp. salt
¼ tsp. sugar
½ c. large pitted black olives, drained
1 Tbs. red wine vinegar

Peel onions and cut in half from top to bottom. Discard the ends and slice crosswise into half circles ½-inch thick. There should be 2 cups of sliced onions. Wash bell peppers and remove the stem ends and seeds. Slice lengthwise into strips a ½-inch wide and 2 to 2½-inches long. There should be 2 cups of prepared bell peppers. Add the olive oil to an electric skillet and heat to 275°. If using a frying pan, place over medium heat. Add the onions and bell peppers to the skillet or frying pan. Cook and stir until the onion is translucent, about 20 to 30 minutes. The vegetables should be tender but not browned. Place the oregano, anise, and black pepper in a mortar and grind into a powder with the pestle. Stir into the vegetables along with the salt and sugar. Add the black olives and red wine vinegar. Continue to cook and stir for 1 to 2 minutes or until the vinegar has cooked down and serve.

LEFTOVER ONIONS AND BELL PEPPERS

Leftover onions and bell peppers from above

Spaghetti Sauce (see Chapter: Sauces and Gravies)

If you happen to have some of the onions and bell peppers left over (which is rare), add ½ cup Spaghetti Sauce to each cup of leftover vegetables in a small saucepan. Stir over medium heat until heated through. Serve over your favorite pasta.

Note: The combined weight of the bell peppers when purchased should be about 1 pound. Although this recipe calls for three different colored bell peppers, any combination of colored peppers will work. If you do not have a mortar and pestle for crushing your herbs, just rub between your thumb and forefinger.

240812-16

PIROSHKI
(Makes 18 piroshki or 4 to 6 servings)

PASTRY DOUGH

1 ½ c. all-purpose flour
¾ c. vegetable shortening

⅓ c. cold water
½ tsp. salt

Prepare the pastry dough before cooking the filling. In a large bowl, combine the flour, shortening, and salt. Mix together with a pastry blender. Stir in the water to form a soft pastry dough. Place on a counter lightly dusted with flour and knead until smooth, no more than 1 minute. Shape into a round ball and set aside until ready to use.

FILLING - Makes 2 ½ cups

2 c. rutabagas, peeled and sliced
  ¼-inch thick (8 oz.)
1 ½ c. potatoes, peeled and diced
  into 1-inch pieces (8 oz.)
3 MorningStar Farms® sausage
  patties (4 oz.)

vegetable oil
1 c. finely chopped yellow onion
  (4 oz.)
2 Tbs. butter
½ tsp. salt
¼ tsp. black pepper

In a 1-quart saucepan, add the rutabagas, cover with water, and boil over medium-high heat until tender, about 10 to 12 minutes. Drain and set aside. In another 1-quart saucepan, add the potatoes, cover with water, and boil until tender, about 8 to 10 minutes. Drain and add to the rutabagas. Mash the two together until free of lumps. In a small frying pan, fry the sausage patties in a small amount of vegetable oil until lightly browned. Remove from pan and chop into small pieces. There should be 1 cup of chopped sausage. In a large frying pan over medium heat, cook and stir the onion in 1 tablespoon vegetable oil until tender, about 5 minutes. Add the butter and sausage and cook for 1 minute. Add the potato and rutabaga mixture, salt, and pepper and stir until well blended. Remove from heat.

ASSEMBLE AND BAKE

Pastry Dough and Filling from
  above

1 egg yolk, lightly beaten with ---
  1 tsp. water

Roll pastry dough to a ⅛-inch thickness and cut into 4-inch rounds. Place a tablespoon of filling on half of a circle of pastry dough. Brush edge with water and fold dough over filling to make a semicircle. Seal edges by pressing with fork tines. Repeat for remaining pastry dough. Arrange on a large cookie sheet and brush with beaten egg yolk. Bake in a preheated 425° oven for 25 to 30 minutes. Allow 3 to 4 piroshki per serving.

Note: These small pastries can be served as an appetizer or with soup. Turnips can be used in place of the rutabagas. You will need to purchase 1 pound rutabagas or turnips and ¾ pound potatoes.

FRESH MASHED POTATOES
(Makes 4 to 6 large servings)

MICROWAVE OVEN METHOD

*2 lbs. russet potatoes, peeled and
    quartered
1 ½ c. water*

*4 to 6 Tbs. butter
1 tsp. salt
¾ to 1 c. whole milk*

Combine potatoes and 1 ½ cups water in a covered casserole dish. Place in a microwave oven and cook at full power for 20 to 25 minutes or until tender. Stop and stir once or twice during cooking. Drain potatoes and mash with a potato masher. For smoother potatoes, run the potatoes through a potato ricer. Add butter and salt and stir until the butter is melted. Slowly add ¾ cup of milk while beating with a wire whisk. If the potatoes are too thick, then slowly beat in more milk until they reach the desired consistency. Keep warm until ready to serve.

STOVETOP METHOD

Same list of ingredients as above   Additional water

Place the quartered potatoes in a 2-quart saucepan. Cover with water and place over high heat. Reduce heat to a simmer when water begins to boil. Cook the potatoes at a gentle simmer for 10 to 15 minutes, or until potatoes are tender when pierced with the point of a sharp knife. Drain the potatoes as soon as they are done cooking. You do not want them to absorb any more water. Mash with a potato masher. For smoother potatoes, run the potatoes through a potato ricer. Add butter and salt and stir until the butter is melted. Slowly add ¾ cup of milk while beating with a wire whisk. If the potatoes are too thick, then slowly beat in more milk until they reach the desired consistency. Keep warm until ready to serve.

Note: You will need a potato masher or potato ricer for this recipe. In spite of the prevalence of instant mashed potatoes at the supermarket, some people still prefer homemade mashed potatoes. If you like lumpy mashed potatoes, use the potato masher instead of the potato ricer.

240812-16

MASHED RUTABAGAS
(Makes 2 cups or 4 servings)

2 lbs. fresh rutabagas
1 tsp. salt
1 Tbs. vegetable oil
2 Tbs. butter

½ tsp. sugar
1 tsp. imitation bacon bits,
   crushed with back of a spoon
dash coarse black pepper

Peel rutabagas and cut from top to bottom into quarters. There should be about 1½ pounds after peeling. Slice crosswise into pieces ¼-inch thick. Place in a 3-quart saucepan, cover with water, bring to a boil, and simmer until tender, about 25 to 30 minutes. Drain and mash with a potato masher. Add the salt and oil to the pan. Cook and stir rutabagas for 5 minutes. The purpose here is to cook down some of the liquid in the rutabagas so that they are not too watery. Add the butter, sugar, crushed imitation bacon bits, and black pepper. Mix everything together until butter is melted and serve.

Note: Rutabagas are an acquired taste. They have a strong flavor that many people do not find desirable. To reduce the dominant flavor they can be mixed with an equal amount of mashed potatoes (from the previous recipe) before serving. Rutabaga devotees will also enjoy leftover cold mashed rutabaga sandwiches.

SAUTÉED ZUCCHINI AND ONIONS
(Makes 4 Servings)

1½ lb. fresh zucchini squash
1 lrg. yellow onion
1 Tbs. vegetable oil
½ tsp. salt

pinch garlic powder
pinch onion powder
½ tsp. dried oregano, crushed

Wash and drain the zucchini. Remove the stem end and blossom end from each squash. Slice crosswise into pieces ⅜ to ½-inch thick. You should have about 5 cups of zucchini when done slicing. For small zucchini or just for variety, you can slice the zucchini at an angle. Peel the onion and dice into 1-inch pieces. There should be 1½ cups of diced yellow onion. Preheat an electric skillet to 250° or use a frying pan over medium-low heat. Add the oil, squash, and onion. Gently cook and stir for about 15 minutes or until the squash is tender. Add the salt, garlic powder, onion powder, and oregano. Stir for about 30 seconds or until seasonings have had a chance to blend well. Keep warm until ready to serve.

Note: You may use yellow squash or scalloped squash in place of the zucchini. As a matter of fact, any one of the myriad of summer squashes available from your garden or farmer's market will work here.

FRIED WHOLE OKRA
(Makes 6 to 8 servings)

1 lb. fresh okra
2 eggs
1 Tbs. milk
1 c. yellow cornmeal
½ c. all-purpose flour
½ tsp salt

¼ tsp. garlic salt
⅛ tsp. black pepper
Vegetable oil for frying
Tartar Sauce or Thousand Island
  Dressing (see Chapter: Salads)

Sort through okra pods. Use only fresh young okra, no more than 3-inches in length. Wash and pat dry. Beat the eggs and milk together in a small bowl. In a separate large bowl mix together the cornmeal, flour, salt, garlic salt, and pepper. Preheat vegetable oil about ¼ inch deep in a frying pan to about 350°. Dip each okra in the beaten egg, then roll in the cornmeal mixture. Fry in the hot oil, about 1 to 1½ minutes on each side until golden, turning once when necessary. Serve warm, using Tartar Sauce or Thousand Island Dressing as a dip.

Note: Frozen okra can be used in place of the fresh. Thaw or defrost and pat dry before cooking. There are about 64 small okra pods in a pound.

OKRA AND GREEN CHILE FRITTERS
(Makes 6 fritters)

8 oz. fresh okra; pods should be
  no more than 4 in. long
1 (4 oz.) can diced green Ortega®
  chiles
½ c. all-purpose flour
2 eggs, lightly beaten

3 Tbs. milk
½ tsp. salt
¼ tsp. black pepper
Oil for frying
Thousand Island Dressing (see
  Chapter: Salads)

Remove stems and slice okra crosswise into pieces about ¼-inch wide. There should be 2 cups of sliced okra. In a 2-quart saucepan bring 6 cups of water to a boil. Blanch the okra in the boiling water for 3 minutes. Drain and rinse the okra thoroughly in a colander and place in a large bowl. Add the diced green chiles to the okra. In a small bowl, make a batter by combining the flour, eggs, milk, salt, and pepper. Stir together until well blended. Stir the batter into the okra and mix well. Use ⅓ cup of the batter for each fritter. Put batter in a frying pan coated with a thin layer of oil heated to 325°. Shape into a round fritter and flatten with the back of a spatula. If you are using a frying pan, heat the oil over medium-high heat. Fry until golden brown, turning once, about 5 minutes on each side. Serve topped with Thousand Island Dressing.

240812-16

SAVORY DRESSING
(Makes 4 to 6 servings)

6 vegetarian sausage links
2 tsp. vegetable oil
1 lrg. apple (6 to 8 oz.)
1 (7 oz.) can button mushrooms, drained
2 c. diced yellow onion
1 c. diced celery
1 c. diced bell pepper
3 Tbs. olive oil, divided (2 Tbs. + 1 Tbs.)

1 ½ tsp. poultry seasoning
1 tsp. sage, crushed
1 tsp. salt
½ tsp. hickory salt
½ tsp. black pepper
¼ tsp. summer savory
½ tsp. rosemary, crushed
½ tsp. paprika
¼ c. butter

In a small frying pan cook the sausage links in 2 teaspoons vegetable oil until lightly browned, about 5 to 6 minutes. Cut into bite-size pieces and reserve. Quarter the apple, peel, and remove seeds. Slice each quarter crosswise into 5 or 6 pieces. Drain the mushrooms and cut each mushroom in half. In a large frying pan, cook and stir the onion, celery, and bell pepper in 2 tablespoons olive oil over medium heat for about 5 minutes. Add the sliced apple and cook for another 3 minutes or until onion is translucent. When the vegetables are done cooking, add the reserved sausage links, mushroom halves, poultry seasoning, sage, salt, hickory salt, black pepper, and summer savory. Continue to cook and stir together for another 1 to 2 minutes. Fold biscuit batter (see below) into vegetables in pan and cook over low heat for 1 to 2 minutes while turning occasionally with a spatula. I know this may sound unusual, but this is the way I learned it, and I am just passing it on to you. Coat the bottom of a 2 quart casserole dish with the remaining 1 tablespoon of olive oil. Pour contents of pan into casserole dish and spread out evenly. Sprinkle rosemary and paprika over top. Cut butter into pieces and distribute evenly over top. Bake, uncovered, in a preheated 400° oven for 40 to 45 minutes. This is usually served with slices of Worthington® Meatless Smoked Turkey and Brown Gravy (see Chapter: Sauces and Gravies) on top.

BISCUIT BATTER

2 c. biscuit mix
2 eggs

¾ c. water

You can prepare this biscuit batter while the vegetables are cooking. In a large bowl, mix together biscuit mix, 2 eggs, and water to make a thick batter. The batter should be slightly thinner than you would make for drop biscuits but thicker than pancake batter. Set aside until ready to use.

Note: This should probably be called Southern Savory Dressing. My guess is that this dressing is frequently prepared in the South in place of the more familiar commercial dressing made from bread crumbs or croûtons. For a gluten free version you can use Bisquick® Gluten Free for the biscuit mix. Add one more egg for a total of three eggs and reduce water to ⅔ cup.

RICE MEDLEY
(Makes 5 ⅓ cups or 8 servings)

2 c. cooked white rice
2 c. cooked Mexican Rice (From
either one of the recipes in this
chapter).
1 ½ c. cooked bulgur wheat

3 Tbs. butter
¼ c. chopped parsley leaves
¼ c. chopped green onions
2 Tbs. water

Quantities are approximate and can be adjusted to accommodate what is available. Combine the white rice, Mexican Rice, bulgur wheat, and butter in a casserole dish. Add the parsley and green onion tops. Heat in the microwave oven, stirring occasionally, until steaming hot and butter is melted, about 6 minutes. Taste and add a little water if it is too dry. To prepare in an electric skillet, melt butter in a skillet set at 275°. Stir and cook the parsley and green onions in the butter for 10 to 15 seconds. Add the white rice, Mexican rice, bulgur, and 2 Tbs. water. Stir continuously until heated through. Keep warm until ready to serve. Allow ⅔ cup Rice Medley per serving.

Note: This recipe was created as a way to use leftover rice and/or bulgur. Any or all of the ingredients can be left from a previous meal. Quantities are approximate and can vary depending on what you have on hand. Cook fresh any ingredients that are missing.

RICE WITH PEAS AND MUSHROOMS
(Makes 4 to 6 Servings)

½ c. frozen peas, cooked and
drained
1 c. long grain rice, uncooked
4 oz. fresh button mushrooms

3 Tbs. butter, divided --- (2 Tbs. +
1 Tbs.)
2 Tbs. chopped parsley
1 tsp. salt

Cook the rice according the to package directions and keep warm until ready to assemble. There should be 3 cups of cooked rice. Gently rinse the mushrooms and drain. Cut each mushroom in half from top to bottom. Lay the mushroom halves flat on the cutting board and slice each half from top to bottom into ¼-inch thick slices. There should be 2 cups of sliced mushrooms when finished. Add 2 tablespoons of the butter to a large frying pan over medium heat. When the butter has melted add the sliced mushrooms. Cook and stir until tender, about 3 to 4 minutes. Stir in the cooked peas, chopped parsley, and remaining 1 tablespoon butter. Cook for 1 minute and add the rice and salt. Stir over medium heat until well blended. Keep warm until ready to serve.

240812-16

SPANISH SAFFRON RICE
(Makes 3 cups or 6 servings)

2 Tbs. butter
⅔ c. finely chopped white onion
1 clove garlic, minced (1 tsp.)
½ tsp. saffron threads

2 c. water
1 tsp. salt
1 c. long grain rice, uncooked

In a 2-quart saucepan combine the butter, white onion, and garlic over medium heat. Cook and stir until the onion is soft and translucent. Crush the saffron threads between your fingers and add to the saucepan along with the water and salt. Bring to a boil, cover, and gently simmer for about 5 minutes. This allows the water to absorb some flavor and color from the saffron. Stir in the rice, cover, and simmer over low heat for 20 minutes or until rice is done. Let stand for 5 minutes before serving. Fluff the rice with a fork and serve.

Note: There is no denying that saffron threads are expensive. You can reduce the cost per meal by buying a larger quantity. They keep well for a very long time when stored in a dark cabinet. For a vegan version of this rice, substitute olive oil for the butter.

SIMPLE BULGUR WHEAT PILAF
(Makes 4 servings)

2 Tbs. butter
1 c. bulgur wheat
¼ c. finely chopped yellow onion

½ tsp. salt
Dash black pepper
2 c. vegetable stock or water

Melt butter in a warm electric skillet or frying pan. Add the bulgur and onion. Stir and cook at 325° until bulgur has turned a golden color. If using a frying pan, cook over medium-high heat. Reduce heat and add the salt, pepper, and vegetable stock or water. Stir and bring to a gentle simmer. Cover and cook for 15 minutes or until all of the water is absorbed. Fluff briefly and serve.

PINTO BEANS COOKED IN A SLOW COOKER
(Makes 3 quarts)

2 lb. dried pinto beans	2 tsp. salt
3 Tbs. onion soup mix	

Sort through the beans and remove any non-bean material. Place in a large pot and cover with water. Stir with a large spoon and drain off the water. Repeat this cleaning process two more times. The water from the last rinsing should be clear. Place the drained pintos in your slow cooker in the evening before retiring. Fill the pot with water until it almost comes up to the top. Place the lid on top and let stand overnight. Turn the pot on first thing in the morning. If your slow cooker has more than one setting, it should be set on low. Stir in the onion soup mix. Cover and cook for 8 to 10 hours or until beans are tender. If your slow cooker has two settings, you can turn it up to the highest setting for the last 2 hours. If possible, stir once after every 2 to 3 hours of cooking. This insures that all of the beans will be cooked evenly. Stir in the salt about 30 minutes before turning off the slow cooker. Conventional wisdom says that adding the salt in the beginning tends to make the beans tough. You can also use this recipe for Anasazi beans or cranberry beans. Most people agree that neither one has the same hearty flavor that you get from pinto beans.

Note: You will need a 4-quart slow cooker for this recipe. If you eat a lot of pinto beans, you may want to consider cooking them in a slow cooker. Beans simmered for a long period of time are easier to digest. Leftovers keep very well in the freezer.

PINTO BEANS WITH JALAPEÑO PEPPERS
(Makes 1 quart)

2 to 4 Jalapeño peppers	1 qt. cooked pinto beans
1 c. diced yellow onion	1 Tbs. + 1 tsp. honey (preferred)
1 Tbs. olive oil	or brown sugar

The number of Jalapeños you use depends on how "hot" you would like your beans. To prepare the Jalapeño peppers, remove the stem and cut in half lengthwise. Remove the seeds and finely mince the peppers. In a 2-quart saucepan cook and stir the yellow onion in the olive oil until the onion is translucent, about 5 minutes. Do not allow the onion to brown. You can use canned pinto beans, beans fresh from being cooked in a slow cooker, or frozen beans that have been thawed or defrosted. Add the pinto beans, Jalapeño peppers, and honey. Stir the beans over medium heat until they just begin to simmer. Allow to simmer for about 5 minutes. You can cook them longer and let the flavors come together even more.

240812-16

NEW MEXICO STYLE REFRIED BEANS
(Makes 1 pint)

1 pt. cooked pinto beans
¼ c. finely chopped yellow onion
1 clove garlic, minced

2 Tbs. corn oil
2 Tbs. all-purpose flour
¼ tsp. hickory salt (opt.)

Place pinto beans in a blender. Do not drain. The bean liquid should almost come to the top of the beans in the blender. Pour off any excess liquid or add water if necessary. Whirl the beans in the blender at a slow speed until smooth, about 1 minute. In a 1-quart sauce pan, placed over medium heat, cook and stir the onion and garlic in the corn oil until tender, about 5 minutes. Stir in the flour and cook for about 1 minute to form a paste. Stir in the pinto beans from the blender and optional hickory salt. Continue to cook and stir over medium heat until beans thicken and just begin to bubble.

Note: If you like, you can forgo the blender and just mash the beans with a potato masher in the pot with the flour paste.

MEXICAN RICE
(Makes 6 to 8 servings)

2 c. water
2 tsp. chili powder
2 Tbs. imitation bacon bits
2 Tbs. olive oil
½ c. finely chopped yellow onion
1 clove garlic

1½ c. long grain rice, uncooked
1½ tsp. salt
2 Tbs. butter
2 Tbs. diced red pimientos (they
    come in a jar)

In a 1-quart saucepan, combine 2 cups water and the chili powder. Bring to a boil and simmer for 5 minutes. Remove chili-water from heat until ready to use. Place the imitation bacon bits on a cutting board and mash with the back of a spoon until it is almost a powder. You can also use a mortar and pestle to crush the bacon bits. In an electric skillet set at 275°, cook and stir the onion, garlic, and bacon bits in the olive oil until the onion is translucent, about 5 minutes. If you are using a frying pan it should be placed over medium-low heat. Remove the clove of garlic and discard but leave the onion in the pan. Stir in the rice and cook for about 2 minutes. Measure the chili-water and add enough water to make 3 cups. Add the chili-water, salt, butter, and pimientos to the vegetables in the skillet. Cover, reduce heat, and simmer gently for 10 minutes. Stir once, return cover to pan, and continue cooking for an additional 10 minutes or until the rice is done.

MEXICAN RED RICE
(Makes 5 cups or 6 large servings)

1 lrg. (about 4 oz.) Roma tomato
¾ c. diced white onion (½-inch dice)
2 Tbs. corn oil

2 cloves garlic, peeled and sliced
1 ¾ c. water, divided (¾ c. + 1 c.)
1 c. long grain rice, uncooked
1 tsp. salt

Peel, chop, and reserve the Roma tomato. There should be about ½ cup chopped tomato. In a medium frying pan, at least 9 inches in diameter, cook and stir the onion in 2 tablespoons of oil for 3 minutes. Add the sliced garlic and continue to cook for 3 more minutes or until onion is translucent. Take pan off burner. Remove onion and garlic with a slotted spoon and put in a blender. Leave as much oil in the pan as possible. Add the reserved diced tomato and ¾ cup of the water to the blender. Run the blender on low for 30 seconds and set aside. Add the rice to the frying pan. Parch the rice by cooking over medium-high heat in the oil in the frying pan while stirring continuously. Cook for 6 to 8 minutes or until rice is lightly browned. Carefully add the blended tomatoes, the remaining 1 cup water, and salt to the frying pan. Stir and heat until mixture comes to a boil. Reduce heat to a simmer and cover. Stir once after ten minutes of cooking. Cook for a total of 20 minutes. Let stand covered for 5 minutes before serving.

HOMEMADE CHEESE NACHOS
(Makes 6 to 8 servings)

HOMEMADE CORN CHIPS

12 corn tortillas
Oil for frying, about 2 c.

popcorn salt (opt.)

Cut tortillas into 8 pie-shaped wedges of the same size. Pour oil into an electric skillet to about ½-inch deep. Heat the oil to medium-high or 350° and add 16 to 24 tortilla pieces. Use a large slotted spoon to separate the chips so that they do not stick together. The chips should be in a single layer in order to cook evenly. After about 1 minute, turn the chips so that they cook evenly on both sides. Total frying time will be about 2 minutes. Drain on paper towel and sprinkle salt on the chips if desired.

HOMEMADE CHEESE NACHOS

Corn chips from above
4 oz. (1 c.) grated cheddar cheese

Fresh chile salsa

Spread the chips out on a large cookie sheet in a single layer. Sprinkle some grated cheese over the chips. Place under a broiler and heat until cheese is melted and begins to bubble. Remove and serve with fresh salsa while they are still warm.

120

SWEET AND SOUR PINEAPPLE WALNUTS
(Makes 6 servings)

PREPARING THE WALNUTS

48 walnut halves
3 c. boiling water
1 c. all-purpose flour
1 egg, lightly beaten

⅓ c. water
Oil for frying, at least ½ inch
    deep (about 2 c.)

First you will need to blanch and roast the walnuts. In a 1-quart saucepan bring 3 cups of water to a boil. Add the walnuts and boil gently for 5 minutes. Drain in the sink, rinse with cold water and spread evenly on a cookie sheet. Bake in a preheated 275° oven for 40 minutes or until walnuts are dry. In a medium bowl, combine the flour, egg, and ⅓ cup water. Beat together to create a smooth batter. Place the oil in an electric skillet and heat to 350°. If using a frying pan, cook over medium-high heat. Dip each blanched walnut half in the batter and fry in the oil, turning once, until they are lightly browned. This will take about 2 minutes for each walnut. Remove from oil, drain, and keep warm in a 250° oven until ready to serve.

PINEAPPLE SWEET AND SOUR SAUCE

1 (8 oz.) can pineapple slices
1 lrg. Roma tomato; seeded and
    diced into 1-inch pieces, (¾ c.)
2 Tbs. peanut oil
½ c. diced yellow onion (¾-inch
    pieces)
½ c. diced green bell pepper ---
    (¾-inch pieces)

⅔ c. sugar
⅔ c. ketchup
½ c. white vinegar
¼ tsp. salt
¼ c. cornstarch dissolved in ----
    ¼ c. water

Drain the pineapple slices and reserve the juice. Cut each slice into 8 pieces. Set aside until ready to use. In a 2-quart saucepan heat 2 tablespoons peanut oil over medium heat and add the onion and bell pepper. Cook and stir until the onion is tender, about 5 minutes. Quickly stir in the sugar, ketchup, vinegar, salt, and ⅔ cup of the reserved pineapple juice. Cook and stir until mixture comes to a gentle boil. Stir in the cornstarch mixture and continue to cook until sauce thickens and bubbles gently. Add the fried walnuts and cook for 15 seconds. Add the pineapple pieces and diced tomato and cook for another 15 to 30 seconds so that everything is evenly heated. Serve.

Note: History says this dish was created by Chinese monks who served only vegetarian meals. The original name of the recipe was Mock Sweet and Sour Pork. The walnuts were supposed to be the substitute for pork. Although usually served as a side dish with Chinese meals, it can also be served over rice as a main dish.

CHINESE EGG ROLLS
(Makes 8 Egg Rolls)

PREPARING THE SHIITAKE MUSHROOMS

2 c. (about 1 oz.) dried, sliced
  Shiitake mushrooms
1 ½ c. water

1 Tbs. soy sauce
½ tsp. sugar

In a 1-quart saucepan, combine the Shiitake mushrooms, 1 ½ cups water, 1 tablespoon soy sauce, and sugar. Stir together, bring to a boil, cover, and remove from heat. Let rest for 10 minutes. When the mushrooms are cool enough to handle, squeeze out and discard as much liquid as possible. Place on a cutting board and remove any tough pieces of stem. Finely chop the mushrooms and measure. There should be ½ cup firmly packed mushrooms for stuffing egg rolls.

PREPARING THE EGG ROLLS

2 c. (about 4 oz.) fresh mung
  bean sprouts
½ c. finely chopped celery
¾ c. peeled and grated carrot
¼ c. chopped green onions
1 egg, lightly beaten
2 tsp. soy sauce

¼ tsp. salt
8 egg roll wrappers (wraps)
Vegetable oil for frying
Ketchup
Fresh mustard for dipping (See
  below)

Rinse the mung bean sprouts, drain and chop into small pieces about ¼ inch long. In a large bowl combine the chopped Shiitake mushrooms, chopped bean sprouts, celery, carrot, green onions, beaten egg, 2 teaspoons soy sauce, and ¼ teaspoon salt. Stir together until well blended. Place one egg roll wrapper on a flat surface so that one of the corners is facing you. Brush water around the edges of the wrapper with a small pastry brush. This will help the egg roll to stay together when rolled up. Spread 2 heaping tablespoons of the mixture from left to right just below the center. Fold the corner that is closest to you over the filling. Fold the left and right corners toward the center over the filling. Firmly roll the wrapper up and press the top corner to seal. Pinch the egg roll, if necessary, to create a round, not flat, sausage-like roll. When all 8 egg rolls have been assembled you can begin frying. Fill an electric skillet with vegetable oil ½ to ¾-inch deep. Heat the oil to 350°. If using a frying pan, place the pan over medium-high heat. Add a few egg rolls at a time to the frying pan. Cook for about 1 ½ to 2 minutes on each side. The egg rolls should be golden brown when done. Remove from oil and drain on paper towel. Serve with ketchup and fresh mustard (see below) in a small condiment dish. Dip the egg roll in the ketchup while picking up a small amount of mustard from the side. Keep in mind that the fresh mustard is very hot.

(continued)

240812-16

2 Tbs. ground mustard   *½ c. ketchup*
1 Tbs. warm water

Place the ground mustard in a small dish. Using a chopstick, slowly stir in 1 tablespoon warm water. The prepared mustard should have the same consistency as ketchup. If it is too thick, slowly stir in some more warm water, a drop at a time, until it reaches the right consistency. Set aside until ready to use. Do not use yellow mustard (from a jar) in place of this freshly blended mustard. The fresh mustard is much more flavorful and spicier. To serve, put 1 tablespoon ketchup in the center of a small condiment dish and place about ½ teaspoon fresh mustard on the edge of the ketchup.

DEEP FRIED WONTON STUFFED WITH TURNIP
(Makes 24 wontons or 4 servings)

1 lb. fresh turnips   *24 wonton wrappers (wraps)*
1 tsp. sugar   *Oil for frying, about ½-inch deep*
½ tsp. salt   *Ketchup and Fresh Mustard for*
pinch white pepper   *Dipping (see previous recipe)*
2 tsp. peanut oil

Peel the turnip, grate on a coarse grater, and measure. You should have 2 cups of firmly packed grated turnips. In a small frying pan, combine the grated turnip, sugar, salt, and white pepper, and cook in the peanut oil for 6 to 8 minutes. The turnips should be tender when done. Let cool slightly before you begin to stuff the wontons. Place a wonton wrapper on a flat surface. Using a pastry brush, moisten the edges with water. Place about 1 teaspoon of the grated turnip in the center of the wrapper. Fold one corner over the filling to create a triangle. Press the edges of the wonton wrapper to seal. Fold the two opposing corners of the wonton over the center to form the traditional shape and press to seal. Set aside until all of the wontons have been filled. Place the oil in a skillet and heat to medium-high or 350°. Fry the wontons for 1 to 2 minutes or until golden brown. Turn once so that both sides are cooked evenly. Drain and keep warm until ready to serve. You can also use a deep fryer to cook the wontons. Serve with ketchup and fresh mustard (see previous recipe) in a small condiment dish. Dip a wonton in the ketchup while picking up a small amount of mustard from the side. Keep in mind that the fresh mustard is very hot.

Note: The "Note" from the following recipe (Deep Fried Stuffed Vegetable Wonton) regarding egg roll wrappers also applies to this recipe.

DEEP FRIED STUFFED VEGETABLE WONTON
(Makes 36 wontons or 6 servings)

2 Tbs. peanut oil
½ c. peeled and finely diced
    carrots
½ c. finely diced yellow onion
½ c. finely diced bell pepper
½ c. finely diced celery
1 Tbs. soy sauce

½ tsp. salt
1 Tbs. cornstarch
36 wonton wrappers (wraps)
vegetable oil for frying
Sweet and Sour Sauce (see
    following recipe)

Add the peanut oil to a 1-quart saucepan. Cook and stir the carrots, onion, bell pepper, and celery in the oil over medium heat until tender, about 5 minutes. Remove from heat and stir in soy sauce, salt, and cornstarch. Place a wonton wrap on a flat surface, brush the edges with a small amount of water, and place a heaping teaspoon of the vegetable filling in the center. Fold the wrapper over the filling to create a triangle and press around the edges to seal. Curl the two opposing corners towards each other, pinch, and seal to make the traditional wonton shape. Repeat until all wonton wrappers are filled. Place vegetable oil in an electric skillet or frying pan about ½-inch deep. Heat to medium high or 350°. Fry the wontons in the hot oil, turning once, until they are golden brown on both sides, about 2 minutes. Drain on paper towel. Keep warm while preparing the Sweet and Sour Sauce which will be used as a dipping sauce.

Note: If you do not have or cannot find wonton wrappers, you can always use egg roll wrappers that have been cut in half in both directions, resulting in 4 wonton wrappers. Some cooks may prefer this method because egg roll wrappers are a little thicker than wonton wrappers. When using a frying pan, you will need 2 to 2½ cups of oil that is about ½ to ⅝-inch deep.

SWEET AND SOUR SAUCE
(Makes ¾ cup)

1 tsp. peanut oil
3 Tbs. sugar
3 Tbs. ketchup
3 Tbs. water

2 Tbs. white vinegar
1 Tbs. cornstarch dissolved in ---
    1 Tbs. water

In a 1-quart saucepan combine the peanut oil, sugar, ketchup, water, and white vinegar. Stir over medium heat until sauce begins to simmer. Remove from heat and stir in cornstarch mixture. Return to heat, stirring constantly, until sauce thickens and begins to boil. Remove from heat and serve with Deep Fried Stuffed Vegetable Wontons or Fried Egg Roll Chips (see previous and following recipes).

FRIED EGG ROLL CHIPS
(Makes 48 chips or 4 servings)

6 egg roll wrappers
Vegetable oil for frying, about ---
  ½ inch deep

Sweet and Sour Sauce (see
  previous recipe)

Place a single egg roll wrapper on a cutting board. Cut in half from top to bottom and then from side to side so that you have four equal-sized square pieces. What you have now are essentially four wonton wrappers. Cut the egg roll wrapper again diagonally from corner to corner in each direction so that you have eight triangles. Repeat for all of the egg roll wrappers. Heat vegetable oil in an electric skillet to 350° or in a frying pan to medium-high. Since the wrappers are fairly thin, your oil only needs to be about ½ inch deep. You can also use a deep fryer. Fry the triangles for two minutes, about 1 minute on each side, or until golden brown. Turn once while frying so that the chips are cooked on both sides. When serving with Asian food, serve with Sweet and Sour Sauce (see previous recipe) as a dip. Extra chips can be served as a snack in place of corn chips. Serve with any dip that you would serve with corn or potato chips. They can also be used to make cheese nachos.

Note: A pizza cutting wheel actually works better at cutting egg roll wrappers than a knife. Leftover egg roll wrappers (and wonton wrappers) keep well in the freezer. If they become dried out, they can still be used in this recipe. You should never have to throw out wrappers because they can always be used to make chips.

PAN FRIED NOODLES
(Makes 4 to 6 servings)

4 green onions
1 lb. Chinese or any other type of
  Asian noodles
2 Tbs. peanut oil (more if needed)

1 Tbs. finely chopped fresh
  ginger
½ tsp. garlic salt

Wash the green onions and slice into ¼-inch pieces, using both the green and white parts. There should be ¾ cup when done. Set aside until ready to use. Cook the noodles according to the package directions and drain. If you do not plan to fry the noodles right away, toss a small amount of peanut oil with the noodles in order to keep them from sticking together. Heat the 2 tablespoons of peanut oil in a wok over medium heat for 15 to 20 seconds. Add the green onions and ginger and stir for about 30 seconds. Add the cooked noodles and sprinkle the garlic salt over top. Stir and toss the noodles until thoroughly heated. These noodles can be served as a side dish or used as the foundation for Sautéed Vegetables on Noodles.

CHINESE FRIED RICE
(Makes 3 to 4 large servings)

1 ½ c. medium grain rice, uncooked
1 egg, lightly beaten
1 Tbs. peanut oil
1 tsp. freshly grated ginger
½ c. yellow onion, sliced top to bottom into ¼ in. thick pieces
3 green onions, cut crosswise into 1-inch pieces
¼ c. sliced bell pepper, about --- 1 ½ inches long

½ c. celery, sliced diagonally into pieces ¼ inch thick
1 ½ c. diced Chinese cabbage leaves
½ tsp. garlic powder
½ tsp. onion powder
¼ c. water
½ c. peas, fresh or frozen
¼ c. soy sauce
½ tsp. sesame oil

Cook the white rice according to package directions and keep warm until ready to use. Scramble the egg in a small frying pan and set aside. Pour the peanut oil around the sides of a wok over medium-high heat. Add the grated ginger and cook for 5 to 10 seconds, just long enough to flavor the oil. Quickly add the yellow onion, green onion, bell pepper, celery, Chinese cabbage, garlic powder, and onion powder. Cook and stir over medium heat for 2 minutes. Add the water and peas and continue to cook until vegetables are tender, about 3 to 4 more minutes. Add the cooked rice, scrambled egg, and soy sauce. Cook and stir for about 1 minute or until everything is well blended. Quickly stir in the sesame oil and serve.

SNOW PEAS AND WATER CHESTNUTS
(Makes 4 to 6 servings)

6 oz. fresh snow peas
2 tsp. peanut oil
¼ tsp garlic salt
1 (8 oz.) can sliced water chestnuts, drained

⅔ c. water
2 Tbs. soy sauce
1 Tbs. cornstarch dissolved in --- 1 Tbs. water
Sesame oil

Remove the strings from the snow peas, rinse under cold water, and drain in a colander. Add the peanut oil to a wok over medium-high heat and add the snow peas and garlic salt. Cook and stir until snow peas are almost tender, about 5 minutes. Add the sliced water chestnuts, ⅔ cup water, and soy sauce. Continue to cook and simmer for 1 to 2 minutes. Reduce heat so that the water in the pan is not boiling and stir in the cornstarch mixture. Return the heat to medium-high and stir until the sauce bubbles and is thickened. Remove from the heat, stir in a few drops of sesame oil, and serve.

Note: Snow peas are easy to grow and can produce a large crop in a very short period of time. This recipe was created one year when there was an abundance of snow peas.

126

Bread

Bread
Baking Powder Breads:

Most baking powder breads are pretty straightforward. Any cook who has had experience baking would probably have made baking powder bread at one time or another. The only comment that needs to be made here is regarding muffin pans. The traditional muffin pan has 12 indentations or cavities for muffins. These have become known as medium sized muffins. At some point a larger muffin gained popularity. This muffin pan has 6 large indentations but requires the same amount of batter as the medium muffin pan. In other words, the large muffins are almost exactly twice as big as the traditional medium muffins. There is also a mini-muffin pan with 24 indentations which makes muffins that are half the size of the medium muffins. Any recipe that fills 12 of the regular muffin tins will also work for large muffin pans and mini-muffin pans. There is no need to adjust a recipe for the different sizes of pans.

Yeast Breads

Yeast: There are two different kinds of dry baker's yeast on the market: regular active dry yeast and instant active dry yeast. The regular yeast was the norm for many years. When the instant yeast came along it made bread baking easier and more reliable. The instant yeast is much more forgiving and becomes active under a much wider set of conditions. Apparently the instant yeast, which does not have to be mixed with liquid to become activated, made it possible for the bread machine to exist.

Instant yeast bubbles: Most recipes here will say to let the dough rest for a minute at the beginning while the yeast becomes active. It is extremely rare for the instant yeast to not become active. However, if you will look closely at the paste that is first formed you will see little bubbles forming and starting to expand. This starts immediately and means that the yeast is working.

How to knead: Kneading is very simple. Once the dough has been placed on a lightly floured surface, press the center of the dough with the heel of your left hand. Turn the dough counterclockwise 90 degrees and fold the top edge over the center of the dough and press again with the heel of your hand. Turn counterclockwise again and repeat. After several repetitions the dough will become a smooth ball that is ready to rest and rise.

When Bread Dough is Rising: There are two factors that have a major influence on how fast bread dough will rise. The age of the yeast and the temperature of the kitchen. The times given in these recipes are for fresh yeast and a warm kitchen.

Cooling rack: When bread is removed from the oven after baking it is still very hot. If you put it on a flat surface while it cools, moisture will form on the bottom of the loaf and make it soggy. By placing bread on a cooling rack, it allows air to circulate all around the loaf and helps prevent the formation of condensation on the bottom.

BREAD

Baking Powder Breads

HOMEMADE BAKING POWDER
(Makes ½ cup)

3 Tbs. baking soda   3 Tbs. cornstarch
3 Tbs. cream of tartar

Sift together the baking soda, cream of tartar and cornstarch. Store in a tightly sealed jar. If the baking powder becomes caked over time, just resift it through a fine mesh strainer and it will be as good as new.

Note: If you are going to be baking your own baking powder breads from scratch, you can also make your own fresh baking powder. Since this recipe does not include phosphate or aluminum compounds, it does not have a bitter aftertaste that some commercial products frequently have.

HOMEMADE BISCUIT MIX
(Makes 40 oz. or 8 cups)

BASIC HOMEMADE BISCUIT MIX

7 c. sifted all-purpose flour (2 lb.)   ½ c. powdered nonfat milk
2 tsp. salt   1 c. shortening
⅓ c. baking powder(5 Tbs.+1 tsp.)

Combine the flour, salt, baking powder, and powdered milk in a large bowl. Add shortening and cut into the flour with a pastry blender until well blended. Store in an airtight container .

MAKING 6 LARGE ROUND BISCUITS FROM HOMEMADE BISCUIT MIX

1 ½ c. Homemade Biscuit Mix   ⅓ c. water

Place the biscuit mix in a large bowl and stir in the water. Gently mix until blended to make a soft dough. Knead gently and roll out on a lightly floured counter top to a thickness of ½ inch. Use a 2 ½-inch diameter biscuit cutter to cut into 6 large biscuits. Place on an ungreased cookie sheet and bake in a preheated 425° oven for 12 minutes or until tops are golden brown.

Note: This recipe makes a large quantity of biscuit mix to keep on hand for quick preparation of homemade biscuits. It can be used in place of the commercial biscuit mixes that you find at the grocery store. This mix will keep in a tightly sealed container for up to 6 months.

CHEESE BISCUITS
(Makes 4 large biscuits)

1 ½ c. Homemade Biscuit Mix (see previous recipe)
¼ c. water
1 c. diced cheddar cheese (5 oz.)

8 strips cheddar cheese, about --- ⅜ x 2½-in. (1 oz.)
Vegetable shortening

Place the Biscuit Mix in a bowl and stir in the water. Knead gently 2 or 3 times until dough forms a solid mass. Divide into 4 equal pieces. Roll or pat each piece into a circle 5 inches in diameter. Put ¼ cup diced cheddar cheese in the center of each. Gently fold the edges over to cover the cheese, leaving a small opening in the center to allow the heat to escape. Arrange two strips of cheese on the top of each biscuit to form an "X". Place on a lightly greased cookie sheet. Bake in a preheated 425° oven for at least 15 minutes or until lightly browned. Remove from oven and serve immediately.

Note: You will need a total of 6 ounces of cheddar cheese for this recipe. Commercial biscuit mix, like Bisquick®, can be used in place of the Homemade Biscuit Mix if you like.

BUTTERMILK BISCUITS
(Makes 8 to 10 biscuits)

2 c. sifted all-purpose flour
2 ½ tsp. baking powder
¼ tsp. baking soda
½ tsp salt

1 Tbs. sugar
⅓ c. vegetable shortening
¾ c. fresh buttermilk (do not substitute)

Sift together the flour, baking powder, baking soda, salt, and sugar in a large bowl. Cut in the shortening with a pastry blender. Add the buttermilk and mix just until the dough follows the fork around the edge of the bowl. Turn out onto a lightly floured board and knead gently for 20 to 30 seconds. Roll or pat to ½-inch in thickness. Use a biscuit cutter to cut into rounds. If you don't have a biscuit cutter, you can use the opening of an empty, clean, fruit can. It should be about 2 ¾ inches in diameter. Place the biscuits on a lightly greased baking sheet. Knead the leftover scraps of dough together and repeat the process until all of the dough has been used. You should have 8 to 10 biscuits when finished. Bake in a preheated 425° oven for 12 to 14 minutes, or until lightly browned on top.

Note: You will need a 2 ½ to 2 ¾-inch diameter biscuit cutter. Buttermilk biscuits are a little different from regular biscuits. The buttermilk reacts with the leavening to make them lighter, and it gives the biscuits a unique flavor.

240812-16

TEA SCONES
(Makes 8 scones)

⅓ c. raisins
2 c. all-purpose flour (do not sift)
¼ c. butter
2 Tbs. sugar

1 tsp. baking powder
¼ tsp. salt
1 egg, lightly beaten
½ c. milk

Plump raisins by soaking in warm water for 5 minutes. Drain and set aside until ready to use. In a large bowl combine the flour, butter, sugar, baking powder, and salt. Cut butter into flour with a pastry blender. In a separate small bowl, stir the milk into the beaten egg. Set aside 1 tablespoon of the milk mixture for the tops of the scones. Stir remainder of milk and plumped raisins into the flour mixture. Turn out onto a lightly floured surface and knead to make a moist dough. Divide dough into two equal pieces. Pat each piece into a circle about 5 inches in diameter and ¾ inch thick. Cut each piece into quarters and arrange on a lightly floured baking sheet. Brush tops with reserved milk mixture. Bake at 425° until lightly browned, about 15 to 18 minutes. Serve warm.

PUMPKIN BREAD
(Makes 2 loaves)

1 c. raisins (opt.)
4 eggs, lightly beaten
2 c. sugar
1 c. oil
1 (15 oz.) can pumpkin (about ---
    1¾ c.)
⅔ c. water
4 c. all-purpose flour

2 tsp. baking soda
1½ tsp. baking powder
1 tsp. salt
1 tsp. nutmeg
1 tsp. cinnamon
½ tsp. cloves
½ tsp. powdered ginger
¾ c. walnuts (opt.)

Plump the optional raisins by soaking them in warm water for 5 minutes. Drain and set aside until ready to use. In a large bowl mix together the eggs and sugar. Add the oil, pumpkin, and water and beat together until well blended. In a separate bowl, sift together the flour, baking soda, baking powder, salt, nutmeg, cinnamon, cloves, and ginger. Add to the pumpkin mixture and beat everything together until you have a smooth batter. Fold in the optional raisins and walnuts. Spread evenly into two greased and floured 9 x 5 x 3-inch loaf pans. Bake in a preheated 350° oven for 1 hour to 1 hour and 10 minutes or until cake tester comes out clean.

BANANA NUT BREAD
(Makes 1 loaf)

⅓ c. shortening
¾ c. sugar
2 eggs, lightly beaten
1 ⅓ c. mashed ripe bananas
¾ c. milk
3 c. sifted all-purpose flour

1 ½ tsp. baking soda
¾ tsp. cinnamon
½ tsp. salt
¼ tsp. ground cloves
¼ tsp. nutmeg
¾ c. chopped walnuts (opt.)

In a large bowl beat together the sugar and shortening. Stir in the beaten eggs, mashed bananas, and milk. In a separate bowl, sift together the flour, baking soda, cinnamon, salt, cloves, and nutmeg. Stir the dry ingredients into the banana mixture until thoroughly blended. Fold in the optional walnuts. Pour into a greased and floured 9 x 5 x 3-inch loaf pan. Bake in a preheated 350° oven for 1 hour to 1 hour and 10 minutes. It is done when a toothpick inserted in the center of the bread comes out clean.

Note: One banana measures about ⅓ cup when mashed. You will need 3 to 4 large ripe bananas for this recipe.

BANANA MUFFINS
(Makes 12 muffins)

¼ c. raisins
¼ c. butter (½ stick), softened
½ c. sugar
2 eggs, lightly beaten
⅔ c. mashed ripe bananas
⅔ c. milk

1 ¾ c. sifted all-purpose flour
2 tsp. baking powder
½ tsp. salt
½ tsp. cinnamon
¼ tsp. nutmeg
¼ c. chopped walnuts

Plump the raisins by soaking in warm water for 5 minutes. Drain and set aside until ready to use. In a large bowl, beat the butter and sugar together until well blended. Add the eggs, mashed bananas, and milk, beating well after each addition. In another large bowl, sift together the flour, sugar, salt, baking powder, cinnamon, and nutmeg. Make a well in the center of the dry ingredients. Pour the mashed banana mixture into the well in the flour. Place the raisins and walnuts on top of the liquid. Stir everything together with a few swift strokes. Fill greased muffin cups about two-thirds full. Bake in a preheated oven at 425° for 20 to 25 minutes. Remove from the muffin pan immediately. Serve warm or allow to cool completely before storing in an airtight container.

Note: You will need two large ripe bananas for this recipe. You will also need a 12-cup muffin/cupcake pan.

240812-16

BRAN MUFFINS
(Makes 12 muffins)

½ c. raisins
¾ c. whole wheat flour
½ c. all-purpose flour
1 c. wheat bran
1 Tbs. brown sugar
1 tsp. baking soda

¼ tsp. salt
1 ¼ c. buttermilk
1 egg, lightly beaten
⅓ c. molasses
1 ½ Tbs. melted butter

Plump raisins by soaking in warm water for 5 minutes. Drain and set aside until ready to use. In a large bowl, combine the whole wheat flour, the all-purpose flour, wheat bran, brown sugar, baking soda, and salt. Mix together until well blended. In a separate bowl, combine the buttermilk, egg, molasses, and melted butter. Beat liquid mixture until well blended. Stir the liquid ingredients into the dry ingredients with a few swift strokes. Fold in the plumped raisins. Grease the muffin cups or line with paper liners. Spoon batter evenly into the 12 prepared muffin tins. Bake at 350° for 20 to 25 minutes. Muffins are done when a toothpick inserted in the center of a muffin comes out clean. Let cool on a rack for 10 minutes before removing from pan.

Note: You will need a regular 12-cup muffin pan for this recipe.

WHOLE WHEAT IRISH SODA BREAD
(Makes one 8-inch round loaf)

2 c. whole wheat flour (do not sift)
1 c. all-purpose flour (do not sift)
¼ c. wheat germ
¼ c. brown sugar
2 tsp. baking soda

2 tsp. baking powder
1 tsp. salt.
1 ½ c. buttermilk (do not substitute)
2 Tbs. melted butter

In a large bowl, combine the whole wheat flour, all-purpose flour, wheat germ, brown sugar, baking soda, baking powder, and salt. Mix together until well blended. Stir in the buttermilk and melted butter until a batter is formed that is still lumpy. Spoon batter into a greased and floured 8-inch round cake pan. Do not smooth surface. Bake in a preheated 425° oven for about 30 minutes. When a toothpick inserted in the center comes out clean, then the bread is done. Cool in the pan for 10 minutes, and then turn out onto a rack to finish cooling.

Note: You will need an 8-inch round cake pan for this recipe. This bread is especially good toasted. Do not substitute for the buttermilk because it reacts with the leavening to make a lighter loaf.

JOHNNY CAKES
(Makes 14 to 16 four-inch cakes)

1 c. yellow cornmeal
1 c. boiling water
½ c. biscuit mix, commercial or
  Homemade Biscuit Mix (see
  earlier recipe)

2 eggs, lightly beaten
2 tsp. sugar
1 tsp. salt
½ c. cold water
vegetable oil for frying

Pour the boiling water over the cornmeal in a large bowl and stir. Let stand for 10 minutes. Add the biscuit mix, eggs, sugar, salt, and cold water. Stir until well blended. You should have a fairly thin batter. Add one more tablespoon of water if batter is too thick. Preheat an electric skillet to 350° or use a frying pan over medium-high heat. Pour batter from a large spoon or ladle into the skillet coated with a thin layer of vegetable oil. The Johnny cakes should be 4 inches in diameter. Fry until golden brown, about 5 to 6 minutes. Turn once and finish cooking on the second side, about 4 to 5 more minutes. Johnny cakes should be crisp around the edges. Keep warm until ready to serve.

Note: Soaking the cornmeal in boiling water helps to make the Johnny Cakes tender in the center. This step can be eliminated in order to save time. Johnny Cakes are considered a comfort food in the South and are served at every opportunity.

CORN PONE
(Makes 12 pieces)

¾ c. yellow cornmeal
⅓ c. biscuit mix, commercial or
  Homemade Biscuit Mix (see
  earlier recipe)
1½ tsp. sugar

¾ tsp. salt
1 egg
⅔ c. water
3 Tbs. butter

In a large bowl mix together cornmeal, biscuit mix, sugar, and salt. In a separate bowl beat egg, and ⅔ cup water together, and stir into cornmeal. Add more water if batter is too thick. Put the butter in a 13 x 9 x 2-inch baking pan, and place in a preheated 400° oven. Remove from oven when butter has melted and covers bottom of pan. This will take 4 to 5 minutes. Be careful not to let the butter burn. Pour the batter into pan and spread evenly over bottom. Return to oven and bake for 40 minutes. Cut into 12 pieces and serve.

Note: You will need a 13 x 9 x 2-inch baking pan. Corn pone has a wide variety of incarnations. It can be flat or shaped into pones, baked or fried, one word or two. This particular variety is tender in the center, and dark brown and crisp around the edges.

240812-16

CORNBREAD
(Makes 12 pieces)

¾ c. yellow corn meal
¾ c. all-purpose flour
3 Tbs. sugar
2 ¼ tsp. baking powder

¾ tsp. salt
2 eggs, lightly beaten
¾ c. milk
¼ c. vegetable oil

In a large bowl mix together the corn meal, flour, sugar, baking powder, and salt. In a separate bowl, beat the eggs together with the milk and oil. Stir the liquid ingredients into the cornmeal mixture until well blended. Pour into a greased and floured 8-inch square baking pan. Bake in a preheated 400° oven for 25 to 30 minutes. A toothpick inserted in the center should come out clean when done. Serve warm with butter.

Note: You will need an 8-inch square baking pan for this recipe.

PANCAKE MIX
(Makes 8 cups)

BASIC PANCAKE MIX

6 c. sifted all-purpose flour
1 ¾ c. instant nonfat dry milk
¼ c. sifted soy flour

3 Tbs. + 1 tsp. baking powder
2 Tbs. sugar
2 tsp. salt

In a large bowl, combine the all-purpose flour, instant nonfat dry milk, soy flour, baking powder, sugar, and salt. Mix well and store in an airtight container until ready to use.

HOW TO PREPARE PANCAKES

2 c. Basic Pancake Mix
2 eggs, lightly beaten

2 to 4 Tbs. vegetable oil
1 ⅓ c. water

Place 2 cups Basic Pancake Mix in a large bowl. Make a small well in the center and add the eggs and vegetable oil. Slowly stir in 1 ⅓ cups of water. For thinner pancakes you can add up to an additional ¼ cup of water. Pour or ladle about ⅓ cup of batter onto a dry, preheated 350° griddle. Cook for three to four minutes on each side or until golden brown. You can also use a frying pan over medium-high heat. Keep warm until ready to serve. Makes eight to ten 6-inch pancakes.

Note: Since this pancake mix does not contain any shortening, it should keep for a long time without getting rancid and spoiling. By adding the oil when you make the pancakes, you can avoid the use of saturated fat and adjust the amount of oil you use to suit your own tastes. You can also use the Homemade Baking Powder from the beginning of this chapter.

AEBLESKIVERS
(Makes 24-28 Aebleskivers)

2 c. sifted all-purpose flour
1 Tbs. granulated white sugar
1 ½ tsp. baking soda
1 tsp. baking powder
½ tsp. salt
2 c. fresh buttermilk

3 eggs, separated
3 Tbs. butter, melted
1 tsp. vanilla
vegetable shortening
Powdered sugar
Plum jam or raspberry jam

In a large bowl sift together flour, white sugar, baking soda, baking powder, and salt. Add buttermilk, egg yolks, melted butter, and vanilla. Mix together thoroughly. Using an electric mixer, beat egg whites in another bowl until stiff but not dry and fold into batter. Preheat aebleskiver pan over medium-high heat for 3 to 4 minutes. Fill each indentation with ½ teaspoon shortening. Pour batter into each indentation until full and reduce heat to medium. Begin turning the aebleskivers a quarter turn with the knitting needle as soon as the outer portion of the aebleskiver develops a hard shell. Continue turning the aebleskivers in quarter turns with the knitting needle. Cook until they are deep brown and the needle comes out clean when inserted. To serve, place aebleskivers on a plate and sprinkle powdered sugar over top. Serve with plum or raspberry jam on the side. Allow 4 aebleskivers per serving.

MAKING AEBLESKIVERS WITH BISQUICK©

2 ¼ c. Bisquick© (do not sift) or
    Homemade Biscuit Mix (see
    earlier recipe)
1 Tbs. granulated white sugar

3 eggs, separated
2 c. fresh buttermilk
1 tsp. vanilla

Mix together the Bisquick© and white sugar in a large bowl. Stir in the buttermilk, egg yolks, and vanilla. Using an electric mixer, beat the egg whites until stiff but not dry and fold into batter. Cook and serve the aebleskivers using the same directions as above. Makes 18 to 20 aebleskivers.

Note: You will need an aebleskiver pan for this recipe. There are no substitutes. Aebleskiver pans are usually made of cast iron and have 7 indentations for the batter. They can be found at kitchen supply stores and catalogs and on the internet. You will also need a metal knitting needle or a metal or wooden skewer. The finished product looks like a spherical pancake.

AMERICAN INDIAN FRY BREAD
(Makes 26 to 28 pieces)

4 ½ c. all-purpose flour
2 tsp. salt
1 ½ Tbs. baking powder

3 Tbs. sugar
2 ¼ c. buttermilk
vegetable oil for frying

In a large bowl mix together the flour, salt, baking powder, and sugar. Add buttermilk and stir until well blended. Turn dough out onto a lightly floured surface. Knead gently for 2 minutes. Dough should be soft and slightly sticky. Let rest for 5 minutes. Tear off a small piece of dough about the size of a ping-pong ball. Flatten with your hand or roll out to no more than ½-inch in thickness. Repeat until all of the dough has been used. Heat oil ⅛-inch deep in an electric skillet or frying pan to 350° (medium high). You should be able to get 8 to 9 pieces in the pan at one time. Fry pieces of bread in the hot oil, turning once, until golden brown on both sides. About 4 to 5 minutes on each side should be enough. Remove from pan and drain on paper towel.

Note: Serve warm at breakfast with jam, butter, and/or peanut butter. They can also be served with soup or chili.

CAKE DOUGHNUTS
(Makes 18 to 22 doughnuts)

2 Tbs. shortening
¾ c. sugar
2 eggs, lightly beaten
¾ c. milk
3 ¼ cups all-purpose flour (do not sift)

1 tsp. salt
5 tsp. baking powder
1 tsp. cinnamon
½ tsp. nutmeg

In a large bowl cream together the shortening and sugar. In a medium bowl beat together the eggs and milk and slowly stir into the sugar mixture. In another medium bowl combine the flour, salt, baking powder, cinnamon and nutmeg. Stir the flour into the milk mixture. This will make a sticky dough. Turn out onto a floured counter top and knead for 1 minute or until dough holds together. Roll to a thickness of ½-inch. The dough may still be slightly sticky. Cut out doughnuts with a floured 2¾-inch doughnut cutter. Knead scraps of dough together and repeat procedure until all of the dough has been used. Fry in a deep fryer preheated to 350°. If using an electric skillet the oil should be about ¾-inch deep. Turn once after frying for 1 minute. Cook for a total of 2 to 2½ minutes. Drain on paper towel. Serve plain or topped with your favorite frosting.

Note: You will need a 2¾-inch doughnut cutter for this recipe. It is recommended that you use a deep fryer for cooking the doughnuts.

FLOUR TORTILLAS
(Makes 12 medium tortillas)

PREPARING THE DOUGH

3 c. sifted all-purpose flour　　3 Tbs. shortening
1 tsp. salt　　1 ¼ c. warm water
2 tsp. baking powder

Combine flour, salt, and baking powder in a bowl. Cut in the shortening with a pastry blender. Add warm water and mix well with a fork. Knead dough 4 to 6 times on a lightly floured surface. The dough will be slightly sticky. Flour and water measurements must be very accurate. If the dough is too dry, the tortillas will be crisp as crackers. This can also happen if the tortillas are cooked too long.

ROLLING INTO A CIRCLE AND COOKING THE TORTILLAS

Divide the dough into 12 equal pieces. Shape each piece into a round ball. On a lightly floured counter top, roll each ball of dough into a circle about 9 inches in diameter. For nicely rounded tortillas, trim edges with a pizza cutter and discard any trimmings. Cook on an ungreased electric skillet set at 350° for 45 seconds to 1 minute on each side. There should be a few pale brown spots on each side of the tortilla. If you are using a frying pan, place the pan over medium-high heat. Place the cooked tortillas on a plate covered with a tea towel. Fold the towel over the tortillas and invert a large bowl over the stack to keep them from drying out.

VARIATION: USING BISCUIT MIX TO MAKE FLOUR TORTILLAS

1 ½ c. Bisquick® or Homemade　　1 ½ c. sifted all-purpose flour
　Biscuit Mix (see earlier recipe)　　1 ¼ c. warm water

Stir together the 1 ½ cups Bisquick® and 1 ½ cups sifted flour in a large bowl. DO NOT add any salt, baking powder or shortening. Stir in 1 ¼ cups warm water to make tortilla dough. Knead, shape, cut the dough, and cook the tortillas as outlined in the above directions.

Note: While you can use a knife to cut your dough into circles, a wheel-type pizza cutter works much better. To make larger tortillas, divide dough into 8 equal pieces before shaping into balls. Roll dough into circles about 10 inches in diameter.

136

TRADITIONAL WAFFLES
(10 to 12 waffles)

1 ½ cups all-purpose flour
1 Tbs. baking powder
½ tsp. salt
1 Tbs. sugar

3 eggs, separated
¼ cup melted butter
1 ½ cups milk

In a large bowl combine flour, baking powder, salt, and sugar. In a separate bowl, stir together the egg yolks and butter until well blended. Slowly stir in the milk. Stir liquid ingredients into flour mixture until you have a batter that is free of lumps. In an electric mixer beat the three egg whites until stiff but not dry. Gently fold the egg whites into the batter. Pour the batter onto a preheated waffle iron. Close the waffle iron and bake 5 to 7 minutes or until waffles are golden brown. Serve with syrup or soft cream cheese (see below) and apple butter.

SOFT CREAM CHEESE FOR WAFFLES

1 (8 oz.) pkg. cream cheese at
   room temperature

¼ c. milk

Beat ¼ cup milk into 8 ounces cream cheese until smooth. Chill thoroughly before serving.

Note: These waffles are easier to prepare than the following Belgian waffles because they use baking powder instead of active dry yeast.

BELGIAN WAFFLES MADE WITH ACTIVE DRY YEAST
(Makes 16 to 18 waffles)

2 ¼ c. sifted all-purpose flour
1 Tbs. instant dry yeast
1 Tbs. sugar
2 c. lukewarm milk, about 110°

4 eggs, separated
½ c. butter, melted
1 tsp. vanilla
½ tsp. salt

Place the flour, instant dry yeast, and sugar in a large bowl. Slowly stir in the warm milk until smooth. In a separate small bowl beat together the egg yolks, melted butter, vanilla, and salt. Stir into flour mixture. In the bowl of an electric mixer beat the egg whites until stiff. Carefully fold them into the batter. Let mixture stand in a warm place for 30 minutes. Fill a preheated waffle iron almost to the edge with batter. Cook waffles until they are golden brown, about 5 to 6 minutes.

Note: Waffle irons come in a wide variety of shapes and sizes, so there may be some variation in the number of waffles that this recipe will make. The instant dry yeast creates more bubbles which makes these waffles crisper and lighter than the previous recipe.

Yeast Breads

TRADITIONAL WHITE BREAD
(Makes 2 loaves)

FIRST RISING

6 c. all-purpose flour, divided ---
  (2 c. + 4 c.)
3 Tbs. sugar
2 Tbs. instant dry yeast

2 ¼ c. warm water
2 Tbs. vegetable oil
1 Tbs. salt

In a large bowl combine 2 cups flour, sugar, and instant dry yeast. Stir in the warm water and mix until smooth and well blended. Let stand for a minute while yeast becomes active. Stir in oil and salt. Add the remaining 4 cups of flour and stir until well blended and the dough is formed. Place on a lightly floured surface and knead until smooth and elastic, about 3 to 5 minutes. Wash the bowl that the dough was prepared in. Lightly oil the bowl and place the dough in the bowl to let the dough rise. In most of the recipes here the bowl that is used for mixing the dough can also be used for letting the dough rise. Let rise in a warm place until double in bulk, about 30 minutes. The cooler the kitchen, the longer it will take for the dough to rise.

SECOND RISING

Turn dough out onto a lightly floured surface, punch down, and knead for about 2 minutes to release some of the air from the dough. Lightly dust the surface with more flour if the dough becomes sticky. Divide into two equal pieces. Roll each piece into a 10 x 15-inch rectangle. Roll up from the narrow side and pinch seams and ends to seal. Place seam side down in lightly greased 9 x 5 x 3-inch loaf pans. Let rise until double in bulk or until the top of the dough rises to about 1 inch above the edge of the pan. This will take 30 to 40 minutes.

BAKING

Bake in a preheated 425° oven for 25 to 30 minutes, or until the loaves are a deep golden brown and sound hollow when tapped. Remove bread from pans and place on rack to cool.

Note: This is your basic, everyday white bread. If you have never baked yeast bread before, you should try this recipe before baking any of the other breads that follow in this section. Please read the section "All About Flour and Yeast" in the Introduction where it describes some of the different flours used in baking bread.

240812-16

BRAN BREAD
(Makes 2 loaves)

1 c. wheat bran
2 c. all-purpose flour
2 Tbs. instant dry yeast
2 ¾ c. warm water

¼ c. vegetable oil
¼ c. honey
1 Tbs. salt
4 ½ c. bread flour

In large bowl combine the wheat bran, all-purpose flour, and instant dry yeast. Stir in the warm water and let stand for 3 minutes to allow the yeast to become active. Add the oil, honey, and salt and stir until well blended. Add the bread flour and stir until a stiff dough is formed. Turn out onto a lightly floured surface. Knead until smooth and elastic, about 5 minutes. Place in a lightly oiled bowl and let rise until double in bulk, about 30 minutes. Turn dough out onto a dry surface and knead for 1 to 2 minutes. Add a small amount of flour if dough becomes too sticky to handle. Divide into two equal pieces. Roll each piece into a 10 x 15-inch rectangle. Roll up from the narrow side to form a loaf. Pinch seams and ends closed and place in greased 9 x 5 x 3-inch bread pans. Let rise until double in bulk, about 30 to 40 minutes. Bake in a preheated 400° oven for 25 to 30 minutes.

SPECIAL BRAN BREAD
(Makes 2 loaves)

2 c. bran-water (from making
   gluten) at room temperature
3 c. all-purpose flour, divided ---
   (1 c. + 2 c.)
2 Tbs. instant dry yeast

1 ½ c. warm water
⅓ c. butter, melted
¼ c. brown sugar
1 Tbs. salt
3 ½ c. bread flour

In a large bowl stir together 1 cup of the all-purpose flour, the yeast, and 1 ½ cups of warm water. Let stand for 3 minutes to allow the yeast to become active. Stir in the bran-water, melted butter, brown sugar, and salt until well blended. Add the remaining 2 cups of all-purpose flour and the bread flour. Stir until a stiff dough is formed. Turn out onto a lightly floured surface and knead until smooth and elastic, about 5 minutes. Place in a lightly oiled bowl and let rise until double in bulk, about 45 minutes. Turn dough out onto a dry surface and knead for 1 to 2 minutes. Add a little flour if dough is too sticky. Divide into 2 equal pieces. Roll each piece into a 10 x 15-inch rectangle. Roll up from the narrow side to form a loaf. Pinch seams and ends closed and place in greased 9 x 5 x 3-inch bread pans. Let rise until the top of the dough is about 1 inch above the edge of the pan, about 1 hour. Bake in a preheated 400° oven for 25 to 30 minutes.

Note: Bran-water is a byproduct of making Fresh Raw Gluten Made From Whole Wheat Flour (see recipe in Chapter: Main Dishes; Gluten). It should be at room temperature when used. DO NOT put it in the microwave. The wheat starch may thicken into a paste making it unusable for baking.

MASHED POTATO BREAD
(Makes 2 loaves)

5½ c. all-purpose flour, divided
  (½ c. + 5 c.)
¼ c. sugar
2 Tbs. instant dry yeast
½ c. warm water
1 c. warm milk

1 c. mashed potatoes made from
  instant flakes
1 egg, lightly beaten
¼ c. butter (½ stick), melted
2 tsp. salt

In a large bowl combine ½ cup of the flour, sugar, and instant dry yeast. Stir in the warm water and let stand for a minute while the yeast becomes active. Stir in the warm milk, mashed potatoes, beaten egg, melted butter, and salt until well blended. Add the remaining 5 cups of flour and stir until a ball of soft dough is formed. Turn out onto a lightly floured surface and knead until smooth and elastic, about 5 minutes. Place in a lightly oiled bowl and let rise in a warm place until double in bulk, about 30 minutes. Turn out onto a lightly floured surface and knead for 1 to 2 minutes. Divide into 2 equal pieces. Roll each piece into a 10 x 15-inch rectangle. Roll each piece up from the narrow end and pinch seams and ends to seal. Place in greased 9 x 5 x 3-inch loaf pans. Let rise until double in bulk, about 45 minutes. The top of the bread should be slightly higher than the edge of the pan. Bake in a preheated 400° oven until lightly browned, about 25 to 30 minutes.

WHEN USING HOMEMADE MASHED POTATOES

1 c. fresh Homemade Mashed
  Potatoes (see recipe in
  Chapter: Side Dishes)

1 c. warm milk

Place the mashed potatoes in a blender. Pour the warm milk over the potatoes and blend together for about 20 seconds. Use in place of the mashed potatoes and milk in the above recipe.

240812-16

DINNER ROLLS
(Makes 15 rolls)

3 ¾ c. all-purpose flour, divided
   (1 ½ c. + 2 ¼ c.)
1 Tbs. instant dry yeast
1 Tbs. sugar

1 ½ c. warm milk
3 Tbs. melted butter, divided ----
   (2 Tbs. + 1 Tbs.)
1 ½ tsp salt

In a large bowl combine 1 ½ cups flour, the instant dry yeast, and sugar. Stir in the warm milk and let stand for 1 minute. Stir in 2 tablespoons of the butter and the salt and mix well. Add the remaining 2 ¼ cups of flour and stir until a soft dough is formed. Turn out onto a lightly floured surface and knead for 3 minutes. Place in a lightly oiled bowl and let rise until double in bulk, about 30 minutes. Punch down, knead gently for 1 minute, and divide into 15 equal pieces. Shape each piece into a ball and place in a greased 13 x 9 x 2-inch baking pan. The rolls should be spaced evenly apart in 3 rows by 5 rows. Let rise until double in bulk, about 45 minutes to one hour. Brush tops with the remaining 1 tablespoon melted butter. Bake in a preheated 400° oven for 25 minutes.

Note: You will need a 13 x 9 x 2-inch baking pan.

OATMEAL AND MOLASSES BREAD
(Makes 2 loaves)

5 ½ c. all-purpose flour, divided
   (½ c. + 5 c.)
2 Tbs. instant dry yeast
¾ c. warm water
1 ¼ c. boiling water

1 c. oats (uncooked oatmeal)
⅓ c. shortening
½ c. molasses
1 Tbs. salt
2 eggs, lightly beaten

In a small bowl combine ½ cup flour and the instant dry yeast. Stir in the ¾ cup warm water and let rest for about a minute while the yeast becomes active. In a separate large bowl, pour boiling water over the oats. Add the shortening, molasses, and salt. Stir together until well blended and shortening has melted. Allow to cool for 5 minutes until lukewarm. Add yeast mixture and beaten eggs to the large bowl and stir well. Add the remaining 5 cups of flour and mix until well blended. Turn out onto a lightly floured surface and knead for about 1 minute until the dough holds together and is smooth on the outside. Place in a lightly oiled bowl and let rise until double in bulk, about 30 minutes. Turn out onto a lightly floured surface and knead the dough, which will be very soft, for about 1 minute. Divide into 2 equal pieces. The dough will be very sticky, so you do not have to roll the dough out before placing in the pans. Shape by hand into 2 loaves and place in greased 9 x 5 x 3-inch loaf pans. Gently press the dough down in the pans until it is flat and reaches all four corners. Let rise in a warm place until dough is about 1 inch above the edge of the pan, about 1 hour. Bake in a preheated 375° oven for about 40 minutes.

WHOLE WHEAT BREAD
(Makes 2 loaves)

2 c. whole wheat flour
2 Tbs. instant dry yeast
2 ½ c. warm water
¼ c. vegetable oil

⅓ c. honey
1 Tbs. salt
4 ½ c. all-purpose flour

In a large bowl combine the whole wheat flour and instant dry yeast. Stir in the warm water, vegetable oil, and honey. Mix together until well blended. Let rest for a minute while the yeast becomes active. Add the 4 ½ cups of all-purpose flour and salt. Stir together until a ball of dough is formed. Turn out onto a lightly floured surface and knead gently for 3 to 4 minutes. Place in a lightly oiled bowl, cover, and let rise until double in bulk, about 30 minutes. Turn out onto a dry surface and knead for 1 to 2 minutes. Dust a little flour on the counter top if the dough becomes too sticky. Divide into two equal pieces. Roll each piece into a 10 x 15-inch rectangle. Roll up from the narrow end and pinch seams and ends to seal. Place in two greased 9 x 5 x 3-inch loaf pans and let rise until double in bulk, about 45 minutes. The dough should rise to at least 1 inch above the top of the pan. Bake in a preheated 400° oven for 30 to 35 minutes. Remove from pans and allow to cool on a rack.

50% WHOLE WHEAT BREAD
(Makes 2 loaves)

3 ½ c. all-purpose flour, divided ---
    (3 c. + ½ c.)
2 Tbs. instant dry yeast
⅓ c. brown sugar

2 ¾ c. warm milk
3 Tbs. vegetable oil
1 Tbs. salt
3 ½ c. whole wheat flour

In a large bowl combine 3 cups all-purpose flour, the instant dry yeast, and brown sugar. Stir in the warm milk and let rest for a minute while the yeast becomes active. Add the oil and salt. Mix together until well blended. Slowly stir in the remaining ½ cup of all-purpose flour and all of the whole wheat flour. Stir until everything holds together to form the dough. Turn out onto a lightly floured surface and knead for 2 to 3 minutes. Place in a lightly oiled bowl and let rise until double in bulk, about 45 minutes. Turn out onto a lightly floured surface and knead for 1 minute. Divide dough into 2 equal pieces. Roll out each piece into a 10 x 15-inch rectangle. Roll up from the narrow side and pinch seams and ends to seal. Place in lightly greased 9 x 5 x 3-inch loaf pans. Let rise for about 45 minutes, or until the dough is about 1 ½ inches above the edge of the pan. Bake at 375° for 35 to 40 minutes.

Note: This has more whole wheat flour than the previous recipe, which makes this loaf slightly heavier.

240812-16

ALMOST 100% WHOLE WHEAT BREAD
(Makes 2 loaves)

7 c. whole wheat flour, divided ---
   (3 c. + 4 c.)
¼ c. vital wheat gluten flour
2 Tbs. instant dry yeast

3 c. warm milk
½ c. honey
½ c. (1 stick) melted butter
1 Tbs. salt

In a large bowl combine 3 cups of the whole wheat flour, the vital wheat gluten flour, and the instant dry yeast. Mix together until well blended. Stir in the warm milk and allow to stand for a minute while the yeast becomes active. Stir in the honey, melted butter, and salt. Slowly add the remaining 4 cups of whole wheat flour. Stir everything together until the dough is formed. Turn out onto a lightly floured surface. Knead for about 5 minutes or until smooth and elastic. Place in a lightly oiled bowl and allow to rise until double in bulk, about 45 minutes. Turn out onto a lightly floured surface, knead for about a minute and divide into two equal pieces. Roll each pieces into a 15 x 10-inch rectangle. Roll up along the narrow edge, pinch seams to seal and place in greased 9 x 5 x 3-inch loaf pans. Let rise until bread is about 1½ inches above the edge of the pan, about 40 to 50 minutes. Bake in a preheated 350° oven for 45 to 50 minutes.

Note: There is a small amount of vital wheat gluten flour in this bread, so technically it does not qualify as pure 100% whole wheat bread. This helps to hold the bread together and keeps it from becoming too crumbly.

OAT FLOUR BREAD
(Makes 2 loaves)

½ c. wheat bran
1½ c. oat flour (not rolled oats)
4 c. all-purpose flour, divided ---
   (1 c. + 3 c.)
2 Tbs. instant dry yeast

2½ c. warm water
¼ c. honey
3 Tbs. vegetable oil
1 Tbs. salt

In a large bowl combine the wheat bran, oat flour, 1 cup of the all-purpose flour, and the instant dry yeast. Stir in the warm water, honey, and vegetable oil. Let stand for a minute while the yeast becomes active. Add the remaining 3 cups of all-purpose flour, and the salt. Mix together until it forms a solid mass of dough. Turn out onto a lightly floured surface and knead for about 5 minutes until smooth and elastic. Place in a lightly oiled bowl and let rise until double in bulk, about 30 minutes. Turn dough out onto a lightly floured surface and knead for about 5 minutes. Add a little more flour if dough becomes too sticky. Divide into two equal pieces. Roll each piece into a 10 x 15-inch rectangle. Roll up from the narrow end and pinch seams and ends to close. Place in lightly greased 9 x 5 x 3-inch loaf pans. Let rise until double in bulk, about 45 minutes. Bake in a preheated 400° oven for 30 to 35 minutes.

SWEDISH ORANGE RYE BREAD
(Makes 1 round loaf)

2 ½ c. all-purpose flour, divided
  (1 ¼ c. + 1 ¼ c.)
1 Tbs. instant dry yeast
2 Tbs. granulated sugar
1 ¼ c. warm water
1 Tbs. butter, melted
1 Tbs. whole caraway seeds

1 Tbs. grated orange peel
1 ½ tsp. salt
1 c. rye flour
1 egg yolk mixed with 1 tsp.
  water
poppy seeds (opt.)

In a large bowl combine 1 ¼ cups all-purpose flour, instant dry yeast, and sugar. Stir in the warm water and let stand for a minute while the yeast becomes active. Add the melted butter, caraway seeds, orange peel, and salt. Stir everything together until well blended. Add the rye flour and the remaining 1 ¼ cups of all-purpose flour. Stir together until the dough is formed. Turn out onto a lightly floured surface. Knead dough until it is soft, smooth, elastic, and not too sticky, about 3 minutes. Place dough in a lightly oiled bowl and and let rise until double in bulk, about 30 minutes. Turn out onto a lightly floured surface and knead for about 2 minutes. Gently fold the top edge of the dough towards the center. Rotate the dough ¼-turn to the left. Fold the top edge towards the center again and rotate another ¼-turn to the left. Repeat this until you have a smooth ball of dough where the center of the top looks like a "belly button." Pinch the center together so that it does not come undone. Turn the dough over and place on a lightly greased large cookie sheet. The bread will be baked on this cookie sheet. Let rise in a warm place until the dough is double in size, about 30 to 40 minutes. Brush the top of the dough with the egg yolk mixture. Sprinkle the optional poppy seeds over top. Make three ¼-inch deep slashes across the top of the dough. Bake in a preheated 400° oven for 30 minutes.

240812-16

CHEESE BREAD
(Makes 2 loaves)

5 c. all-purpose flour, divided ---
  (2 c. + 3 c.)
1 ½ Tbs. instant dry yeast
2 Tbs. sugar
2 c. warm water
1 ⅓ c. firmly packed, freshly
  grated cheddar cheese (5 oz.)
⅔ c. firmly packed, freshly grated
  Kasseri cheese (2 ½ oz.)

1 Tbs. olive oil
2 tsp. salt
1 egg yolk lightly beaten with ----
  1 tsp. water
2 Tbs. freshly grated Parmesan
  cheese

In a large bowl, combine 2 cups of the flour, the instant dry yeast, and sugar. Stir in the warm water and let rest for a minute while the yeast becomes active. Stir in the grated cheddar cheese and the grated Kasseri cheese. Stir until well blended and there are no lumps of cheese left from being well packed. Stir in the olive oil and salt. Add the remaining 3 cups of flour and mix until a soft ball of dough is formed. Turn out onto a lightly floured surface and knead until smooth and elastic, about 3 minutes. Add more flour to the kneading surface if the dough becomes too sticky. This dough tends to be a little softer than regular bread dough. Place in a large, lightly oiled bowl and let rise in a warm place until double in bulk, about 30 minutes. Punch down and turn dough out onto a very lightly floured surface. Knead for about 1 minute. Add a little flour if the dough becomes sticky. Divide dough into two equal pieces. Roll each piece into a 10 x 15-inch rectangle. Roll up from the narrow end and pinch seams and ends to close. Place in greased 9 x 5 x 3-inch loaf pans and let rise until double in bulk, or until dough is about 1 inch above the edge of pan. This will take 40 to 50 minutes. Brush the top of each loaf with the beaten egg yolk. Sprinkle 1 tablespoon of freshly grated Parmesan cheese evenly over each loaf. Gently rub the back of a large soup spoon over the top of each loaf to help hold the Parmesan cheese in place. Bake in a preheated 400° oven for 30 to 35 minutes.

Note: Kasseri cheese is a Greek sheep's milk cheese with a firm texture and a sharp, salty flavor. It gives this bread its cheesy flavor and fragrance. Since it is a specialty cheese, it may be difficult to find. This bread also makes excellent croutons.

SALLY LUNN BREAD
(Makes 1 loaf)

2 ½ c. all-purpose flour, divided ---
  (1 c. + 1 ½ c.)
1 Tbs. sugar
1 ½ tsp. instant dry yeast
½ c. milk

⅓ c. water
2 Tbs. butter
2 eggs, lightly beaten
1 tsp. salt

In a large bowl combine one cup flour, sugar and instant dry yeast. Combine the milk, water, and butter in a small saucepan. Heat until it is just slightly warm and the butter has melted, about 110° to 120° F. Stir the warm milk into the flour mixture. Let stand for a minute while the yeast becomes active. Stir in the beaten eggs and mix well. Add the remaining 1 ½ cups flour and salt and stir until well blended. The dough will be very sticky. Cover the bowl and allow to rise until double in bulk, about 45 minutes. Stir the dough down. Transfer the dough to a greased 9 x 5 x 3-inch bread pan. Spread the dough out so that it is an even thickness and reaches all four corner of the pan. Let rise for 45 minutes or until dough almost reaches the top of the pan. Bake in a preheated 350° oven for 35 to 40 minutes. The bread should be dark brown and have a nice crust when done.

Note: This batter bread does not require kneading. You can double this recipe to make two loaves of bread, but dividing the sticky dough into two equal pieces before placing in the bread pans can be a challenge.

BASIC EGG BREAD
(Makes 2 loaves)

6 c. all-purpose flour, divided ---
  (2 c. + 4 c.)
2 Tbs. sugar
2 Tbs. instant dry yeast
1 ¾ c. warm water

3 eggs, lightly beaten
2 Tbs. honey
2 Tbs. melted butter
1 Tbs. salt

In a large bowl combine two cups of the flour, the sugar, and instant dry yeast. Stir in the warm water until well blended. Let stand for a minute while yeast becomes active. Add the eggs, honey, butter, and salt. Stir until smooth. Add the remaining 4 cups of flour and stir until a stiff dough is formed. Turn out onto a lightly floured surface and knead until smooth and elastic, about 5 minutes. Place in a lightly oiled bowl and let rise until double in bulk, about 30 minutes. Turn out onto a lightly floured surface and divide into two equal pieces. Roll each piece into a 10 x 15-inch rectangle. Roll up from the narrow end and pinch seams and ends to seal. Place in greased 9 x 5 x 3-inch bread pans. Let rise until double in bulk, about 45 minutes. Dough should rise at least 1 inch above the top of the pan. Bake in a preheated 400° oven for 25 to 30 min.

240812-16

TWISTED EGG BREAD LOAF
(Makes 2 loaves)

5¾ c. all-purpose flour, divided --
(1 c. + 4¾ c.)
⅓ c. sugar
2 Tbs. instant dry yeast
1 c. warm water
5 whole eggs

1 egg, separated
¼ c. (½ cube) butter, melted
2 Tbs. honey
2 tsp. salt
1 tsp. water
1 Tbs. sesame seeds

In a large bowl combine 1 cup flour, ⅓ cup sugar, and instant dry yeast. Stir in the 1 cup warm water and let rest for a minute while yeast becomes active. In a medium bowl, beat together 5 whole eggs and 1 egg white. Set aside and reserve the 1 egg yolk. Stir in the butter, honey, and salt. Add the egg mixture to the yeast mixture in the large bowl. Gradually add the remaining 4¾ cups of flour. Turn out onto a lightly floured surface and knead until smooth and elastic, about 5 minutes. Dough will be slightly sticky. Place dough in lightly oiled bowl, cover, and let rise until double in bulk, about 1 hour.

BRAIDING AND BAKING THE LOAVES

Punch down and divide into 8 equal pieces. Roll each piece into a rope 15 inches long. For each loaf place 4 ropes on a floured surface so that the ends meet in the center forming a "+" sign and overlap slightly. Pinch the ends together. Bring opposite ends up, cross over and lay down on opposite sides of board. Bring the remaining 2 ropes (perpendicular to the first two ropes) up, cross over and lay down on board. Repeat until the entire loaf is braided. Then lay on its side and pinch ends together and tuck under. Place in a greased 9 x 5 x 3-inch loaf pan. Repeat for second loaf. This is not the traditional way to make a 4-strand braid, but it makes a loaf with bigger lumps on the top. Cover and let rise in a warm place until double in size. Beat together the reserved egg yolk with 1 teaspoon water and brush onto tops of loaves. Sprinkle ½ tablespoon sesame seeds over each loaf. Bake in a preheated 375° oven for 25 minutes.

Note: Most braided egg breads are baked on a cookie sheet to create a free-form loaf. Ours is baked in bread pans so that they can be sliced for sandwiches. This recipe makes a very rich bread that some people have described as almost being like cake. It is prepared mostly for special occasions. The previous Basic Egg Bread recipe is for everyday use.

ITALIAN FLAT BREAD
(Makes 1 round flat loaf)

1 ¾ c. all-purpose flour, divided
   (¾ c. + 1 c.)
¾ tsp. instant dry yeast
½ tsp. sugar
¾ c. warm water

½ tsp. salt
1 Tbs. + 1 tsp. olive oil
Additional salt
Black pepper

In a medium bowl combine ¾ cup of the flour, the instant dry yeast, sugar, and warm water. Mix well and allow to stand for a minute while the yeast becomes active. Add ½ teaspoon salt and 1 tablespoon of olive oil. Mix well and add the remaining 1 cup of flour. Stir until the dough holds together. Turn out onto a lightly floured surface and knead for about 5 minutes or until smooth and elastic. Place in a lightly oiled bowl and let stand until double in bulk, about 45 minutes. Turn out onto a dry surface and roll into a circle about ½-inch thick and 10 inches in diameter. Rub the top of the dough with the remaining 1 teaspoon of olive oil. Sprinkle a small amount of salt and pepper over the top of the bread. Place on a lightly greased baking sheet and allow to rise for 30 minutes or until it has doubled in height. Bake in a preheated 400° oven for 18 minutes or until lightly browned. Remove from oven and allow to cool until it can be comfortably handled. Tear into pieces (do not cut) and serve with your choice of pasta.

FRENCH BREAD
(Makes 1 large long loaf)

1 c. unbleached flour
3 ¼ c. bread flour, divided (½ c. +
   2 ¾ c.)
5 tsp. sugar

1 Tbs. instant dry yeast
1 ½ c. warm water
2 Tbs. olive oil
2 ½ tsp. salt

In a large bowl combine the unbleached flour, ½ cup of the bread flour, sugar, and instant dry yeast. Stir in the warm water and let stand for a minute while the yeast becomes active. Stir in the olive oil and salt. Add the remaining 3 cups of bread flour and mix until the dough comes together. Turn out onto a lightly floured surface and knead for about 5 minutes. Place in a lightly oiled bowl and let rise until double in bulk, about 1 hour. Punch dough down and knead for one minute on a lightly floured surface. Roll into a 12 x 10-inch rectangle. Roll up from the narrow end, pinch seams closed, and place on a greased cookie sheet with the seam side down. If you prefer, you can shape the loaf by hand into a free form loaf. Let rise until double in bulk, about 40 to 45 minutes. Cut 4 or 5 slashes diagonally across the top of the loaf ¼-inch deep and 2 inches apart. Bake in a preheated 400° oven for 25 to 30 minutes. This makes one 12 to 13-inch long free-form loaf

240812-16

BAGUETTE
(Makes 2 loaves)

1 c. unbleached flour
4 tsp. sugar
1 Tbs. instant dry yeast
1 ⅓ c. warm water
1 ½ Tbs. olive oil

2 tsp. salt
2 ½ c. all-purpose flour
1 tsp. cornstarch dissolved in ---
½ c. water
Cornmeal

In a large bowl combine the unbleached flour, sugar, and instant dry yeast. Add the warm water and stir until smooth. Let stand for 3 minutes while yeast becomes active. Stir in olive oil and salt and mix until well blended. Add the all-purpose flour and stir together until a stiff dough is formed. Turn out onto a lightly floured surface and knead for 5 minutes or until dough is smooth and elastic. Add more flour if dough becomes too sticky. Place in a lightly oiled bowl and let rise in a warm place until double in bulk, about 45 minutes. Punch down and divide into two equal pieces. Roll each piece into a 5 x 14-inch rectangle. Roll up from the widest edge and pinch seam to seal. Place loaves with the seam side down on a large cookie sheet that has been dusted with cornmeal. Cover and let rise for 20 to 25 minutes or until puffy looking, but not quite double in size. While dough is rising, heat cornstarch and water in a small saucepan and let cool slightly. Cut slashes diagonally across each loaf ¼-inch deep and 2 inches apart. Bake in a preheated 400° oven. Brush each loaf evenly with cornstarch mixture before putting in the oven. Repeat brushing with cornstarch after 10 and 20 minutes of baking. Bake for a total of 25 to 30 minutes or until golden brown and makes a hollow sound when tapped.

FRENCH ROLLS
(Makes 9 rolls)

1 ½ c. all-purpose flour
2 Tbs. sugar
1 Tbs. instant dry yeast
1 ¼ c. warm water

1 ½ Tbs. olive oil
1 ½ tsp. salt
1 ½ c. bread flour

In a large bowl combine the all-purpose flour, sugar, and instant dry yeast. Stir in the warm water until smooth and well blended. Let stand for a minute while the yeast becomes active. Stir in the olive oil and salt. Add the bread flour and stir until a stiff dough is formed. Turn out onto a lightly floured surface and knead until smooth and elastic, about 5 minutes. Place in a lightly oiled bowl and let rise until double in bulk, about 30 minutes. Punch dough down and divide into 9 equal pieces on a lightly floured surface. Knead and turn each piece about 6 times until smooth on the outside. Shape into round rolls and pinch bottom closed. Place the rolls on a large lightly oiled cookie sheet. Let rise until double in bulk, about 30 minutes. Using a sharp knife, slash across the top of each roll 3 times to form a star. Bake in a preheated 400° oven for 20 to 25 minutes.

ENGLISH MUFFINS
(1 dozen 3 ½-inch muffins)

BASIC ENGLISH MUFFINS

1 c. milk
¾ c. water
¼ cup shortening
1 Tbs. instant dry yeast

4 c. all-purpose flour, divided ---
(2 c. + 2 c.)
1 Tbs. sugar
1 ½ tsp. salt

In a small saucepan combine the milk, water, and shortening. Heat over low heat until the shortening is melted. Remove from heat and allow to cool to about 110°. In a large bowl combine 2 cups flour, instant dry yeast, and sugar. Slowly pour the warm milk mixture into the flour and stir until well blended. Let this sponge rest for 1 hour or until the sponge collapses, whichever comes first. Add the remaining 2 cups of flour and salt. Mix until you have a soft dough. Turn out onto a lightly floured surface and knead until smooth and elastic, about 2 to 3 minutes. Place in a greased bowl and let rise until double in bulk, about 45 minutes. Turn dough out onto a lightly floured surface. DO NOT KNEAD. Gently pat into a 12-inch square (with rounded corners) about ¾-inch thick. Cut into 9 rounds with greased muffin rings. Leave rings in place and set on a lightly floured surface or cookie sheet to rise. Gently knead leftover pieces of dough together. Pat out by hand and fill remaining three rings. Let rise until dough comes to the top of the rings, about 45 minutes to 1 hour. Using a spatula, lift each muffin with ring and gently slide onto a dry electric skillet that has been preheated to 350° or a frying pan on medium-high heat. A large skillet should be able to accommodate six muffins at a time. Otherwise, cook four at a time. Remove rings after muffins have cooked for about 2 minutes. Cook for 10 to 12 minutes on each side. Place on wire rack to cool. Repeat for remaining muffins.

OVEN-BAKED ENGLISH MUFFINS

Basic English muffin dough from above

Cornmeal (opt.)

Prepare the English muffin dough following the above instructions. Once you have patted out the dough after the first rising, cut the dough into rounds using a cookie cutter or recycled can that is 3 ¼ to 3 ¾-inches in diameter. Place the circles of dough on a cookie sheet that has been lightly dusted with flour or optional corneal. Allow to rise until double in bulk, about 45 minutes. Bake in a preheated 350° oven for 10 minutes. Turn the muffins with a spatula and bake for an additional 20 minutes.

Note: Although these can be made without English muffin rings, they make the job much easier. English muffin rings can be found at kitchen supply stores and on the Internet. They are usually 3 ¾ x 1-inch in size. Directions for oven-baked English muffins are included for anyone who can't find or does not want to use the rings.

240812-16

RAISIN BREAD
(Makes 2 loaves)

1 c. raisins
5 ¾ c. all-purpose flour, divided ---
   (1 ¾ c. + 4 c.)
¼ c. sugar
2 Tbs. instant dry yeast
1 ¾ c. warm water

2 eggs, lightly beaten
¼ c. butter, melted
2 tsp. salt
1 beaten egg (keep separate from
   2 beaten eggs from above)
¼ c. sugar with 1 tsp. cinnamon

Plump raisins by soaking in warm water for about 5 minutes. Drain and set aside. In a large bowl combine 1 ¾ cups flour, sugar, and instant dry yeast. Stir in the warm water and let rest for a minute to let the yeast become active. Stir in the 2 beaten eggs, melted butter, salt, and plumped raisins. Mix until well blended. Slowly add the remaining 4 cups of flour. Turn out onto a lightly floured surface and knead until smooth. Place in a lightly oiled bowl and let rise until doubled in bulk. Punch dough down and divide into two equal pieces. Roll each piece on a lightly floured surface into a 10 x 15-inch rectangle. Brush each with the remaining beaten egg and sprinkle cinnamon sugar evenly over each piece of dough. Roll dough up starting from the narrow edge and pinch seam and end to seal. Place each loaf in a greased 9 x 5 x 3-inch loaf pan. Let rise until doubled in bulk, about 45 minutes. Bake in a preheated 400° oven for 25 to 30 minutes.

BAGELS
(Makes 12 bagels)

1 ½ c. bread flour
4 Tbs. sugar, divided --- (3 Tbs. +
   1 Tbs.)
2 Tbs. instant dry yeast
1 ¾ cups warm water

2 Tbs. butter, melted
1 Tbs. + 2 tsp. salt
2 ¾ c. all-purpose flour
1 egg beaten with 1 Tbs. water

In a large bowl combine the bread flour, 3 tablespoons sugar, and instant dry yeast. Stir in the warm water and let stand for a minute to allow the yeast to become active. Add the butter and 1 tablespoon salt. Slowly stir in the all-purpose flour. Turn out onto a lightly floured surface and knead for 5 minutes. Place in a greased bowl and let rise until double in bulk, about 45 minutes. Punch dough down and let rest 15 minutes. Divide into 12 pieces and shape each into a smooth ball. Poke a 1-inch hole in each and work with thumb until smooth and doughnut shaped. Let rest for 15 minutes. In a large skillet, heat 1 inch of water, the remaining 1 tablespoon sugar, and 2 teaspoons salt to a simmer. Drop 6 bagels at a time into simmering water. Cook for 3 minutes, turn and cook 2 minutes, turn again and cook 1 minute more. Drain on paper towels. Place 6 bagels on a large greased cookie sheet and brush with the beaten egg mixture. Bake in a preheated 400° oven for 25 to 30 minutes. You may sprinkle the bagels with sesame, caraway, or poppy seed before baking.

BASIC SWEET YEAST DOUGH

2⅔ c. all-purpose flour, divided
   (⅔ c. + 2 c.)
3 Tbs. sugar
1 Tbs. instant dry yeast
¼ c. warm water

⅓ c. warm milk
¼ c. butter (½ stick), melted
2 eggs, lightly beaten.
½ tsp. salt

In a large bowl combine ⅔ cup of the flour, the sugar, and instant dry yeast. Stir in the warm water and warm milk. Let stand for a minute while yeast becomes active. Stir in the melted butter, eggs, and salt. Add the remaining 2 cups of flour. Mix together until you have a soft ball of dough. Turn out onto a lightly floured surface. Knead for 2 to 3 minutes or until it is smooth and elastic. Add more flour if dough becomes too sticky. Place in a lightly oiled bowl and let rise until double in bulk. This will take about 45 minutes. Use in any of the following pastry recipes that call for Basic Sweet Yeast Dough.

PECAN STICKY ROLLS
(Makes 12 rolls)

Basic Sweet Yeast Dough (see
   previous recipe)
2 Tbs. melted butter

¼ c. firmly packed brown sugar
¼ c. chopped pecans

Prepare Sweet Yeast Dough according to directions. Prepare Pecan Topping (see below) while dough is rising. Punch dough down when double in bulk and roll into a 12 x 16-inch rectangle. Brush with 2 tablespoons melted butter. Sprinkle brown sugar and chopped pecans evenly over the top. Roll up from the narrow end and pinch seam to seal. Cut into twelve 1-inch pieces. Arrange, cut side up, in the prepared muffin pans. Let rise until at least double in bulk, about 45 minutes. Bake in a preheated 375° oven for 20 to 25 minutes or until lightly browned. Let stand for 1 minute and invert onto a large plate or cookie sheet and remove muffin pans. Allow to cool before serving.

PECAN TOPPING

½ c. (1 stick) butter
1 c. firmly packed brown sugar

2 Tbs. light corn syrup
¾ c. pecan halves and pieces

Combine butter, brown sugar and corn syrup in a 1-quart saucepan. Heat and stir until butter is melted and sugar is dissolved. Stir in pecans. Coat the muffin tins with non-stick spray. Divide the pecan topping evenly between the 12 muffin tins. Set aside until ready to use.

Note: You will need two 6-cup large muffin pans.

240812-16

DANISH COFFEE CAKE
(Makes 8 to 10 servings)

Basic Sweet Yeast Dough (see earlier recipe)
²⁄₃ c. finely ground roasted almonds
¼ c. white sugar

¼ c. firmly packed brown sugar
1½ tsp. cinnamon
3 Tbs. butter, melted
Glaze (see below)

Prepare Basic Sweet Yeast Dough as directed. In a small bowl, mix together the ground roasted almonds, white sugar, brown sugar, and cinnamon. Set aside until ready to use. After the dough has doubled in bulk, punch down and turn out onto a dry surface. Knead dough 4 or 5 times and roll into a 12 x 22-inch rectangle so that the widest side faces you. Brush the 3 tablespoons of melted butter evenly over the top. Spread the finely ground almond mixture evenly over the butter on the dough. Roll up the dough from the long side and pinch the seam along the edge to seal. With the seam side facing up, fold the ends of the roll around to face each other so that they are on top. The long seam should be hidden on the inside. Pinch the ends together and roll the dough towards you so that the ends are now on the bottom. Place the dough on a lightly greased large 11 x 17-inch cookie sheet. Slice the dough about two-thirds of the way through, lengthwise down the middle to expose the center. Gently spread apart and lay flat so that the center and filling are exposed. Let rise until double in bulk, about 45 minutes to 1 hour. Bake in a preheated 350° oven for 20 to 25 minutes. Drizzle glaze over coffee cake after it has cooled.

GLAZE

1⅓ c. powdered sugar
1 Tbs. + 1 tsp. butter, melted

Warm water

Mix the glaze together just before you are ready to pour it over the coffee cake. In a medium bowl combine the powdered sugar and melted butter. Slowly add warm water while beating the sugar. Continue to beat in warm water, a few drops at a time, until the glaze is the consistency of thick syrup. Drizzle over the cooled coffee cake.

CINNAMON ROLLS
(Makes 9 large rolls)

Basic Sweet Yeast Dough (see earlier recipe)
½ c. raisins
2 Tbs. melted butter

1 egg lightly beaten
1½ Tbs. sugar combined with ---
½ tsp. cinnamon
Glaze (See below)

Prepare the Sweet Yeast Dough as directed and let rise until double in bulk. Plump the raisins by soaking them in warm water for 5 minutes. Drain and set aside until ready to use. Punch the dough down and knead gently on a dry surface for about one minute. If the dough is too sticky, you can add a very small amount of flour (about 1 tablespoon) to the work surface. Roll into an 18 x 12-inch rectangle so that the widest side faces you. Spread the melted butter over the upper two thirds of the dough. Brush the remaining third, which is closest to you, with some of the beaten egg so that the dough is slightly moist. You do not need to use all of the beaten egg. Spread the plumped raisins evenly over the dough. Sprinkle the cinnamon sugar over top. Starting with the wide edge that is away from you, roll up the dough and pinch to seal. The portion of the dough with the beaten egg should be along the seam. Cut into 9 pieces that are 2 inches long. Place each piece upright in a greased 8-inch square baking pan. Let rise for 45 minutes or until double in bulk. Bake in a preheated 375° oven for 25 to 30 minutes. Remove from the pan and place on a cookie sheet or large flat serving plate to cool. Drizzle glaze over top and serve.

GLAZE

1 c. powdered sugar
1 Tbs. melted butter

1 Tbs. warm water
Additional warm water

In a medium bowl stir together the powdered sugar, 1 tablespoon melted butter, and 1 tablespoon warm water. Slowly beat in additional warm water until the glaze reaches the right consistency for drizzling over the top of the cinnamon rolls.

HOW TO MAKE 15 SMALL ROLLS

Follow the above directions for large rolls with the following changes. Roll the dough into a 15 x 12-inch rectangle so that the widest side faces you. Spread the butter, egg, raisins, and cinnamon sugar over the dough as directed above. Once the dough has been rolled up, cut into 15 pieces that are 1-inch long. Place upright in a greased 13 x 9 x 2-inch baking pan in 3 rows by 5 rows. Let rise until double in bulk and then bake in a preheated 375° oven for 20 to 25 minutes.

Note: You will need an 8-inch square pan for this recipe. If you would like to make the small rolls, then you will need a 13 x 9 x 2-inch baking pan.

154

DANISH SNAILS
(Makes 8 snails)

Basic Sweet Yeast Dough (see earlier recipe)
2 Tbs. butter, melted
2 Tbs. sugar

½ tsp. cinnamon
Oil for deep frying
Confectioners' Glaze (see below)

Prepare Sweet Yeast Dough as directed. Punch down after it has risen to almost double in bulk. Roll out to an 8 x 20-inch rectangle. Brush the butter evenly over the dough. Mix together the sugar and cinnamon to make cinnamon sugar. Sprinkle evenly over the dough. Roll up from the narrow end and pinch the edge to seal to help keep from unrolling. Slice into 8 equal 1-inch thick pieces. Pat each by hand on a lightly floured surface to about 4 inches in diameter. Then use a rolling pin to roll the snails to 5 inches in diameter. Place on a large, lightly oiled, cookie sheet to rise. You should be able to get 4 snails on a single 15 x 10 x 1-inch cookie sheet. Let rise for about 45 minutes.

FRIED DANISH SNAILS

The most frequently used method for cooking snails is to fry them. Fry each snail in oil at least ½-inch deep that has been heated to 350°. Fry for 1 to 1½ minutes on each side. Remove from frying pan and drain on paper towel.

BAKED DANISH SNAILS

If you like, you can bake the snails after they have risen instead of frying them. Bake on the same cookie sheets that the snails have risen on. Bake in a preheated 350° oven for 12 to 14 minutes or until lightly browned.

CONFECTIONERS' GLAZE

1½ c. powdered sugar
1½ Tbs. butter, melted

About 1½ Tbs. warm water

Prepare the Confectioner's Glaze while the snails are cooling. Allow the snails to cool for 10 to 15 minutes before adding glaze. Place the confectioner's sugar in a large bowl and stir in the melted butter. Slowly stir in the warm water until the glaze reaches the right consistency. Quickly drizzle glaze over snails.

Note: You will need two 15 x 10 x 1-inch cookie sheets. These are also known as Pershings. For a variation you can dip the snails in the Thin Glaze from the following Glazed Doughnuts recipe instead of using the Confectioners' Glaze.

GLAZED DOUGHNUTS
(Makes 10 large doughnuts)

DOUGHNUTS

2 ¾ c. bread flour, divided --- (1 c.
   + 1 ¾ c.)
2 Tbs. sugar
1 ½ Tbs. instant dry yeast
½ c. water
½ c. milk

¾ tsp. salt
2 eggs, lightly beaten
2 Tbs. melted butter
Thin Glaze (see below)
Oil for deep frying

In a large bowl combine 1 cup of the bread flour, instant dry yeast, and sugar. Stir in the warm water and warm milk and let rest for a minute while the yeast becomes active. Add the salt, beaten eggs, and 2 tablespoons melted butter. Mix together until well blended. Slowly stir in the remaining 1 ¾ cups flour to form the dough. Turn out onto a lightly floured surface and knead for 3 minutes. The dough should be soft and elastic. Place in a lightly oiled bowl and let rise until double in bulk, about 30 to 45 minutes. Prepare the Thin Glaze (see below) while the dough is rising. Turn the dough out onto a lightly floured surface. Do not punch down or knead. Gently pat and roll dough into a ½-inch thickness. Use a 4-inch doughnut cutter to cut into doughnuts. Gently knead scraps of dough together and repeat process. Let doughnuts rise for 30 minutes. Fry in hot oil at 350° that is at least ½-inch deep. Cook for 2 minutes on each side or until golden brown. Drain for one minute and quickly dip in glaze. Be sure to cover the whole doughnut. Place them on a rack so that any excess glaze can drip off.

THIN GLAZE

2 c. powdered sugar
2 Tbs. melted butter
2 Tbs. canned milk

½ tsp. vanilla
Warm coffee, about 2 Tbs.

Prepare glaze just before you begin to fry the doughnuts. In a large bowl combine the powdered sugar, melted butter, canned milk, and vanilla. Mix together until well blended. Stir until smooth and all of the lumps are gone. Slowly add warm coffee, a few drops at a time, until you have a thin glaze that the doughnuts can be dipped in.

Note: You will need a doughnut cutter about 4 inches in diameter. You can also use a lid from a tea kettle (or an empty vegetable can) for the outside of the doughnut and an empty spice jar to cut the center doughnut hole. A deep fryer is ideal for this recipe, but a frying pan will also work. These doughnuts do not keep well because the glaze gets watery after a short time.

240812-16

Desserts

Desserts

When preparing any of these desserts, please keep in mind the timing. Some recipes are best when served while they are still warm, like Apple Dumplings. Yet some recipes must be chilled before serving. New York Cheesecake is probably the best example. You should prepare the cheesecake a day ahead of time, because it needs to be thoroughly chilled before serving. Then there are Sweet Potato Turnovers, which are good either warm or chilled.

Equipment Suggestions

Pastry blender: This will help you cut shortening into flour when making pastry dough. It is not mandatory, but they are so reasonably priced that they are very much worth the investment. If you do not have one you can still "cut" the shortening into flour with a pair of knives using a criss-crossing motion to evenly distribute the shortening throughout the flour.

Electric stand mixer: This probably qualifies as a luxury item. A portable hand mixer will frequently work just as well. If you do not have an electric mixer of any kind, all of the recipes here can just as easily be mixed by hand.

DESSERTS

Cakes

BANANA SPICE CAKE
(Makes one single layer 9-inch round cake)

½ c. raisins
¾ c. sugar
½ c. butter (1 stick), softened
2 eggs
1 c. mashed ripe bananas
⅓ c. milk
1 tsp. vanilla extract
2 ¼ c. all-purpose flour

¾ tsp. baking soda
½ tsp. baking powder
½ tsp. cinnamon
¼ tsp. salt
⅛ tsp. nutmeg
⅛ tsp. allspice
powdered sugar (opt.)

Plump raisins by soaking in warm water for 5 minutes. Drain and set aside until ready to use. In a large bowl, beat the sugar and softened butter together until light and creamy. Add the eggs and beat until smooth. Add the mashed bananas, milk, and vanilla. Mix until well blended. In a separate bowl sift together the flour, baking soda, baking powder, cinnamon, salt, nutmeg, and allspice. Add the flour to the banana mixture and beat until smooth, about 5 minutes. Gently stir the plumped raisins into the batter. Pour batter into a greased and floured 9-inch round cake pan. Bake in a preheated 350° oven for 45 to 50 minutes. The cake is done when a toothpick inserted in the center comes out clean. Let cool on wire rack and use a sifter to sprinkle the optional powdered sugar over the top. If you prefer, you can spread the following Butter Cream Frosting over the cake.

BUTTER CREAM FROSTING

6 Tbs. butter (¾ stick), softened,
   do not melt
1 tsp. vanilla extract

2 c. powdered sugar, sifted
1 - 2 Tbs. milk

Beat the softened butter in a large bowl until smooth. Stir in the vanilla extract. Slowly mix in the sifted powdered sugar. The sugar needs to be sifted in order to help prevent lumps from appearing in the frosting. Stir in 1 tablespoon of the milk. If the frosting is too thick, slowly stir in more milk until it reaches the right consistency for spreading on the cake.

Note: You will need 3 large bananas in order to get one cup of mashed bananas. You will also need a 9-inch round cake pan for this recipe.

NEW YORK CHEESECAKE
(Makes one 9-inch cake or 12 to 16 servings)

CRUST

1 ¾ c. graham cracker crumbs   6 Tbs. melted butter

Combine the graham cracker crumbs and butter in a large bowl. Mix with a fork until well blended. Using the backside of a spoon, press the crumbs evenly into bottom and around the sides of a buttered 9-inch spring form pan.

FILLING

3 (8 oz.) pkg. cream cheese at   1 ½ tsp. vanilla extract
  room temperature   ¼ tsp. salt
1 ½ c. sugar   6 eggs
3 Tbs. freshly squeezed lemon
  juice

Beat softened cream cheese until fluffy and smooth, about 3 minutes. Gradually blend in the 1 ½ cups sugar, lemon juice, vanilla and salt. Add the eggs, two at a time, beating well after each addition. Do not beat too long after adding the eggs, 3 minutes at the most. You do not want to beat a lot of air into the batter. Pour filling into the prepared crumb crust. Bake in a preheated 325° oven for 55 to 60 minutes, or until just set. Be careful not to overcook it, or it will become cake-like and lose its flavor. Remove from oven and cool for 30 to 45 minutes before adding topping. If you add the topping any sooner than this, the cream cheese filling will collapse in the center from the weight of the topping. As a result, the topping will be thicker towards the center than around the edges.

TOPPING

3 c. sour cream   1 ½ tsp. vanilla extract
6 Tbs. sugar

In a large bowl stir together the sour cream, 6 tablespoons sugar, and vanilla until well blended. Spread evenly over top of baked cheesecake. Bake for exactly 12 minutes in a preheated 325° oven. Chill overnight before serving. Remove outer ring of pan before slicing. Leftover cheesecake, if there is any, can be sliced and stored in the freezer for 3 to 4 months.

Note: You will need a round 9-inch springform pan for this recipe. This cake requires advanced planning, because it will need to be chilled in the refrigerator overnight, or about 12 hours, before serving. One lemon usually yields 2 tablespoons of juice so you will need to purchase 2 medium lemons. The finished cake will weigh about 5 pounds.

PINEAPPLE UPSIDE-DOWN CAKE
(Makes 6 large servings)

PREPARING THE TOPPING

6 Tbs. butter (¾ stick)
1 c. brown sugar
1 (20 oz.) can pineapple slices

24 pecan halves
6 maraschino cherries

Grease only the sides of a 13 x 9 x 2-inch cake pan. Dust the sides of the pan with flour. In a 1-quart saucepan melt the butter over medium heat. Stir in the brown sugar until well blended and remove from heat. Spread the sugar mixture evenly over the bottom of the cake pan. Remove 6 pineapple slices from the can and arrange on top of the brown sugar mixture evenly spaced in 2 rows of 3 slices in each row. Place 4 pecan halves upside down around each pineapple slice. Place a maraschino cherry in the center of each pineapple slice. Set the cake pan aside while preparing cake batter.

MIXING BATTER AND BAKING THE CAKE

5 eggs, separated
1 c. granulated white sugar
1⅔ c. sifted all-purpose flour
1¾ tsp. baking powder

¼ tsp. salt
½ c. pineapple juice (from the can
  of pineapple rings)

In the large bowl of an electric mixer cream together the 5 egg yolks and 1 cup granulated sugar for 3 minutes. In a separate bowl combine the flour, baking powder, and salt. Add the flour to the mixing bowl with the egg yolks alternately with ½ cup of pineapple juice from the can of pineapple rings. Mix together at medium speed for 3 minutes. Pour all of the batter from the mixer into a large bowl. Wash the bowl from the mixer and add the 5 egg whites. Beat the egg whites until they are stiff and form peaks. Gently fold the egg whites into the batter mixture in the large bowl until well blended. Pour batter into prepared cake pan. Bake in a preheated 350° oven for 40 to 50 minutes, or until wooden toothpick inserted in center of cake comes out clean.

TURNING THE CAKE UPSIDE-DOWN

Let the cake cool for 10 minutes. Invert cake onto a 14 x 10-inch platter or a large cookie sheet. Let rest for a minute before removing pan. Cool to room temperature before serving.

Note: You will need a 13 x 9 x 2-inch cake pan. In addition you will need a 14 x 10-inch platter or large cookie sheet to invert the finished cake onto. And finally, you will also need to purchase a 20-ounce can of pineapple slices in juice. You will use 6 slices in this recipe and have 4 slices left over for other meals.

TRADITIONAL POUND CAKE
(Makes 1 cake)

BASIC POUND CAKE

1 c. butter (2 sticks), softened at
  room temperature, Do Not
  substitute margarine

1 c. + 1 Tbs. sugar
4 lrg. eggs
2 c. sifted all-purpose flour

The butter should be soft but not melted. Beat the butter in the bowl of an electric mixer until smooth. Add the sugar and continue beating for 2 to 3 minutes. Add the eggs one at a time and beat until well blended. Finally, slowly add the flour. Continue beating until thoroughly blended and the batter has a smooth, even texture, about 3 minutes. Pour the batter into a greased and floured 9 x 5 x 3-inch loaf pan. Bake in a preheated 325° oven for about 1 hour. The cake is done when the edges begin to pull away from the sides of the pan and the center of the cake springs back when gently pressed. Allow the cake to cool in the pan for about 3 to 5 minutes. Then turn the cake out onto a cookie sheet to finish cooling.

LEMON POUND CAKE

Basic pound cake ingredients
  from above

1 Tbs. fresh lemon juice
1 ½ Tbs. finely grated lemon rind

Follow the directions above for the Basic Pound Cake. Before pouring the batter into the baking pan, add the lemon juice and lemon rind. Beat at a low speed for 1 to 2 minutes. Pour into prepared loaf pan and follow the same baking instructions as above.

Note: The original recipe for pound cake has only four ingredients: 1 pound each of butter, sugar, eggs, and flour. This will make two cakes, each weighing 2 pounds. The weights have been converted so that you can use dry measuring cups to make a single cake. This is a heavy cake so please do not expect a light feathery loaf. You will need a 9 x 5 x 3-inch loaf pan.

240812-16

SEED CAKE
(Makes one 9-inch round cake)

1 recipe Basic Pound Cake (from
   previous recipe)
1 Tbs. chopped orange zest
1 Tbs. whole caraway seeds

1 tsp. finely grated lemon rind
1 tsp. mace
½ tsp. nutmeg

Prepare the batter for Basic Pound Cake from the previous recipe. Stir in the orange zest, caraway seeds, lemon rind, mace, and nutmeg. Pour the batter into a greased and floured 9-inch round cake pan. Bake in a preheated 325° oven for about 1 hour. The cake is done when the center springs back after being gently pressed.

Note: You will need one 9-inch round cake pan for this recipe.

MARBLE POUND CAKE
(Makes 1 cake)

2 oz. semi-sweet baking
   chocolate
1 c. butter (2 sticks), softened at
   room temperature; Do Not
   substitute margarine

1 c. + 1 Tbs. sugar
4 lrg. eggs
2 c. sifted all-purpose flour

Melt the chocolate in the top of a double boiler and set aside. The butter should be soft but not melted. Beat the butter with an electric mixer until smooth. Add the sugar and continue beating for 2 to 3 minutes. Add the eggs one at a time and beat until well blended. Finally, slowly add the flour. Continue beating until thoroughly blended and the batter has a smooth even texture, about 3 minutes. Put half of the batter in a separate bowl. Stir the melted chocolate into the batter in the bowl of the electric mixer. Mix until well blended. Grease and dust with flour a 9 x 5 x 3-inch loaf pan. Place large spoonfuls of batter in the bread pan alternating the dark and light batter. When done, run a knife or chopstick down the length of the pan in a circular motion 2 or 3 times to give it the traditional marbled pattern. Bake in a preheated 325° oven for about 1 hour. Test the cake by using a toothpick or by gently pressing the center of the cake. If the cake immediately returns to its original shape, it is done. Remove the cake from the pan after it has cooled on a rack for 3 to 5 minutes and place on a cookie sheet.

Note: You will need a double boiler for melting the chocolate. You will also need a 9 x 5 x 3-inch loaf pan. This is identical to the earlier recipe for Traditional Pound Cake except that chocolate has been added to half of the batter in order to make the marbled pattern in the cake.

LIGHT FRUITCAKE
(Makes 1 large fruitcake, about 3 ½ lb.)

1⅔ c. raisins (9 oz.)
¼ c. diced dates (1 ½ oz.)
1⅓ c. pecan halves (5 oz.)
1 c. candied cherries (8 oz.)
1 c. candied pineapple (8 oz.)
¾ c. butter (1 ½ sticks), softened
   at room temperature

⅞ c. sugar (¾ c. + 2 Tbs.)
3 lrg. eggs
1⅔ c. sifted all-purpose flour
1 Tbs. white wine (opt.)

Plump raisins by soaking in hot water for 5 minutes. Drain and set aside until ready to use. Set aside 6 to 8 large pieces of candied fruit and 8 pecan halves for decorating the top of the cake. In a large bowl, stir together the dates, the remaining pecan halves, candied cherries, candied pineapple, and plumped raisins. Set aside while preparing batter. Beat the softened butter in the bowl of an electric mixer until creamy. Add sugar, eggs and flour, beating well after each addition. Pour the batter over the candied fruit mixture and mix until well blended. Pour into a greased and floured 9 x 5 x 3-inch bread pan. Place in a preheated 325° oven. After 15 minutes of baking, decorate the top of cake with the extra fruit and pecans that were set aside earlier. Bake for an additional 1 to 1 ¼ hours. The cake is done when the center of the cake springs back when gently pressed. Remove from oven and slowly pour the optional white wine over the cake. Let stand until wine is absorbed, about 30 minutes. Remove from pan and allow to cool completely on a cookie sheet. Wrap tightly in aluminum foil so that it does not dry out.

FOR 3 SMALL FRUITCAKES

Fruitcake batter from above.

To make three small fruitcakes from this recipe, you will need three small mini-loaf pans that measure about 5 ½ x 3 x 2-inches. Prepare the batter following the above instructions. Grease and dust with flour each of the small loaf pans. Divide the batter evenly between the three pans. Place in a preheated 325° oven. After 15 minutes of baking, decorate the top of each fruitcake with the extra fruit and pecans that were set aside earlier. Bake for an additional 45 minutes to one hour. The cakes are done when the center of the each cake springs back when gently pressed. Remove from oven and slowly pour one teaspoon of the optional white wine over each cake. Let stand until wine is absorbed, about 20 minutes. Remove from pans, allow to cool completely on a cookie sheet, and wrap in aluminum foil. Each cake will weigh a little over 1 pound when finished.

Note: There are no fence sitters when it come to fruitcake. You either love it or you hate it. This recipe is essentially a pound cake batter filled with dried fruit, candied fruit, and nuts. The word "light" in the recipe title refers to the color of the cake and not its weight. I hope that some of the fruitcake lovers out there will find this recipe worthwhile.

240812-16

DARK FRUITCAKE
(Makes 1 large fruitcake, about 3 ¼ lb.)

2 c. raisins (10 oz.)
½ c. butter (1 stick), softened
1 c. firmly packed brown sugar
2 eggs, separated
2 Tbs. dark molasses
2 Tbs. wine
1⅓ c. sifted all-purpose flour
½ tsp. baking soda

½ tsp. cinnamon
¼ tsp. mace
¼ tsp. cloves
¼ tsp. nutmeg
1 c. walnut pieces (¼ lb.)
1 c. candied cherries (6 oz.)
½ c. chopped dates (3 oz.)
1 c. candied pineapple (6 oz.)

Plump the raisins by soaking in warm water for 5 minutes. Drain and set aside until ready to use. In a large bowl beat together the butter and sugar. Add 2 egg yolks, molasses, and wine. Beat again until well blended and smooth. In a separate large bowl, sift together flour, baking soda, cinnamon, mace, cloves, and nutmeg. Stir the flour mixture into the egg batter until thoroughly blended. Fold in the plumped raisins, walnuts, cherries, dates, and pineapple. In a medium bowl beat the egg whites with an electric mixer until stiff. Gently fold the egg whites into the batter. Grease and dust with flour a 9 x 5 x 3-inch loaf pan. Line the bottom of the pan with a piece of parchment paper. Spread the batter evenly in the pan. Bake in a preheated 300° oven for 3 to 3½ hours. Place a pan of hot water on the bottom rack of the oven for the first 2 hours. Remove the fruitcake from the oven when done and let cool for 30 minutes before removing from pan. Remove parchment paper from the fruitcake. Once the fruitcake has cooled to room temperature, wrap it tightly in aluminum foil before storing.

Note: This recipe creates a fruitcake that is closer to what most people are familiar with. You can also follow the directions in the previous recipe for making 3 small fruitcakes. Neither one of these fruitcake recipes calls for citron or candied orange peel which tends to give fruitcake a bitter flavor.

YELLOW CAKE WITH CHOCOLATE FROSTING
(Makes one round 10-inch double layer cake)

1 c. butter (2 sticks), softened
2 c. sugar
1 tsp. vanilla extract
5 eggs
3 ¾ c. sifted all-purpose flour

4 tsp. baking powder
1 ¼ c. whole milk
Basic Chocolate Frosting (see
   following recipe)

In the bowl of an electric mixer combine the butter, sugar, and vanilla. Beat until smooth, about 3 minutes. Add eggs, one at a time, beating well after each addition. In a separate large bowl, mix together the flour and baking powder. Add flour to butter mixture in three parts, adding about a third of the milk after each addition. Continue to beat until smooth, about 3 minutes. Pour into two round greased and floured 10-inch cake pans. Bake in a preheated 350° oven for 30 to 35 minutes. The cake is done when the center springs back after being gently pressed or a cake tester comes out clean. Cool for 5 minutes and remove from pans. Allow to come to room temperature before spreading Chocolate Frosting (see following recipe) on cake.

Note: You will need two 10-inch round cake pans for this recipe.

BASIC CHOCOLATE FROSTING
(Will frost a 10-inch double layer cake)

4 c. powdered sugar
4 (1 oz.) squares unsweetened
   baking chocolate
6 Tbs. butter or margarine ------
   (¾ stick)

2 tsp. vanilla
¼ c. whole milk
Warm water

Place the powdered sugar in a large non-metallic bowl and set aside until ready to use. In a 1-quart saucepan combine the chocolate, butter, and vanilla. Place over a very low heat and stir until melted and the mixture is smooth. Quickly stir the chocolate and milk into the powdered sugar. Slowly stir in enough warm water, adding a few drops at a time, to bring the frosting to a spreading consistency. Immediately spread on yellow cake from the previous recipe. If frosting begins to get too stiff before you are finished, place in a microwave for 3 to 5 seconds.

Note: This is your basic everyday chocolate frosting that can be used on the previous yellow cake, on cupcakes, or anything else that requires a rich and creamy chocolate frosting.

164

WHITE CAKE WITH PINEAPPLE FROSTING
(Makes one round 8-inch double layer cake)

½ c. butter (1 stick), softened
1 c. sugar
1¼ c. sifted cake flour
1 c. sifted all-purpose flour
4 tsp. baking powder
¼ tsp. salt

1 c. milk
1 tsp. vanilla extract
4 egg whites
Pineapple Frosting (see following recipe)

In a large bowl of an electric mixer beat the butter and sugar together. Add the cake flour, all-purpose flour, baking powder, salt, milk, and vanilla extract. Beat at a slow speed until blended. Increase to medium and beat for 2 to 3 minutes. In a separate bowl beat the egg whites until stiff. Fold into the batter until well blended. Pour an equal amount of the batter into each of two round 8-inch cake pans that have been greased and dusted with flour. Bake in a preheated 350° oven for 25 to 30 minutes. The cake is done when it springs back after being gently pressed in the center. Remove from pans and allow to cool before spreading frosting.

Note: You will need two round 8-inch cake pans for this recipe.

PINEAPPLE FROSTING
(Enough for one 8-inch double layer cake)

8 pineapple slices from a 20 oz. can (or two 8-oz. cans)

4 c. powdered sugar
¼ c. butter (½ stick), melted

Prepare this pineapple frosting and quickly spread on white cake from previous recipe. Finely chop the pineapple slices and place in a large wire mesh strainer. Press out as much liquid as possible with the back of a spoon. In a large non-metallic bowl combine the powdered sugar, butter, and pineapple. Stir together until well blended. The juice in the pineapple should provide enough moisture to make the frosting spreadable. Heat in a microwave for 5 to 10 seconds and spread frosting on cake. Start with the top of the bottom layer and then place the second layer on top. Spread frosting over the top of the cake before frosting the sides. If the frosting becomes too thick then place in a microwave oven for about 5 seconds. This will help to make the frosting more manageable. Since this frosting contains pineapple, it will not keep well at room temperature. Refrigerate any leftover cake that will not be used within 24 hours.

Note: You will need to purchase a 20-ounce can (or two 8-ounce cans) of pineapple slices. You will only need to use 8 of the 10 slices of pineapple that will come in the large can. The biggest challenge for this frosting is not to make it too thin. It should be thick enough to spread and stick to the cake but not so thin that it runs down the side.

CHOCOLATE MAYONNAISE CAKE
(Makes one single layer 13 x 9-inch cake)

3 c. sifted all-purpose flour
1 ¼ c. sugar
¾ c. unsweetened cocoa
   (powder)
2 ¼ tsp. baking powder
1 ½ tsp. baking soda

pinch salt
1 ½ c. mayonnaise
1 ½ tsp. vanilla extract
1 ½ c. warm water
Basic White Frosting (see recipe
   on next page)

Lightly grease and dust with flour a 13 x 9 x 2-inch cake pan. In a large bowl combine the flour, sugar, unsweetened cocoa, baking powder, baking soda, and salt. Stir together until well blended. Add the mayonnaise, vanilla extract, and warm water. Beat vigorously by hand or with an electric mixer for 2 to 3 minutes. Pour batter into the prepared cake pan and spread batter to an even thickness. Bake in a preheated 350° oven for 40 to 45 minutes or until toothpick inserted in center of cake comes out clean. Cool on rack for 15 minutes. Remove from pan and place on a cookie sheet lined with wax paper or parchment paper. Frost the cake with Basic White Frosting (see next page) after it has cooled completely. You can also frost the cake with the Basic Chocolate Frosting that appears earlier in this chapter.

Note: You will need a 13 x 9 x 2-inch cake pan. For a smaller cake, cut the recipe in half and use an 8-inch square baking pan.

CHOCOLATE MAYONNAISE CUPCAKES
(Makes 24 cupcakes)

Cake batter from previous recipe,
   Chocolate Mayonnaise Cake

In a large bowl mix together the ingredients for the batter from the above recipe. Line the cups of two standard (12-cup) muffin tins with paper liners. Divide the batter evenly among the 24 muffin cups. Each muffin cup should be about two-thirds full. Bake the cupcakes in a preheated 350° oven for 20 to 25 minutes. Cupcakes are done when a toothpick inserted in the center of a cupcake comes out clean. Let the cupcakes cool for 5 minutes before removing from tins. Frost with your favorite frosting if desired.

Note: You will need two standard 12-cup muffin tins and paper liners.

240812-16

BASIC WHITE FROSTING
(Makes enough for a single layer 13 x 9-inch cake)

3 c. powder sugar
⅜ c. butter (¾ stick), melted
½ tsp. vanilla extract

¼ c. canned milk
Warm water

In a large nonmetallic bowl combine the powdered sugar, butter, vanilla, and canned milk. Mix together until well blended. Add a few drops of warm water at a time, if needed, to make frosting spreadable. Place frosting in microwave for 3 to 5 seconds if it becomes too stiff while spreading on cake.

LEMON FROSTING
(Makes enough for 12 regular cupcakes)

2 Tbs. butter, melted
2 drops yellow food coloring
2 tsp. lemon juice

¾ tsp. finely grated lemon peel
1 ½ c. powdered sugar
warm water

In a small bowl stir together the melted butter, food coloring, lemon juice, and grated lemon peel. Sift the powdered sugar into a large bowl. Form a well in the center of the sugar and add the melted butter mixture. Mix together until well blended. Slowly stir in drops of warm water until the frosting reaches the desired consistency. Spread on cupcakes immediately.

Note: This recipe also makes enough frosting for 6 jumbo cupcakes. You can double this recipe to frost an 8-inch double layer yellow cake.

ORANGE FROSTING
(Makes enough for 12 regular cupcakes)

2 Tbs. melted butter
2 drops yellow food coloring
1 drop red food coloring
1 Tbs. + 1 tsp. freshly squeezed
   orange juice

1 tsp. finely grated orange peel
1 ½ c. powdered sugar
Warm water

In a small bowl stir together the melted butter, yellow food coloring, red food coloring, and orange juice. Stir in the grated orange peel. Sift the powdered sugar into a large bowl. Form a well in the center and add the melted butter mixture. Stir until well blended. If the frosting is too thick, slowly stir in drops of warm water until the frosting reaches the desired consistency. Spread on cupcakes immediately.

Note: This recipe also makes enough frosting for 6 jumbo cupcakes. You can double this recipe to frost an 8-inch double layer yellow cake.

CUPCAKES
(Makes 12 regular cupcakes)

⅓ c. butter (⅔ stick), softened
⅔ c. sugar
1 ½ c. sifted cake flour
2 ½ tsp. baking powder

¼ tsp. salt
⅔ c. milk
¼ tsp. vanilla extract
2 egg whites and pinch salt

Line the cups of a standard (12-cup) muffin tin with paper liners. In a large bowl beat the softened butter until smooth. Slowly beat in the sugar. Add the cake flour, baking powder, salt, milk and vanilla. Beat everything together until smooth and free of any lumps, about 3 minutes. In a separate bowl beat the egg whites and salt until stiff. Gently fold the beaten egg whites into the batter until well blended. Pour an equal amount of batter into each cup. Each mold should be about two-thirds full. Bake in a 350° oven for 20 to 25 minutes or until the center of a cupcake springs back when gently pressed.

Note: You will need a standard 12-cup muffin tin and paper liners.

PINEAPPLE-WALNUT CAKE
(Makes 12 pieces)

¼ c. butter (½ stick), softened
1 ½ c. sugar
2 eggs
1 (20 oz.) can crushed pineapple,
    undrained (2 ¼ c.)
1 tsp. vanilla extract
2 ½ c. sifted all-purpose flour

2 tsp. baking soda
⅛ tsp. salt
1 ¼ c. chopped walnuts, divided
    (1 c. + ¼ c.)
Cream Cheese Frosting (see
    below)

Beat together the butter, sugar, and eggs until creamy. Stir in the crushed pineapple, and vanilla. Add the flour, baking soda, and salt. Mix together by hand or with an electric mixer until well blended. Fold in 1 cup walnut meats. Pour into a greased and floured 13 x 9 x 2-inch cake pan. Bake in a preheated 350° oven for 35 to 40 minutes or until cake springs back after being gently pressed in the center. Allow to cool for 10 minutes. Turn the cake out onto a cookie sheet. Let cool completely before spreading frosting (see below) on top and sides of cake. Sprinkle the remaining ¼ cup walnut meats over top and refrigerate.

CREAM CHEESE FROSTING

1 (8 oz.) pkg. cream cheese,
    softened

¼ c. butter (½ stick), softened
3 c. powdered sugar

In a large bowl combine the cream cheese, margarine, and powdered sugar. Stir together until smooth and creamy.

Note: You will need a 13 x 9 x 2-inch cake pan.

168

MARBLE TUBE CAKE
(Makes one 8-inch tube cake)

1 c. sugar
½ c. butter (1 stick), softened
2 ¼ c. cake flour
1 Tbs. + 1 tsp. baking powder
1 c. milk

1 tsp. vanilla extract
4 egg whites
2 oz. semi-sweet baking
  chocolate
Powdered sugar

Beat the sugar and butter together with an electric mixer until smooth. In a separate bowl sift together the flour, baking powder, and salt. Add the flour to the butter mixture along with the milk and vanilla. Mix together until well blended, about 3 minutes. Divide the batter into two equal parts. Melt the chocolate in the top of a double boiler. Thoroughly mix the melted chocolate into one part of the batter. In a separate bowl beat the egg whites at high speed until stiff. Fold half of the egg whites into the chocolate batter and the other half into the plain batter. Grease and dust the tube pan with flour. Add the batter to the pan in large spoonfuls, alternating the dark and light batter. Run a chopstick or butter knife in a circular motion in the batter so that it circles the batter 2 or 3 times. This will give the batter its marbled look. Bake in a preheated 350° oven for 45 to 50 minutes. The cake is done when it springs back after being gently pressed in the center. Remove from pan and dust the top of the cake with powdered sugar.

Note: You will need an 8-cup tube pan, about 8 x 3 ¾-inches deep. A small Bundt® pan of about the same size will also work.

RAISIN AND SPICE TUBE CAKE
(Makes one 8-inch tube cake)

1 c. raisins
1 ½ c. water
⅓ c. shortening
1 c. sugar
2 eggs
2 ⅓ c. sifted all-purpose flour

1 tsp. baking soda
¾ tsp. baking powder
¾ tsp. nutmeg
¾ tsp. cinnamon
⅔ c. raisin water
Powdered sugar

Grease and dust with flour an 8-inch tube pan. Set aside until ready to use. In a 1-quart saucepan combine the raisins and 1 ½ cups water. Bring to a boil, turn off heat, and let stand for 5 minutes. Drain the raisins and reserve the raisin water. In a large bowl beat together the shortening and sugar. Add the eggs and beat until creamy. In a separate bowl combine the flour, baking soda, baking powder, nutmeg, and cinnamon. Add to the sugar mixture alternately with ⅔ cup of the warm raisin water. Fold in the drained raisins. Pour batter into prepared tube pan and bake for 50 minutes to 1 hour at 350°. Dust with powdered sugar before serving.

Note: See "Note" in previous recipe for the appropriate pan for this cake.

CARROT CAKE
(Makes one single layer 8-inch round cake)

½ c. butter (1 stick), softened
¾ c. white sugar
¼ c. brown sugar
2 eggs
¼ c. fresh orange juice
½ tsp. vanilla flavoring
1 ½ c. sifted all-purpose flour

1 ½ tsp. baking powder
½ tsp. cinnamon
¼ tsp. nutmeg
¼ tsp. salt
1 c. grated carrots
¼ c. finely chopped walnuts

In a large bowl combine the butter, the white sugar, and brown sugar. Beat together by hand or with an electric mixer until smooth. Mix in the eggs, orange juice, and vanilla. Stir together until well blended. Add the flour, baking powder, cinnamon, nutmeg, and salt. Beat until well blended and smooth, about 3 minutes. Fold in the grated carrots and walnuts. Pour into a greased and floured round 8-inch cake pan. Spread the batter to an even thickness. Bake in a 350° oven for 40 to 45 minutes, or until center of cake springs back when lightly touched.

Note: A large (10-ounce) orange should provide enough juice for this cake. You will need a round 8-inch cake pan for this recipe.

ARKANSAS APPLE CAKE
(Makes one 13 x 9-inch cake)

1 ½ c. sugar
3 eggs, lightly beaten
1 c. vegetable oil
1 tsp vanilla
2 ½ c. sifted all-purpose flour
2 tsp. baking powder
1 tsp. baking soda

½ tsp. salt
3 c. peeled and diced apples
  (about ½-inch pieces)
1 c. chopped walnuts
1 Tbs. sugar
1 tsp. cinnamon

In a large bowl combine 1 ½ cups sugar, the eggs, oil, and vanilla. Beat together until well blended, about 3 minutes. Stir in the flour, baking powder, baking soda, and salt until well blended. Fold in apples and walnuts. The batter will be stiff. Lightly grease and dust with flour a 13 x 9 x 2-inch baking pan. Pour batter into pan and spread to an even thickness. In a small dish stir together 1 tablespoon sugar and 1 teaspoon cinnamon. Sprinkle evenly over the top of the cake batter. Bake in a preheated 350° oven for 50 minutes to 1 hour.

Note: You will need a 13 x 9 x 2-inch baking pan. You will also need to purchase 2 pounds of apples to make this cake.

240812-16

Cookies and Bars

STRAWBERRY OATMEAL BARS
(Makes 24 bars)

1 ½ c. all-purpose flour
1 tsp. baking powder
¼ tsp. salt
1 ½ c. rolled oats (uncooked oatmeal)

¾ c. brown sugar
¾ c. butter (1 ½ sticks), at room temperature
2 c. strawberry jam

In a large bowl sift together the flour, baking powder and salt. Stir in oats and sugar, and cut in the butter with a pastry blender until crumbly. There will be about 4 cups of oat crumb mixture. Firmly pat two-thirds of the crumb mix (2⅔ cups) into a greased 13 x 9 x 2-inch baking pan. Place the strawberry jam in a medium bowl. Mash with a fork until it is smooth in order to make it easier to spread. Spread strawberry jam evenly over the crumbs in the baking pan. Make sure the jam is spread right up to the sides of the pan. Sprinkle the remaining crumb mixture over the jam. Bake in a preheated 375° oven for 35 minutes or until lightly browned. Cool before cutting into 24 (1 ½ x 3-inch) bars.

CRANBERRY BARS

1 (14 oz.) can jellied cranberry sauce
½ c. sugar

2 tsp. cornstarch dissolved in --- 2 tsp. water.

Place the jellied cranberry sauce in a 1 or 2-quart saucepan. Mash with a potato masher until smooth. Add the sugar and cornstarch mixture. Stir and cook over medium heat until it reaches a gentle simmer. Remove from heat and allow to cool. Use in the above recipe in place of the strawberry jam.

Note: You will need a 13 x 9 x 2-inch baking pan for this recipe. You can use apricot, peach, seedless raspberry, plum, fig, or any other jam in place of the strawberry jam. The fig jam in this cookbook (see Chapter: Jellies, Jams, Marmalades and Fruit Butters) makes an especially good fruit bar. One-half of this recipe will fill an 8-inch square baking pan.

CHINESE ALMOND COOKIES
(Makes 24 to 30 cookies)

2 ¼ c. all-purpose flour, sifted
¼ tsp. baking powder
⅔ c. sugar
1 c. shortening

1 ½ tsp. almond extract
1 egg
1 beaten egg yolk
30 blanched almonds (see below)

Sift together flour and baking powder into a large bowl. Add sugar and cut in the shortening with a pastry blender. In a small bowl, beat together the almond extract and 1 egg. Stir the egg mixture into the flour with a fork. Knead until pliable. Let stand for 5 minutes in a cool place. Roll the dough out to ¼-inch in thickness. Cut the cookies with a 2-inch diameter cookie cutter and place on a lightly greased cookie sheet. You should be able to get 12 to 15 cookies on a cookie sheet. Brush the tops of the cookies with beaten egg yolk. Press a blanched almond in the center of each cookie. Bake at 350° for 18 to 22 minutes or until cookies have turned light brown around the edges.

HOW TO BLANCH ALMONDS

30 Almonds   1 c. water

Bring 1 cup water to a boil in a small saucepan. Add almonds and allow to simmer for 1 minute. Drain and rinse in cold water. Slip skins from almonds, and they are ready to use.

Note: These are just as good as, if not better than, the commercially made cookies.

PECAN SHORTBREAD COOKIES
(Makes 24 to 28 cookies)

1 c. (2 sticks) butter at room
    temperature
1 tsp. vanilla extract
¾ c. powdered sugar

2 c. sifted all-purpose flour
¼ tsp. baking powder
⅔ c. chopped pecans

Place the butter and vanilla extract in a large bowl and beat together until creamy. Sift the powdered sugar into the butter and mix until well blended. Stir in the sifted flour and baking powder. Mix together well and fold in the chopped pecans. Place in the refrigerator for 10 to 15 minutes or until dough is firm enough to work with. Roll the dough out on a lightly floured surface to a thickness of ⅜-inch. Cut into 1 ½-inch squares. Place on a lightly greased cookie sheet with a space of at least ¾-inch between each cookie. Bake in a preheated 375° oven for 12 to 15 minute or until cookies are lightly browned around the edges.

CHOCOLATE COATED COOKIES
(Makes 48 cookies)

BASIC COOKIES

¾ c. butter (1 ½ sticks), softened
¾ c. sugar
1 egg, lightly beaten
1 Tbs. milk

1 tsp. vanilla extract
2 ½ c. sifted all-purpose flour
1 tsp. baking soda
1 tsp. cream of tartar

The butter should be at room temperature so that it is softened but not melted. Mix together the butter and sugar. When well blended, stir in the egg, milk, and vanilla extract. Add the flour, baking soda, and cream of tartar. Stir until well blended. Place the dough in a pastry bag with an opening that is about ½-inch in diameter. Squeeze the dough onto a greased cookie sheet in strips about 3 inches long. Allow a 1 ½-inch space between each strip of cookie dough. A large cookie sheet will hold at least 12 cookies. If the dough is too stiff, remove any metal tips from the pastry bag and place the entire bag in a microwave oven. Warm on the high power setting for 6 to 8 seconds at the very most. This should soften the dough enough to make it easier to squeeze. If you do not have a pastry bag, you can drop heaping teaspoons of cookie dough on the cookie sheet to create round cookies. Bake the cookies in a preheated 375° oven for 8 to 10 minutes, or until edges are lightly browned. Remove from oven and let cool. See directions below for adding chocolate to the backs of the cookies.

ADDING CHOCOLATE COATING TO COOKIES

1 lb. (16 oz.) Hershey's® Special
  Dark Chocolate

Cookies from above recipe

Melt the chocolate bars in the top of double boiler. Turn off the heat once the chocolate is melted. Line a cookie sheet with waxed paper. Spoon some of the chocolate on the back of a cookie and spread out almost to the edge. The chocolate does not have to go all of the way to the edge of the cookie. Place the cookie on the wax paper with the CHOCOLATE SIDE DOWN. Gently press on the cookie until you can see the chocolate around the edge. Continue spreading chocolate on more cookies until the cookie sheet is full. Place the cookies in the freezer for 10 to 15 minutes in order to harden the chocolate. Remove from the freezer, and repeat until all of the cookies have been coated.

Note: You will need a pastry bag to properly shape the cookie dough and a double boiler to melt the chocolate. You can also use milk or dark chocolate wafers mentioned in the chapter on candy. If you are allergic to chocolate or would just like something a little different, you can melt butterscotch morsels to spread on the back of the cookies in place of the chocolate.

MEXICAN SUGAR COOKIES
(Makes 20 - 24 Biscochitos)

BASIC SUGAR COOKIE

1 tsp. cinnamon	1 ½ tsp. anise extract
3 Tbs. sugar	2 Tbs. orange juice
1 ¼ c. vegetable shortening -----	3 c. sifted all-purpose flour
(½ lb.)	1 ½ tsp. baking powder
¾ c. sugar	½ tsp. salt
1 egg, lightly beaten	24 walnut halves (opt.)

Combine the cinnamon and 3 tablespoons sugar to make cinnamon sugar and set aside until ready to use. Beat the shortening in a large bowl until creamy. Add ¾ cup sugar, egg, anise extract, and orange juice, beating well after each addition. In a separate bowl sift together flour, baking powder, and salt. Add the flour to the shortening mixture and beat until well blended. Take a slightly heaping tablespoon of dough, roll into a ball, and place on a greased cookie sheet. Flatten to 2 ½ to 3 inches in diameter. Continue until cookie sheet is full. You should be able to put 12 to 15 cookies on a standard 15 x 10-inch cookie sheet. Bake in a preheated 350° oven. After 5 minutes, sprinkle some of the cinnamon sugar over the cookies. Press an optional walnut half gently in the center of each cookie. Return to oven and bake for a total of 15 to 20 minutes, or until edges of cookies are lightly browned.

LEMON COOKIES

2 Tbs. lemon juice	Granulated white sugar
1 tsp. finely grated lemon rind	

For lemon cookies, omit the anise extract. Use 2 tablespoons lemon juice in place of the orange juice and add the grated lemon rind. Sprinkle tops of cookies with granulated white sugar in place of the cinnamon sugar.

ALMOND COOKIES

2 tsp. almond extract	Granulated white sugar
2 Tbs. water	

For almond flavored cookies, use 2 teaspoons almond extract in place of the anise extract. Use 2 tablespoons water in place of the orange juice and sprinkle tops of cookies with granulated white sugar.

TO MAKE VERY LARGE COOKIES

Use 3 to 4 tablespoons of dough for large cookies instead of the rounded tablespoon mentioned above. Flatten the cookies on the cookie sheet to at least 4 inches in diameter. This will make 12 very large cookies. The directions for adding the sugar topping and optional walnuts will be the same. Bake for 20 to 24 minutes or until lightly browned around the edges.

240812-16

CHOCOLATE CHIP COOKIES
(Makes 4 dozen cookies)

⅔ c. butter (1⅓ sticks), softened
⅔ c. shortening
½ c. brown sugar
½ c. white sugar
2 eggs
3 c. sifted all-purpose flour

1½ tsp. baking soda
½ tsp. salt
1 (12 oz.) pkg. chocolate morsels
  (2 cups)
1 c. chopped walnuts or pecans
  (opt.)

In a large bowl mix together the butter, shortening, brown sugar, and white sugar. Stir together until creamy and beat in the eggs. In a separate bowl, sift together flour, baking soda, and salt. Stir the flour into the butter mixture until well blended. Stir in the chocolate morsels and the optional nuts. Place by heaping teaspoonfuls on a greased 15 x 10-inch cookie sheet. There should be room for about twelve cookies on each cookie sheet. Bake in a preheated 350° oven for 12 to 14 minutes or until lightly browned around the edges. Cookies are done when they spring back from being gently pressed in the center. For cookies that are thinner and crunchier, add 1 tablespoon water to the dough along with the beaten eggs.

VARIATION: CHOCOLATE CHIP BARS

Same ingredients as above.   2 c. large dark chocolate wafers

Follow the same directions from above for making the cookie dough. The chocolate wafers are the same ones used in candy making (see Chapter: Candy) and are about 1 inch in diameter. Cut the chocolate wafers into quarters. Use the quartered chocolate wafers in place of the chocolate morsels in the above recipe. Spread the cookie dough to an even thickness onto a greased 15 x 10 x 1-inch cookie sheet. Bake for 20 to 25 minutes. Bars are done when they spring back from being gently pressed in the center. Cut into bars when cool.

Note: These cookies and bars are thicker and have more of a cake-like texture than the traditional chewy chocolate chip cookies. You will need a 15 x 10 x 1-inch cookie sheet to make the chocolate chip bars.

NUTMEG COOKIES
(Makes 28 to 30 large cookies)

½ c. butter (1 stick), softened
1 c. sugar
1 egg, lightly beaten
½ tsp. vanilla
⅓ c. sour cream

2 c. all-purpose flour
1 tsp. baking powder
1 tsp. nutmeg
½ tsp. baking soda
¼ tsp. salt

Beat butter in a large bowl while gradually adding sugar. Stir in the egg, vanilla, and sour cream. In a separate bowl, mix together the flour, baking powder, nutmeg, baking soda, and salt. Add the flour to the butter mixture and beat until smooth. Chill the cookie dough in a refrigerator for about 30 minutes before baking. Take a level tablespoon of dough, shape into a ball, and place on a lightly greased cookie sheet. Allow 2½ inches of space between each ball of dough. You should be able to get 8 to 12 cookies on a 15 x 10-inch cookie sheet. Using a damp hand or glass-bottom, flatten each cookie to about 2 inches in diameter. Bake in a preheated 350° oven for 12 to 15 minutes. The cookies should be lightly browned around the edges and the center should spring back when gently touched.

BISCOTTI ITALIAN ANISE COOKIES
(Makes 24 to 30 biscotti)

¼ c. butter (½ stick), softened
1 c. sugar
3 eggs, lightly beaten
½ tsp. vanilla extract
½ tsp. anise extract
2¼ c. all-purpose flour

½ c. coarsely chopped roasted
  almonds
1½ tsp. baking powder
1 tsp. anise seed, crushed
½ tsp. salt
½ tsp. cinnamon

In a large bowl beat the butter and sugar together until smooth. Add eggs, vanilla extract, and anise extract and mix well. In a separate bowl, combine the flour, chopped almonds, baking powder, anise seed, salt, and cinnamon. Add the flour mixture to the egg mixture and stir together to make a soft dough. Knead on a very lightly floured surface 4 or 5 times so that the dough is not too sticky. Divide dough into two equal parts. Shape each into a log about 12 inches long. Place the two logs, side by side, on a large greased cookie sheet, about 4 inches apart. Bake in a preheated 375° oven for 25 to 30 minutes or until lightly browned. Remove from oven and allow to cool enough so that they can be easily handled, about 10 minutes. Slice diagonally crosswise, into strips ½ to ¾-inches wide. Lay on the cookie sheet with the cut side down and return to the oven. Bake for 7 to 8 minutes and flip to bake on second side for an additional 7 to 8 minutes. Biscotti should be lightly browned on both sides when done.

240812-16

MADELEINES
(Makes 22 to 24 Madeleines)

2 Tbs. melted butter for pans
2 lrg. eggs
½ c. sugar
1 ½ tsp. finely grated lemon rind

1 c. sifted cake flour
½ tsp. baking powder
½ c. butter (1 stick), melted

Brush the Madeleine molds with the 2 tablespoons of melted butter. Set aside until ready to use. Beat eggs thoroughly. Stir in sugar and lemon rind. Add cake flour and baking powder and beat with an electric mixer until ribbons form in the batter when beaters are lifted. Slowly drizzle in ½ cup melted butter while beating the batter continuously. Fill each mold about two-thirds full with batter. Fill both pans at the same time as soon as you are done mixing the batter. As the butter cools it causes the batter to get stiff, making it difficult to fill a pan later. Bake in a preheated 350° oven for 12 to 14 minutes, or until Madeleines are light brown around the edges and the center springs back when lightly touched.

Note: You will need 2 Madeleine pans for this recipe. Although Madeleines may look like a cookie, they are more traditionally known as French Butter Cakes. The pans can be found at most kitchen specialty shops or on the internet. Each pan usually has 12 molds or indentations that are oval shaped and ribbed on the bottom to give the Madeleines their classic shell pattern.

LEMON COOKIES
(Makes 4 dozen cookies)

½ c. butter (1 stick), softened
1 ¼ c. sugar
2 eggs, lightly beaten
2 Tbs. lemon juice
2 tsp. finely grated lemon rind
½ c. sour cream

2 ½ c. all-purpose flour
1 tsp. baking powder
½ tsp. baking soda
½ tsp. salt
Additional granulated white sugar

Beat the softened butter while adding the sugar. Stir in the eggs, lemon juice, lemon rind, and sour cream. In a separate bowl, combine the flour, baking powder, baking soda, and salt. Add the flour to the butter mixture and stir until smooth. Drop batter by heaping teaspoons onto a lightly greased cookie sheet. Bake in a preheated 350° oven. Sprinkle white sugar over the cookies after 5 minutes of baking. A shaker filled with granulated white sugar will make this step easier. Bake for a total of 12 to 15 minutes. Cookies are done when they are lightly browned around the edges and spring back when gently pressed in the center.

PIZZELLES
(Makes 12 - 14 pizzelles)

PLAIN PIZZELLES

3 eggs
¾ c. sugar
½ c. butter (1 stick), melted (do not substitute oil)

1 Tbs. vanilla extract
1 ¾ c. all-purpose flour
2 tsp. baking powder

In a medium bowl beat the eggs while gradually adding the sugar. Stir in cooled butter and vanilla. In a separate bowl sift the flour and baking powder together. Blend flour into egg mixture until smooth. Dough will be sticky so it is best to drop it onto the griddle with a large spoon. Place a heaping tablespoon of dough in the center of the bottom grid of the preheated pizzelle baker. The batter does not have to cover the entire bottom of the baker. It will spread out when you close the top. Close top and cook for about 1½ minutes. Remove the pizzelle from the griddle. Quickly trim the edge and cut the pizzelle into quarters with a knife or pizza cutter so that they are easier to serve with tea. Any trimming/cutting must be done while the pizzelle are still warm. Once they cool off they are crisp and may shatter if you try to trim them. Store in an airtight container.

LEMON PIZZELLES

1 Tbs. finely grated lemon rind   *1 ½ tsp. lemon juice*

Use the lemon rind and lemon juice in place of the vanilla extract in the plain pizzelle recipe above.

Note: You will need a Pizzelle Griddle Iron to make pizzelle. Look for the griddle at a kitchen supply store or on the internet. A pizza wheel works best and fastest for trimming the pizzelle. These go perfectly with green tea.

240812-16

OATMEAL COOKIES AND BARS
(Makes about 4 dozen)

OATMEAL COOKIES

1 c. dried cranberries
½ c. butter (1 stick), softened
½ c. vegetable shortening
⅔ c. light brown sugar
⅔ c. white sugar
2 eggs, lightly beaten
1 tsp. vanilla

1 ½ c. sifted all-purpose flour
½ tsp. salt
1 tsp. baking soda
1 tsp. cinnamon
¼ tsp. nutmeg
2 ½ c. oats, uncooked
1 c. chopped pecans

Plump the cranberries by soaking in warm water for about 10 minutes. Drain and set aside until ready to use. In a large bowl, beat together the softened butter, shortening, brown sugar, white sugar, eggs, and vanilla. Stir together until smooth. In a separate large bowl, sift together flour, salt, baking soda, cinnamon, and nutmeg. Add to the sugar mixture in the first bowl and mix until well blended. Stir in the oats, cranberries, and pecans. Drop a heaping teaspoon of dough onto a greased cookie sheet for each cookie. You should be able to get about 12 cookies on a 15 x 10-inch cookie sheet. Bake in a preheated 350° oven for 15 to 18 minutes, or until the center of a cookie springs back after being pressed gently.

OATMEAL BARS

Cookie dough from above.

Spread the prepared dough out evenly on a greased 15 x 10 x 1-inch inch cookie sheet. The back of a fork works best for spreading out the dough. Bake in a preheated 350° oven for about 20 minutes. The bars are done when the dough springs back when gently pressed in the middle. Allow to cool for 15 to 20 minutes before cutting into bars. The dough should be warm but not cold. Cut into bars about 1 ½ x 2 ¾-inches long.

Note: For more traditional oatmeal cookies, replace the dried cranberries and pecans with an equal amount of raisins and chopped walnuts. You will need a 15 x 10 x 1-inch cookie sheet to make the oatmeal bars.

Pies

DOUBLE 9-INCH PIE CRUST
(Makes a double crust for a 9-inch pie)

2 c. all-purpose flour
1 c. vegetable shortening
¾ tsp. salt

½ c. cold water
1 egg yolk, lightly beaten with --
½ tsp. water (opt.)

Combine the flour, vegetable shortening, and salt in a large bowl. Cut the shortening into the flour with a pastry blender until mixture resembles fine crumbs. Stir in the cold water with a fork. The pastry dough will be sticky at this point. Turn out onto a floured surface and knead a few times until the dough is soft and no longer sticky. Shape into a ball. Cut into two pieces with one piece slightly larger than the other. Roll the larger piece out first so that it is 1 inch larger than the 9-inch pie pan. Place the dough in the pan and trim the edge so that it is even with the edge of the pan. Combine the trimmed pieces with the remaining half of the dough. Knead gently into a single piece of dough. Roll into a circle that is a ½-inch larger than the pie pan. Fill the pie by following the instructions for the pie filling that you are making. Place the top crust over the filling. Fold the edge of the top crust over and under the edge of the bottom crust. Seal the crust by fluting the edge or pressing it with a fork. Now is the time to brush the top pie crust with the optional beaten egg yolk if you like. This will give the crust more of a glossy golden color. Finish preparing the pie according to the directions for the particular pie that you are baking.

Note: You will need a 9-inch pie pan and a pastry blender to prepare this pie crust.

BLUEBERRY PIE
(Makes one 9-inch pie)

Double 9-inch Pie Crust (see
   previous recipe)
4 c. fresh blueberries (about --
   1½ lbs.)

¾ c. sugar
3 Tbs. tapioca
1½ Tbs. lemon juice
1 Tbs. butter

Prepare the double 9-inch pie crust and set aside. Rinse blueberries in a colander and allow to drain. In a large bowl, stir together the blueberries, sugar, tapioca, and lemon juice. Pour into the 9-inch pie pan that has been lined with pie crust. Cut butter into small pieces and place on top of the blueberries. Cover with the top crust and seal. Cut a decorative pattern in the top crust to allow steam to escape. Bake in a preheated 425° oven for 45 to 50 minutes or until crust is golden brown in color.

240812-16

APPLE PIE
(Makes one 9-inch pie)

5 to 6 large Granny Smith or Fuji apples (approx. 1 ½ lbs.)
1 c. sugar
¼ c. cornstarch
¼ tsp. cinnamon
⅛ tsp. nutmeg
dash salt
1 ½ c. water
Double 9-inch Pie Crust (see earlier recipe)

Peel, quarter, and remove the cores of the apples. Slice each quarter crosswise into 5 or 6 pieces and set aside. There should be 1 ¼ pounds of apple slices or 4 ½ cups. In a 2-quart saucepan, stir together the sugar, cornstarch, cinnamon, nutmeg, and salt. Add the water to the saucepan. Place over medium heat and stir continuously until the sugar mixture thickens to form a syrup and begins to boil. Stir in the apples and cook over low heat for 1 to 2 minutes. You do not need to have the mixture come to a boil. You just want to warm the apples slightly and not cook them. Remove from heat and let cool while preparing pie crust. Prepare pie crust and pour apples into a pastry-lined 9-inch pie pan. Cover with the top pastry, fold the edge of the top crust over the bottom crust, and pinch edge to seal. Make some small cuts in the top crust with a knife to allow steam to escape. Bake in a preheated 425° oven for 45 minutes. Serve topped with a generous amount of the following Vanilla Sauce.

VANILLA SAUCE

2 in. of fresh vanilla bean
2 Tbs. cornstarch
⅓ c. sugar
1 ½ c. water
3 Tbs. butter
⅛ tsp. imitation rum extract
⅛ tsp. salt

Cut open the vanilla bean lengthwise. Combine cornstarch, sugar, water, and vanilla bean in a small saucepan. Stir continuously over medium heat until it thickens and begins to boil. Remove from heat. Take out the vanilla bean and, using a small knife, scrape the very small seeds from the center of the bean and add to the sauce. Add the butter, imitation rum extract, and salt. Stir until well blended and serve warm over apple pie.

Note: This method for preparing apple pie is slightly different from the more traditional methods. It involves adding the apples to a syrup before assembling the pie.

APRICOT PIE
(Makes one 9-inch pie)

2 ½ lbs. fresh apricots
1 ½ c. sugar
Pinch nutmeg
⅛ tsp. orange extract

¼ c. + 1 Tbs. cornstarch
¼ c. + 1 Tbs. water
Double 9-inch Pie Crust (see
earlier recipe)

Halve, pit, and do not peel, about 2 ¼ pounds of fresh apricots. Cut each apricot half in half. There should be 4 cups of quartered apricots that will weigh about 2 pounds when done. Place the apricots in a 2-quart saucepan over low heat. Stir and cook the apricots until juice begins to flow. This should take less than 5 minutes. Add the sugar, nutmeg, and orange extract to the saucepan. Heat and stir over medium heat until the apricot juice just begins to simmer. Dissolve the cornstarch in the water. Stir the cornstarch mixture into the apricots in the saucepan. Continue cooking and stirring until the mixture begins to thicken and boil. Let cool while preparing pie crust. Prepare double pie crust for a 9-inch pie. Apricots should be cooled to almost room temperature. Pour apricots into the pastry lined 9-inch pie pan. Cover with the top crust and pinch edge to seal. Cut holes in top crust to allow steam to escape. Bake in a preheated 425° oven for 45 minutes.

DRIED APRICOT PIE
(Makes one 9-inch pie)

3 c. (18 oz.) dried apricots
3 c. water
1 ¼ c. sugar
¼ c. cornstarch

¼ tsp. nutmeg
¼ tsp. orange extract
Double 9-inch Pie Crust (see
earlier recipe)

Cut each apricot in half and place in a 2-quart saucepan. Add 3 cups of water and bring to a boil. Reduce heat, cover, and simmer for 20 minutes. When done, the apricots should be tender when tested with a fork. If not, continue to simmer for another 10 minutes. In a medium bowl mix together the sugar, cornstarch, and nutmeg. Stir the sugar mixture and orange extract into the apricots. Cook and stir over medium heat until mixture begins to bubble. Set aside and allow to cool while you prepare a Double 9-inch Pie Crust. Pour the apricots into the pastry lined 9-inch pie pan. Cover with the top crust and pinch edge to seal. Cut holes in top crust to allow steam to escape. Bake in a preheated 425° oven for 45 minutes.

240812-16

CHERRY PIE
(Makes one 9-inch pie)

2 lbs. cherries
1 Tbs. water
1 ¼ c. sugar
¼ c. + 2 Tbs. cornstarch (⅜ c.)

1 Tbs. butter
Double 9-inch Pie Crust (see
    earlier recipe)

Remove stems, wash, pit, and measure cherries. There should be about 5 cups of pitted cherries. Place in a 2-quart saucepan over low heat. Add the 1 tablespoon of water. Gently cook over low heat until juice begins to form. In a medium bowl, stir together the sugar and cornstarch until well blended. Add sugar mixture and butter to the cherries. Cook over medium heat until sugar is dissolved. Increase heat to medium high and continue to cook until juices begin to bubble. Remove from heat and allow to cool to room temperature while you prepare pastry dough. You can speed the cooling process by placing pan with cherries in a large bowl of ice water. Prepare the Double 9-inch Pie Crust. Line a 9-inch pie plate with pie crust. Place the cooled cherries in the pie crust. Cover cherries with upper crust. Fold upper crust over edge of bottom crust and pinch to seal. Cut slits in top crust to allow steam to escape. Bake in a preheated 425° oven for 45 to 50 minutes. Let cool to room temperature before serving.

PEACH PIE
(Makes one 9-inch pie)

3 lb. fresh peaches
¾ c. sugar
¼ c. cornstarch
⅛ tsp. cinnamon
pinch nutmeg

pinch salt
1 Tbs. lemon juice
Double 9-inch Pie Crust (see
    earlier recipe)

Pit, peel, and slice peaches. There should be about 5 cups of sliced peaches. Place the peaches in a large bowl. In a separate medium bowl combine the sugar, cornstarch, cinnamon, nutmeg, and salt. Add the sugar mixture and lemon juice to the peaches. Stir the sugar into the peaches and let stand for about 10 minutes to allow peach juice to begin to flow. Stir once again after 5 minutes. Prepare the pie crust while the peaches are resting. Pour the peaches into a 9-inch pie pan lined with pastry. Cover peaches with the second piece of pastry over top. Fold top edge over and seal. Cut slits in top crust to allow steam to escape. Bake in a preheated 425° oven for 50 minutes.

SINGLE 9-INCH PIE CRUST
(Makes a single crust for one 9-inch pie)

SINGLE 9-INCH PIE CRUST, UNBAKED

1 ¼ c. all-purpose flour	scant ½ tsp. salt
⅝ c. vegetable shortening -------	¼ c. cold water
(½ c. + 2 Tbs.)	

Combine the flour, vegetable shortening, and salt in a large bowl. Follow the same directions listed for the Double 9-inch Pie Crust (see earlier recipe) except that you do not divide the dough in half. Roll the ball of dough into a circle about 1 inch larger than the pie pan. Place the dough in the pan. Fold the excess dough under so that it is even with the edge of the pan. Flute the edge of the pastry before filling the pie shell.

SINGLE 9-INCH PIE CRUST, BAKED

Single 9-inch pie crust, see above   About 1 qt. of clean, dried beans

Prepare a pie crust according to the directions above. Prick the bottom of the pie with a fork to help prevent bubbles from forming during baking. Line the pie crust with a sheet of aluminum foil. Fill the pie with any variety of dried beans to use as pie weights. This will help the pie crust to keep its shape. Bake the pie in a preheated 425° oven for 15 minutes. Remove the foil and beans and cook for an additional 5 to 7 minutes or until crust is a light brown. Allow the shell to cool before filling with pie ingredients.

Note: The beans used as "pie weights" can be reused but not eaten.

WALNUT PIE
(Makes one 9-inch pie)

Single 9-inch Pie Crust, unbaked (see previous recipe)	¼ tsp. ground ginger
1 c. sugar	1 c. light corn syrup
3 Tbs. all-purpose flour	3 Tbs. melted butter
½ tsp. nutmeg	3 eggs
½ tsp. cinnamon	1 c. coarsely chopped walnuts

Prepare the pie shell first and set aside until ready to use. In a large bowl stir together sugar, flour, nutmeg, cinnamon, and ginger. Add syrup and melted butter and mix well. Beat in eggs one at a time. Gently stir in chopped walnuts. Pour filling into unbaked pie shell. Bake in a preheated 400° oven for 15 minutes. Lower to 325° and bake an additional 30 to 40 minutes, or until filling is fairly firm. Cool thoroughly before serving. For best results, the pie should be made a day in advance in order to let it cool and set up properly.

240812-16

LEMON MERINGUE PIE
(Makes one 9-inch pie)

LEMON PIE FILLING

Single 9-inch Pie Crust, baked
  (see earlier recipe)
1 c. sugar
¼ c. plus 3 Tbs. cornstarch
⅛ tsp. salt
2 c. water

3 beaten egg yolks
3 Tbs. butter
⅓ c. fresh lemon juice
1 ½ tsp. grated lemon rind
2 drops yellow food coloring

Bake the pie crust and set aside until ready to fill. Combine in the top of a double boiler the cornstarch, sugar, salt, and water. Cook and stir directly over low heat (not over boiling water) until the mixture thickens and begins to bubble. Cover and place over the boiling water in the bottom of the double boiler. Cook for 10 minutes. Slowly beat some of this mixture into the egg yolks. Stir the egg yolk mixture back into the mixture in the double boiler. Cook and stir over boiling water for 3 minutes. Remove from heat. Add the butter and stir until melted. Stir in the lemon juice, lemon rind, and yellow food coloring. Spread the lemon filling evenly in the cooked pie shell. Set aside to cool. You can speed up the cooling process by placing the pie in the refrigerator or freezer. Keep an eye on the pie if you use the freezer because you do not want the filling to freeze. Prepare the meringue and spread evenly over the top of the cooled pie filling. Make sure that the meringue is spread all of the way to the crust. Place the pie on the middle shelf under the broiler of an electric oven for about 2 minutes, or until meringue is evenly browned. If you like, you can bake the pie in a preheated 350° oven for 15 to 20 minutes or until the meringue is golden.

MERINGUE TOPPING

4 egg whites
½ c. sugar

⅛ tsp. salt

Place the egg whites and salt in the bowl of an electric mixer. Beat at high speed until stiff peaks form. Reduce mixer speed to medium and slowly add the sugar. Continue beating at high speed for 2 minutes.

Note: You will need to purchase 2 medium lemons (total weight of at least 8 ounces) for this recipe. You will also need a double boiler. The recipe requires 4 eggs that have been separated. The extra egg yolk should be refrigerated until used in another recipe.

MIXED FRUIT GALETTE
(Makes one 7-inch galette)

2 lrg. plums (6 to 8 oz. total)
1 lrg. peach (8 to 10 oz.)
1 c. pitted cherries (about 20
  cherries)
⅔ c. sugar
2 Tbs. water

1 Tbs. butter
2 Tbs. cornstarch dissolved in --
  2 Tbs. water
1 egg yolk, lightly beaten
Pastry dough for Single 9-inch
  Pie Crust (see earlier recipe)

Halve, pit, do not peel, and slice plums. Pit, peel, and slice peach. Remove pits from cherries. There should be a total of about 1 ¼ pounds (1 quart) of prepared fruit. In a 2-quart saucepan combine ⅔ cups sugar and 2 tablespoons water. Heat and stir until sugar is dissolved. Add butter and prepared fruit. Cook and stir until fruit begins to simmer. Remove from heat and stir in cornstarch mixture. Return to stove and cook until juice boils and begins to thicken. Set aside to cool. The fruit can be refrigerated to speed up the cooling process. Prepare the pastry dough for a single 9-inch pie crust. Roll the ball of pastry dough into a 14-inch circle. Line the 7-inch fluted tart pan with pastry dough, letting the extra dough hang over the edge. Pour the cooled fruit into the lined tart pan. Neatly fold the extra dough over the fruit, leaving an opening in the center about 2 inches in diameter. Brush the top of the galette with beaten egg yolk. Place the tart pan on a large cookie sheet lined with parchment paper. Bake in a preheated 425° oven for 40 minutes. Remove from oven and cool before serving. Remove the outer ring of the pan before cutting into pieces.

Note: You will need a 7-inch fluted tart pan with removable bottom, a large cookie sheet, and parchment paper for this recipe.

DOUBLE 8-INCH PIE CRUST
(Makes a double crust for an 8-inch pie)

1 ⅓ c. all-purpose flour
⅔ c. vegetable shortening

½ tsp. salt
¼ c. cold water

In a large bowl combine the flour, vegetable shortening, and salt. Cut the shortening into the flour with a pastry blender. Stir in the cold water with a fork. The pastry dough will be sticky at this point. Turn out onto a lightly floured surface and knead a few times until the dough is no longer sticky. Shape into a ball. Cut into two pieces with one piece slightly larger than the other. Roll the larger piece out first so that it is 1 inch larger than the 8-inch pie pan. Place the dough in the pan and trim the edge so that it is even with the edge of the pan. Combine the trimmed pieces with the remaining half of the dough. Knead gently into a single piece of dough. Roll into a circle that is about a ½ inch larger than the pie pan. Follow the instructions for the pie you are preparing. See additional instructions in the earlier recipe for Double 9-inch Pie Crust.

240812-16

APRICOT PIE FROM CANNED APRICOT HALVES
(Makes one 8-inch pie)

Double 8-inch Pie Crust (see
  previous recipe)
2 (15 oz.) cans apricot halves
⅔ c. sugar
2 Tbs. cornstarch

⅛ tsp. of nutmeg
2 Tbs. apricot syrup (from canned
  apricots)
⅛ tsp. orange extract

Prepare the Double 8-inch Pie Crust and set aside. Drain the apricots in a colander, reserving 2 tablespoons of the syrup. Put the apricots in a large bowl. There should be about 2½ cups of apricots. In a small bowl, mix together the sugar, cornstarch, and nutmeg. Add the 2 tablespoons of reserved apricot syrup and orange extract to the sugar and mix together until well blended. Add the sugar mixture to the apricots. Gently fold together until everything is well blended. Pour apricots into the pastry lined 8-inch pie pan. Cover apricots with the top pastry. Fold top pastry over the edge of bottom pastry and pinch edge to seal. Poke holes in the top with a knife to allow steam to escape. Bake in a preheated 400° oven for 45 minutes.

Note: For someone who likes apricots, the season for fresh apricots is very short. Here is an apricot pie you can prepare any time of year.

PEACH PIE FROM CANNED SLICED PEACHES
(Makes one 8-inch pie)

Double 8-inch Pie Crust (see
  earlier recipe)
1 (29 oz.) can, sliced peaches
½ c. sugar
2 Tbs. cornstarch

¼ tsp. cinnamon
⅛ tsp. nutmeg
2 Tbs. peach syrup (from canned
  peaches)

Prepare the Double 8-inch Pie Crust and set aside. Drain the sliced peaches in a colander, reserving 2 tablespoons of the syrup. Combine sugar, cornstarch, cinnamon and nutmeg in a small bowl. In a large bowl stir together the peaches, sugar mixture, and reserved peach syrup. Line the 8-inch pie pan with pastry dough. Pour the peaches into the pastry lined pie pan and spread the peach filling evenly in the pan. Place the remaining pie dough over the top. Fold the top pastry over the edge of the bottom pastry and crimp to seal. Cut holes in the top of the pie to let steam escape. Bake in a preheated 425° oven for 45 to 50 minutes.

FOUR 4-INCH TART SHELLS
(Makes 4 small pastry tart shells)

UNBAKED TART SHELLS

⅔ **c. all-purpose flour**   **2 Tbs. cold water**
⅓ **c. vegetable shortening**   **¼ tsp. salt**

In a medium bowl combine the flour, vegetable shortening, and salt. Cut the shortening into the flour with a pastry blender. Stir in the cold water with a fork. The pastry dough will be slightly sticky at this point. Turn out onto a floured surface and knead a few times until the dough is soft and no longer sticky. Shape into a ball. Divide the dough into 4 equal pieces. Roll each piece into a circle about 6½ inches in diameter. Line each tart pan with dough. The dough should come to the edge of the pans. Trim any excess dough that hangs over the edge. Press the dough that rests on the top edge of the pans with a fork. The tart shells are now ready to be filled.

BAKED TART SHELLS

Four unbaked tart shells from   **2 c. of clean, dried beans.**
  above

Before making the tart shells you will need an empty tart pan to use as a mold to shape the foil for the dried beans. Remove exactly 12 inches of foil from a roll of aluminum foil. This will give you a square piece of foil that is 12 x 12-inches. Fold the foil in half in both directions. Cut the foil along the folds so that you have 4 sheets of foil that are 6-inches square. Press each piece of foil into an empty tart pan so that the foil takes on the shape of the inside of the pan. Set aside until ready to use. Shaping the foil like this ahead of time will help to keep the pastry dough from getting damaged when lining the pastry with foil before adding the beans. Prepare the dough for the tart shells according to the directions above. Prick the bottom of each shell with a fork to help prevent bubbles from forming during baking. Line each tart pan with the foil that has been set aside. Fill each tart with any variety of dried beans to use as pie weights. You will need ½-cup of dried beans for each tart shell. This will help the tart shells to keep their shape. Bake in a preheated 425° oven for 15 minutes. Remove foil and beans and cook for an additional 3 to 5 minutes or until the bottom of the crust is a light brown. The beans used as "pie weights" can be reused but not eaten

Note: You will need four 4-inch disposable aluminum tart pans for this recipe. Although these pans are "disposable", if you are careful they can be washed and reused several times before being sent to the recycler. For the baked tart shells you will need aluminum foil (12 inches wide) and about 2 cups of dried beans to use as pie weights.

188

PECAN TARTS
(Makes four 4-inch tarts)

Four unbaked 4-inch tart shells
  (see previous recipe)
¼ c. butter, softened
½ c. + 1 Tbs. brown sugar
2 eggs, lightly beaten

¾ c. light corn syrup
2 Tbs. all-purpose flour
1 c. coarsely chopped pecans
¾ tsp. vanilla extract
⅛ tsp. salt

Prepare the unbaked tart shells according to the previous recipe and set aside. In a large bowl stir together the butter and brown sugar until creamy. Mix in the beaten eggs and corn syrup. Stir in the flour, pecans, vanilla extract, and salt. Fill each tart shell with an equal amount of pecan filling. Bake in a preheated 375° oven for 45 minutes. Allow the tarts to cool completely, preferably overnight, before serving.

FRESH PEACH TARTS
(Makes four 4-inch tarts)

PEACHES

4 lrg. peaches (2 to 2½ lb.)
⅓ c. sugar

4 baked tart shells (see earlier
  recipe)

Pit, peel, and slice peaches. You should have about 1 quart of prepared sliced peaches (1¼ pounds) when done. Place the peaches in a large bowl and stir in ⅓ cup sugar. Let marinate for at least 30 minutes. Stir the peaches once or twice while they are marinating. Prepare the baked tart shells while the peaches are being marinated. Drain the peaches in a colander over a bowl and reserve the juice. Measure the juice and add enough water so that you have a total of 1 cup of juice.

GLAZE AND FINISHED TARTS

1 c. peach juice from above
3 Tbs. cornstarch

¼ c. sugar
Whipped topping

Prepare the glaze after the peaches are done marinating. In a 2-quart saucepan combine the peach juice, cornstarch, and ¼ cup sugar. Cook and stir over medium heat until the resulting glaze begins to boil. Remove from heat and add the peaches. Stir until all of the peaches are coated. Spoon an equal amount of peaches into each tart shell. Spread any glaze left in the pan over the peaches. Place in a refrigerator for 1 or more hours to chill the tarts. It may take 2 to 4 hours for the glaze to set. To serve, gently slide the tart from the pan onto a small plate. Serve with whipped topping. These tarts do not keep very well so they should be served the same day they are prepared.

FRESH STRAWBERRY TARTS
(Makes four 4-inch tarts)

STRAWBERRIES

2 lb. fresh strawberries	**4 baked tart shells (see earlier**
½ c. sugar	**recipe)**

Stem the strawberries, rinse under cold water, and drain. Set aside and reserve 4 small strawberries (do not marinate). Quarter or slice the remaining strawberries and place in a large bowl. There should be about 1 quart of prepared fresh strawberries (1 ¼ pounds). Stir in the ½ cup sugar and refrigerate while juices develop. The berries should marinate for at least 1 hour, and preferably 2 hours. Stir the strawberries once or twice while they are marinating. Prepare the baked tart shells while the strawberries are marinating. Drain the strawberries for about 10 minutes in a colander over a bowl and reserve the juice. Measure the juice and add enough water so that you have a total of 1 cup of juice.

GLAZE AND FINISHED TARTS

1 c. strawberry juice from above	**¼ c. sugar**
3 Tbs. cornstarch	**Whipped topping**

Prepare the glaze after the strawberries are done marinating. In a 2-quart saucepan combine the strawberry juice, cornstarch, and sugar. Stir until the cornstarch is dissolved. Use a whisk if necessary. Cook and stir over medium heat until the resulting glaze begins to boil. Remove from heat and add the strawberries. Stir until all of the strawberries are coated. Spoon an equal amount of strawberries into each tart shell. Spread any glaze left in the pan over the strawberries. Place in the refrigerator for at least 1 hour to chill the tarts. It may take 2 to 4 hours for the glaze to set. To serve, gently slide the tart from the pan onto a small plate. Pipe a generous amount of whipped topping over the tart. Place one of the reserved strawberries stem-side down on the whipped topping.

Note: This recipe is very similar to the previous recipe for fresh peach tarts.

240812-16

SWEET POTATO TURNOVERS
(Makes 10 to 12 turnovers)

Pastry Dough (see below)
1 (29 oz.) can sweet potatoes
½ c. brown sugar
⅓ c. white sugar
¼ c. canned evaporated milk, undiluted
1 egg, lightly beaten
½ tsp. finely grated orange rind
1 Tbs. orange juice
2 Tbs. melted butter
½ tsp. cinnamon
¼ tsp. salt
vegetable oil for frying

Prepare the pastry dough (see below) and set aside until ready to use. Drain and mash the sweet potatoes in a large bowl. There should be about 2⅓ cups of mashed sweet potatoes. Add the brown sugar, white sugar, canned milk, beaten egg, orange rind, orange juice, butter, cinnamon, and salt. Mix together until well blended. Roll the pastry dough out on a lightly floured surface. Cut into circles 6" to 6½" in diameter. Using a pastry brush, wet the edge of a circle of dough with water. Place ¼ cup of sweet potato filling on half of a circle of dough. Fold over to form a half circle. Press edge closed with a fork. Gently flatten turnover to an equal thickness. Cover bottom of frying pan with a thin layer of vegetable oil. Fry at 375° (medium-high heat) until golden brown, about 7 to 8 minutes on each side.

PASTRY DOUGH

3 c. all-purpose flour
1 c. vegetable shortening
1 tsp. salt
⅔ c. cold water

In a large bowl combine the flour, shortening, and salt. Cut the shortening into the flour with a pastry blender. Stir in the cold water with a fork. The pastry dough will be sticky at this point. Turn out onto a lightly floured surface and knead a briefly until the dough is smooth and no longer sticky.

PEACH COBBLER
(Makes 6 servings)

1 (29 oz.) can sliced peaches
4 Tbs. butter, melted and divided (2 Tbs. + 2 Tbs.)
⅓ c. sugar
1 Tbs. cornstarch
½ tsp. nutmeg
¼ tsp. cinnamon
1 c. Bisquick®
⅓ c. milk
1 Tbs. sugar

Drain the peaches, reserving ⅓ cup of the juice. Put 2 tablespoons of the butter in an 8 x 8 x 2-inch baking dish. In a large bowl, stir together the peaches, ⅓ cup sugar, ⅓ cup reserved juice, cornstarch, nutmeg, and cinnamon. Pour the peaches into the baking dish. In a medium bowl stir together the Bisquick®, ⅓ cup milk, the remaining 2 tablespoons melted butter, and 1 tablespoon sugar. Spoon the Bisquick® over the peaches in 6 large dollops. Bake in a preheated 375° oven for 40 to 45 minutes.

Miscellaneous Desserts

PEACH SHORTCAKE
(Makes 4 servings)

FRESH PEACH SHORTCAKE

4 slices of Traditional Pound
Cake (see recipe in this chapter
under "Cakes"), each about ---
¾ to 1 inch thick

2 lbs. fresh peaches
¼ c. sugar
Whipped cream topping

Bake the Traditional Pound Cake ahead of time. It can be baking while the peaches are marinating in the refrigerator. Peel, pit, and slice the peaches. There should be about 1 ⅓ pounds of prepared peaches or 1 quart. Place in a large bowl and stir in the sugar. Marinate for 2 to 3 hours in the refrigerator or until juices begin to flow. To serve, place a slice of pound cake on a plate. Spoon marinated peaches over cake and top with a generous amount of whipped cream.

PEACH SHORTCAKE MADE WITH FROZEN PEACHES

2 lb. fresh peaches   ¼ c. sugar

Pit, peel, and slice the peaches. Place in a bowl and stir in the sugar. Let stand just long enough for the juices to begin flowing and the sugar to dissolve completely. Place in a plastic bag, expel as much air as possible, and seal. Place the peaches in the freezer. To serve, remove from the freezer and allow the peaches to thaw overnight in the refrigerator. They can also be defrosted in a microwave oven. It is all right if a few ice crystals remain. Use the peaches in the above recipe for Fresh Peach Shortcake.

Note: For anyone who does not like strawberries or is looking for a little variety, this peach shortcake should hit the spot. By freezing peaches in the summer when they are plentiful, you can have peach shortcake during the winter when there is a shortage of fresh fruit. A large peach will weigh 5 to 6 ounces. So you will need to purchase about 6 peaches for this recipe.

STRAWBERRY SHORTCAKE
(Makes 4 servings)

4 slices of Traditional Pound
Cake (see recipe in this chapter
under "Cakes"), each about ---
¾ to 1 inch thick

1 ½ lb. fresh strawberries (two
baskets)
⅓ c. sugar
Whipped cream topping

Bake the Traditional Pound Cake ahead of time. Stem the strawberries, rinse under cold water, and drain. Set aside 4 of the whole strawberries. Quarter or slice the remaining strawberries and place in a large bowl. There should be about 1 quart of fresh strawberries. Stir in the sugar and refrigerate while juices develop. The berries should marinate for at least 1 hour and preferably 2 hours. Stir the strawberries once or twice while they are marinating. To serve, place a slice of pound cake on a plate and spoon marinated strawberries over the cake. Cover with whipped topping and place one of the reserved strawberries on top of the whipped cream with the stem end down.

Note: Traditional Pound Cake makes a great substitute for the standard sponge cake when making shortcake desserts. Pound cake is easy to make and keeps well in the freezer. It also will not fall apart easily when it absorbs the juice from marinated fruit. The general rule for marinating strawberries is to add 1 Tablespoon sugar to each 4 ounces (¾ cup) of cleaned strawberries.

PINEAPPLE SHORTCAKE
(Makes 4 servings)

4 slices of Traditional Pound
Cake (see recipe in this chapter
under "Cakes"), each about ---
¾ to 1 inch thick

1 fresh pineapple (about 4 lb.)
⅓ c. to ½ c. sugar
Whipped cream topping

Bake the Traditional Pound Cake ahead of time. Remove the crown and the base of the pineapple. Cutting from top to bottom, cut off wide strips of the peel, and remove the eyes in the next step. Use whatever method you find easiest to remove the eyes. You can use a knife, a small scoop, or a strawberry huller to remove the eyes. Cutting again from top to bottom, cut the pineapple into 6 or 8 wedges. Remove the center tough "heart" from each wedge. Lay the wedges flat on a cutting board and cut across the wedges in a perpendicular direction into chunks. You should have about 1 quart or 1 ¼ pounds of pineapple chunks. Place the chunks of pineapple in a large bowl and stir in ⅓ to ½ cup sugar depending on the tartness of the pineapple. Allow to marinate for 1 to 2 hours or overnight. Serve over a slice of pound cake and top with whipped cream.

CHOCOLATE ÉCLAIRS AND CREAM PUFFS
(Makes 6 éclairs or cream puffs)

1 (3.4 oz.) pkg. instant vanilla
   pudding
1⅔ c. whole milk
½ c. sifted all-purpose flour

⅛ tsp. salt
2 lrg. eggs, unbeaten
¼ c. shortening
½ c. boiling water

In a medium bowl stir together the instant pudding and milk for 1 minute. Refrigerate until ready to use. Sift the flour and salt together and set aside. Break the eggs into a bowl and set aside. This preparation is necessary because once you begin to cook the batter it comes together very quickly. In a 1-quart saucepan combine the shortening and water. Bring to a gentle simmer (do not boil) and remove from heat. Quickly stir the flour into the water. Stir vigorously until mixture forms a solid lump around the spoon, leaving the sides of the pan clean. Quickly add eggs, one at a time, beating thoroughly after each addition. Continue to beat until mixture is smooth and the batter sticks to the side of the pan. Use a large spoon to drop batter in 6 equal portions on a lightly greased baking sheet. Carefully spread each piece of dough into a rectangle about 3½ x 1½-inches, rounding the corners and sides and piling the dough on top. Bake in a preheated 450° oven for 20 minutes and then 350° for 20 minutes. Let cool on a rack. When filling eclairs, cut an opening three quarters of the way around the center of the shell, leaving the back intact to serve as a hinge. Fill only the number of eclairs that you plan to serve right away. Fill each shell with ¼ cup of vanilla pudding. Prepare the chocolate glaze. Spread about 1 tablespoon glaze over the top of each éclair and serve. The pastry shells do not stay fresh for very long, generally less than 24 hours. If you would like to use left-over shells that have lost their crispness, simply place in a preheated 250° oven for 5 minutes.

CHOCOLATE GLAZE

1 oz. unsweetened dark chocolate
1 Tbs. butter

1 c. powdered sugar
2 Tbs. canned milk

Melt the unsweetened chocolate and butter in the top of a double boiler. Add the powdered sugar and 2 tablespoons canned milk. Stir until well blended and spread over éclairs. If the glaze becomes too stiff, quickly beat in a few more drops of canned milk until it reaches the right consistency.

VARIATION: CREAM PUFFS

Powdered sugar

Cream puffs are essentially chocolate eclairs without the chocolate. When making cream puffs from the above recipe, omit the chocolate glaze and sprinkle powdered sugar over top in its place.

(continued)

240812-16

The biggest problem that cooks have in making the shells for chocolate éclairs is that they do not puff up very much when baked. This is usually caused by too much flour or cooking the batter too long. Be very careful when measuring the flour. When preparing the batter do not let the water come to a hard boil. You just want it to begin to simmer gently and then remove it from the heat immediately before adding the flour.

Note: You will need a double boiler for this recipe if you plan to make the chocolate éclairs. This recipe uses instant pudding for the filling instead of the more traditional vanilla pastry cream made with whipped cream.

BREAD PUDDING
(Makes 6 servings)

½ c. raisins	¼ tsp. salt
6 slices firm white bread	¼ tsp. ground cardamom
4 c. milk	6 eggs, lightly beaten
¾ c. sugar	¼ tsp. ground nutmeg
2 Tbs. butter (¼ stick)	Whole milk or cream
1 tsp. vanilla	

Plump the raisins by soaking them in warm water for 5 minutes. Drain and set aside until ready to use. Toast the bread in a 250° oven for 25 minutes or until lightly browned. In a 2-quart saucepan combine the 4 cups milk, sugar, butter, vanilla, and salt. Cook and stir the milk over medium heat until bubbles begin to appear around the edge of the pan. Do not allow the milk to boil. While the milk is heating, break the toasted bread into pieces and layer with the plumped raisins in a 2-quart baking dish. Slowly stir the milk into the beaten eggs. Pour the milk mixture over the bread in the baking dish and allow to stand for 15 minutes. Sprinkle the nutmeg over the top of the pudding. Set the baking dish in a larger pan containing enough hot water to come about halfway up the sides of the baking dish. Bake in a preheated 350° oven until set, about 45 minutes. Serve hot or cold with milk or cream.

VARIATIONS

1 (6 oz.) box Zwieback ---- OR ----   24 Graham cracker squares

To add a little variety to your bread pudding you can use 1 box of Zwieback in place of the white bread. You can also use 24 Graham cracker squares. Neither of these has to be toasted like the bread in the above recipe. They can be used straight out of the box

Note: You will need a 2-quart baking dish for this recipe. You will also need a larger pan for the baking dish to sit in. The baking dish should be able to rest comfortably in the larger pan. A 13 x 9 x 2-inch cake pan usually works best.

SPICY APPLE DUMPLINGS
(Makes 6 servings)

PREPARE SYRUP AND APPLES

6 medium apples (about 2 lb.)
1 (12 oz.) can lemon-lime soda
1 c. sugar
¼ tsp. nutmeg
¼ tsp. cinnamon

¼ c. butter (½ stick)
1 Tbs. "Red Hots"® candy
¼ c. sugar
1 tsp. cinnamon

In a 1-quart saucepan combine the lemon-lime soda, 1 cup sugar, ¼ teaspoon nutmeg, ¼ teaspoon cinnamon, butter, and 1 tablespoon of Red Hots® candy. Stir over medium heat until butter, sugar and candy are dissolved. Set aside until ready to use. Peel and core the apples. Steam the apples for 3 to 5 minutes or until tender almost all of the way through. In a small bowl combine ¼ cup sugar and 1 teaspoon cinnamon. After they have cooled, roll each apple in the cinnamon sugar in the bowl so that it is completely covered. Reserve the remaining cinnamon sugar for the last step.

PREPARE PASTRY DOUGH

2 c. all-purpose flour
1 tsp. salt

¾ c. vegetable shortening
⅔ c. milk

In a large bowl combine the flour, salt, and shortening. Cut the shortening into the flour using a pastry blender. Add the milk and stir to make a soft pastry dough. Place on a lightly floured surface and roll the pastry into a 14 x 21-inch rectangle. Cut into six 7-inch square pieces.

ASSEMBLE AND BAKE APPLE DUMPLINGS

6 candied cherries

Additional whole milk

Place an apple in the center of each piece of pastry. Pour a teaspoon of the remaining cinnamon sugar in the center of each apple followed by a candied cherry. Fold the pastry dough over the apples and pinch the seams along the sides to seal. Leave the top of the dumpling open so that steam can escape. Arrange in the 13 x 9 x 2-inch baking dish and pour the syrup into the bottom of the dish. Bake in preheated 425° oven for 35 to 40 minutes. To serve, place each dumpling in a shallow bowl. Pour any syrup remaining in the bottom of the baking dish over the dumplings. Serve warm with whole milk on the side.

Note: You will need a 13 x 9 x 2-inch baking dish for this recipe. You will also need a steamer for the apples. For a variation you can replace the cinnamon sugar and cherry in the center with about 8 pieces of Red Hots® candy.

240812-16

Jellies, Jams, Marmalades and Fruit Butters

Jellies, Jams, Marmalades, and Fruit Butters

Please see the Introduction for instructions on how to use a boiling water bath.

Making your own jellies and jams is a good way to preserve extra fruit from the summer. Since these recipes have not been tested in a professional kitchen, I should probably warn you to use these recipes at your own risk. Most of the recipes use equal amounts of juice/fruit and sugar, which is not recommended by the pectin manufacturers. We have adjusted and increased the amount of pectin accordingly so that the recipes that use powdered pectin work very well. This is not an issue for recipes like apple butter that do not use pectin. The recipes that use pectin specify "powdered fruit pectin." While we usually use Sure-Jell® Fruit Pectin, other brands of powdered pectin may work as well.

Notes on Cooking

Some of the recipes call for cooking the jelly for one minute and others require two minutes. The extra cooking time in some recipes was necessary in order to get the jelly to set up properly. When extracting juice from the cooked fruit, most of the recipes call for a colander lined with a pressing cloth. We recommend this method in place of the traditional jelly bag because filling the jelly bag with hot cooked fruit without making a mess is a bit of a challenge.

Equipment Suggestions

Generally speaking, if you have never canned jellies or jams before, you can probably get by with the supplies that you have in your kitchen. If you plan to do a lot of canning, you may want to consider getting some of the following items.

Canning Jar Lifter: You can use a large set of tongs for removing jars from a pot of boiling water or putting the jars of jellies in the water bath. The jar lifter is made specifically for this job and makes it easier and safer to handle hot jars.

Pressing cloth: Most cookbooks recommend using 4 layers of cheesecloth or a jelly bag for straining juice for jelly. Two layers of a regular plain white dish towel will work just as well. Unlike cheesecloth, it can be washed and reused. You can also make a pressing cloth from coarse muslin fabric.

Asparagus cooker or similar tall pot: Cooking jams and jellies can be especially messy if they boil over. Most recipes recommend using a 6 to 8 quart pot for cooking jellies. Experience has shown that a tall asparagus cooker or similar pot, with the insert removed, does the best job. They are tall enough to prevent boiling over, and they are smaller in diameter, which means that there is less foam to skim before pouring into jars.

Steam Juicer: This is strictly for the person who plans to juice a large quantity of fruit. It is expensive but a time saver for juicing large quantities, especially soft fruit like grapes and berries. It also does not make the same mess that you sometimes get from using a pressing cloth or jelly bag. It consists of a large pot with three sections that stack on top of each other. The bottom section contains water for creating steam, the top section holds the fruit, and the center section is where the juice is collected. **They are available in several different sizes.**

JELLIES, JAMS, MARMALADES, AND FRUIT BUTTERS

Jellies

BLACKBERRY JUICE FOR MAKING JELLY
(Makes 3 cups)

PREPARING BLACKBERRIES

7 (6 oz.) baskets of blackberries

There are two methods for extracting blackberry juice for the following blackberry jelly recipe. The first is the fastest but creates a bigger mess. The second requires a steam juicer and takes longer but is not as messy. Begin by rinsing off the blackberries and draining them in a colander.

PRESSING CLOTH METHOD

Place the blackberries in a large bowl and mash with a potato masher. Place a colander lined with a damp pressing cloth on top of a large pot. Place the mashed berries in the pressing cloth and let the juice drain through the cloth and into the pot. After the mashed berries have drained for 15 to 20 minutes, raise the four corners of the cloth over the top of the berries and twist to close. Continue to twist and press the cloth to remove as much juice as possible.

STEAM JUICER METHOD

Place the prepared whole berries in the top basket of a steam juicer. The berries do not have to be mashed. Fill the bottom pan of the juicer with water and simmer for about 30 minutes. Turn off the heat and let stand for an additional 30 minutes. The berries will continue to lose juice while they are at rest. Measure the resulting juice. You should have about 3 cups.

Note: Here are two ways for extracting juice from blackberries for making jelly. One method requires a pressing cloth and the other uses a steam juicer. Both methods can also be used for raspberries, boysenberries and most other soft berries that are used for making jelly. If you do not have a steam juicer, then the pressing cloth technique will be your best option.

BLACKBERRY JELLY
(Makes 4 half-pints)

3 c. blackberry juice (see previous recipe)
1 (1.75 oz.) box powdered fruit pectin

3 c. sugar

Combine 3 cups blackberry juice and powdered pectin in a tall pot. Stir over medium-high heat until the pectin is dissolved and the juice comes to a full boil. Add sugar and return to a full rolling boil. Boil hard for 1 minute. Remove from heat, skim foam, pour into hot, sterilized jars, and seal. Process in a boiling water bath for 10 minutes.

Note: Please read the previous recipe for instructions on how to juice your blackberries.

RASPBERRY JELLY
(Makes 4 half-pints)

RASPBERRY JELLY

8 (6 oz.) baskets raspberries
1 (1.75 oz.) box powdered fruit pectin

3 c. sugar

Follow the method outlined in the earlier "Blackberry Juice for Making Jelly" recipe to get the juice that you will need to make this jelly. Measure 3 cups raspberry juice into a tall pot and stir in the powdered pectin. Continue to stir over medium-high heat until the pectin is dissolved and the juice comes to a full boil. Add sugar and return to a full rolling boil. Boil hard for 1 minute. Remove from heat, skim foam, pour into hot, sterilized jars, and seal. Process in a boiling water bath for 10 minutes.

240812-16

RASPBERRY-APPLE JELLY
(Makes 4 half-pints)

4 (6 oz.) baskets raspberries
1 ½ c. unsweetened apple juice
3 c. sugar

1 (1.75 oz.) box powdered fruit
   pectin

Prepare raspberry juice following directions in the earlier "Blackberry Juice for Making Jelly" recipe. You can use freshly made apple juice from the recipe in this chapter, or you can use unsweetened apple juice from the grocery store. Measure raspberry and apple juices into a tall pot and stir in powdered pectin. Bring to a full boil over medium-high heat while stirring frequently. Add sugar and return to a full rolling boil. Boil hard for 2 minutes. Remove from heat, skim foam, pour into hot, sterilized jars, and seal. Process 10 minutes in a boiling water bath.

Note: Raspberries are expensive and can be difficult to grow for the home gardener. Adding apple juice to the jelly helps to stretch the raspberry juice that you have, with little loss of flavor.

RASPBERRY-GRAPE JELLY
(Makes 4 half-pints)

4 (6 oz.) baskets raspberries
1 ½ c. bottled white grape juice
1 (1.75 oz.) box powdered fruit
   pectin

3 c. sugar

Prepare raspberry juice following directions in the earlier "Blackberry Juice for Making Jelly" recipe. You will need 1 ½ cups of prepared raspberry juice when done. Combine raspberry juice and white grape juice in a tall pot. Stir in the powdered pectin and bring to a full boil over medium-high heat while stirring frequently. Stir in the sugar and return to a rolling boil. Boil hard for 2 minutes. Remove from heat, skim foam, pour into hot, sterilized jars, and seal. Process in a boiling water bath for 10 minutes.

Note: This is another recipe that will help you stretch your supply of raspberry juice.

GRAPE JUICE FOR CANNING AND MAKING JELLY
(Makes 4 cups)

PRESSING CLOTH METHOD

3½ lbs. grapes   **1½ c. water**

Select 3½ pounds fully ripe, fresh Concord-type grapes. Wash, remove stems, and measure. There should be 2 full quarts of prepared grapes. Crush grapes in a 3-quart or larger pot. Add 1½ cups water. Cover and simmer for 10 minutes. Line a colander with a large pressing cloth and place on top of a 2 to 3-quart saucepan. Pour the cooked grapes into the lined colander. Drain and collect juice for 15 to 20 minutes. Twist the four corners of the cloth together and squeeze to collect the remaining juice.

STEAM JUICER METHOD

2 qt. prepared grapes

Place prepared grapes in the top of a steam juicer. Fill bottom pan with water and bring to a boil. Reduce heat and simmer for 60 to 70 minutes. Remove from heat and let stand for one hour while juice drips into pan.

CANNING GRAPE JUICE

Grape juice from above

In order to can juice, put juice in a pot and bring to a simmer. Pour into hot, sterilized jars, leaving ¼-inch head space, and seal. Process pints and quarts for 15 minutes in a boiling water bath.

Note: You will need two 2 to 3-quart saucepans, a colander, and a large pressing cloth for juicing the grapes. You can also use a steam juicer.

GRAPE JELLY
(Makes 3 pints)

4 c. Concord grape juice   **4 c. sugar**
1 (1.75 oz.) box + 1½ tsp.
powdered fruit pectin

Measure grape juice and powdered pectin into a tall pot. Bring to a full boil over medium-high heat while stirring continuously. Add sugar all at once. Return to a full rolling boil. Boil hard for 2 minutes. Remove from heat, skim foam, pour into hot, sterilized jars, and seal. Process in a boiling water bath for 10 minutes.

Note: This recipe may seem a little unusual but by using an additional 1½ teaspoons pectin, it makes it possible to make exactly 3 pints of jelly.

APPLE JUICE FOR MAKING JELLY
(Makes 3 to 4 cups juice)

TRADITIONAL BOILING METHOD

3 lbs. apples   *3 c. water*

Wash and drain the apples. Remove stems and blossom ends. Do not peel or core the apples. Cut into 1-inch pieces. Place in a 4-quart pot and add 3 cups water. Bring to a boil, cover, and reduce heat to a simmer. Continue to simmer for 10 minutes. Remove lid and mash cooked apples. Return lid and continue to simmer for an additional 10 minutes while stirring occasionally. Place a colander over a 3-quart saucepan. Line the colander with a large pressing cloth. Pour the cooked apples into the lined colander so that the juice is collected in the pot below. Allow to stand until juice stops flowing. Draw the four corners of the cloth together above the apples and twist to close. Squeeze out as much juice as possible. For the clearest possible juice, do not squeeze the apples as directed in this last step.

EXTRACTION JUICER METHOD

3 lbs. apples

Wash and drain the apples. Remove stems and blossom ends. Do not peel or core the apples. Cut the apples into wedges that will fit into your juicer. Run all of the apples through the juicer. Since the juice will contain a small amount of pulp, you must heat the juice in a 2-quart saucepan until it just begins to simmer. Remove from heat. Strain the juice through a pressing cloth lined colander that is resting over a 3-quart saucepan. The juice will be collected in the saucepan below. This should produce about 3 cups of juice.

APPLE JUICE FROM STEAM JUICER

5 lbs. apples

Wash and drain the apples. Remove stems and blossom ends. Do not peel or core apples. Quarter apples and place in the top basket of the steam juicer. Fill the bottom pan with water and bring to a boil. Simmer for 1 ½ to 2 hours or until juice stops flowing. You can refrigerate the juice for up to a week before using. To can juice for longer storage time, bring juice to a gentle boil in a saucepan. Pour into jars and seal. Process in a boiling water bath for 15 minutes. Five pounds of apples will make about 1 quart of juice.

Note: You will need a colander and large pressing cloth at least 20-inches square for the first two methods. You will need a steam juicer for the third method. This juice is used in the following recipe for Apple-Cinnamon jelly. The "Extraction Juicer Method" makes the clearest juice.

APPLE-CINNAMON JELLY
(Makes 4 half-pints)

3 c. apple juice (see previous recipe)
½ tsp. cinnamon

1 (1.75 oz.) box powdered fruit pectin
3 c. sugar

Combine 3 cups apple juice, ½ teaspoon cinnamon and powdered pectin in a tall pot. Stir to dissolve pectin and bring to a boil over medium-high heat. Stir in sugar and bring to a hard boil that cannot be stirred down. Reduce heat, if necessary, to keep from boiling over. Boil hard for 1 minute. Remove from heat, skim foam, pour into hot, sterilized jars, and seal. Process 10 minutes in a boiling water bath.

Note: You can use commercial unsweetened apple juice if you like. You will have the best tasting results if you use apple juice made from fresh apples.

MANZANITA BLOSSOM JELLY
(Makes 4 half-pints)

8 c. manzanita blossoms
4 c. water
1 (1.75 oz.) box powdered fruit pectin

2⅔ c. sugar

Soak manzanita blossoms in cold water for 5 minutes. Drain the blossoms in a colander and place in a 3-quart saucepan with 4 cups of water. Bring water to a boil and simmer for 20 minutes while stirring occasionally. Place a colander lined with a pressing cloth over a large pot or saucepan. Pour the cooked blossoms into the colander so that the juice is collected in the pot below. Bring the four corners of the pressing cloth together over the colander, twist to close, and squeeze out any extra juice. Measure the juice to make sure that there is 2⅔ cups. If there is not enough juice, add up to ⅓ cup water to make up the difference. If there is too much, continue to simmer gently until it is reduced to 2⅔ cups. Place the juice in a tall pot. Stir powdered pectin into the juice until dissolved, and bring to a full boil while stirring. Add 2⅔ cups of sugar and return to a rolling boil. Boil hard for 1 minute. Remove from heat, skim foam, pour into hot, sterilized jars, and seal. Process 10 minutes in a boiling water bath.

Note: Manzanita grows wild along much of the western U. S. It is particularly plentiful in the Sierra foothills. It has clusters of small pink blossoms that bloom from about mid-March to mid-May, depending on the elevation. Manzanita jelly has a unique flavor and a beautiful deep red color.

240812-16

PEACH JUICE FOR MAKING JELLY
(Makes 3 cups)

PRESSING CLOTH METHOD

3 ½ to 4 lb. fresh peaches   *1 c. water*

Wash, halve, and pit the peaches. You do not need to peel them. Chop the peaches into 1-inch pieces. There should be about 7 cups or 3 pounds of prepared fruit. Place in a 3-quart saucepan with 1 cup of water. Cook over medium heat, while stirring occasionally, until peaches come to a boil. Reduce heat and simmer gently for 15 minutes. Place a colander on top of a 2-quart or larger saucepan. Line the colander with a pressing cloth. Pour the cooked peaches into the colander and let the juice drip into the pot below. There should be 3 cups of juice when done. If there is not enough juice, join the four corners of the pressing cloth together above the peaches and twist to close. Squeeze to remove any additional juice. If there is still not enough juice, add water to make up the difference. Use the juice to make the jelly in the recipe below.

STEAM JUICER METHOD

4 lb. fresh peaches

Wash, halve and pit the peaches. They do not have to be peeled. Place in the top basket of a steam juicer. Heat water in the bottom pan of the juicer to a gentle boil and steam peaches for 45 minutes to 1 hour. Let rest for 30 minutes, or until juice stops dripping from peaches. Drain juice from steamer and measure; there should be 3 cups of peach juice. Use the juice in the following recipe.

Note: You may use nectarines in place of the peaches. The steam juicer method will produce a clearer jelly than the first method.

PEACH JELLY
(Makes 4 half-pints)

3 c. peach juice from above   *3 c. sugar*
1 (1.75 oz.) box powdered fruit
  pectin

Place the 3 cups of peach juice from above in a tall pot. Stir in the powdered fruit pectin and bring to a full boil over medium-high heat while stirring frequently. Add sugar and return to a rolling boil. Stir well to make sure that all of the sugar is dissolved. Boil hard for 2 minutes. Remove from heat, skim foam, pour into hot, sterilized jars, and seal. Process 10 minutes in a boiling water bath.

PLUM JELLY
(Makes 5 half-pints)

3 lbs. fully ripe plums (cherry, Japanese or large)
1 ½ c. water

1 (1.75 oz.) box powdered fruit pectin
3 ⅓ c. sugar

Wash the plums and crush with a potato masher to break the skins. In a 3-quart pot combine plums and 1 ½ cups water. Bring to a boil, reduce heat to a simmer, and cook covered for 20 minutes. Place a colander, lined with a pressing cloth, on top of a 2-quart saucepan. Pour the cooked plums into the colander and let the juice drip into the pot below. There should be 3 ⅓ cups of juice. Add water or cook juice down as needed. Place juice in a tall pot, stir in powdered pectin and bring to a hard boil. Add sugar and return to a rolling boil. Boil hard for 1 minute. Remove from heat, skim foam, pour into hot, sterilized jars, and seal. Process 10 minutes in a boiling water bath. May take up to one week to set up completely.

STEAM JUICER METHOD

3 lbs. fresh plums

Place 3 pounds washed plums (do not crush) in the top basket of a steam juicer. Bring water in the bottom pan to boil. Simmer for 30 minutes. Let rest for an additional 30 minutes. Measure juice and use in above recipe.

POMEGRANATE JELLY
(Makes 4 half-pints)

3 c. bottled pomegranate juice
1 (1.75 oz.) box powdered fruit pectin

3 c. sugar

Place 3 cups pomegranate juice in a tall pot. Stir in the powdered pectin and bring to a full boil while stirring frequently. Add the sugar and return to a rolling boil. Stir to make sure that all of the sugar is dissolved. Boil hard for 1 minute. Remove from heat, skim foam, pour into jars, and seal. Process in a boiling water bath for 10 minutes.

POMEGRANATE JUICE FROM FRESH POMEGRANATES

8 Pomegranates (about 6 lbs.)

Be sure to wear gloves when preparing pomegranates. Cut the fruit into quarters. Flip the quarters inside out and separate the seeds from the pulp. You should have about 6 cups of seeds when done. Discard the pulp and place the seeds in a 3-quart saucepan. Place over medium heat and cook until the juices begin to flow. Mash the seeds with a potato masher and strain through a pressing cloth. Twist the four corners together and mash to release juice. Measure juice and use in the above recipe.

240812-16

STRAWBERRY JUICE FOR MAKING JELLY
(Makes 3 cups)

PRESSING CLOTH METHOD

4 (12 oz.) baskets strawberries   *1 c. water*
(about 3 lbs.)

Remove stems of strawberries and rinse under cold water. Cut each strawberry into 3 or 4 pieces. There should be 2 quarts of prepared strawberries. Place in a 3-quart saucepan with 1 cup water. Cook and stir over medium heat until strawberries come to a simmer. Reduce heat and simmer gently for 10 minutes while stirring occasionally. Line a colander with a pressing cloth and place over a large pot. Pour strawberries into the pressing cloth in colander and let juice drain into the pot below. Bring corners of cloth together over strawberries and twist to close. Press gently to remove as much juice as possible. There should be about 3 cups of juice. Adjust the juice so that you have exactly 3 cups. Add water if there is not enough juice or cook down if there is too much.

STEAM JUICER METHOD

4 (12 oz.) baskets strawberries

Stem, wash, and drain 4 baskets (about 3 pounds) of strawberries. There should be about 2 quarts of prepared fruit. Place berries in the top of a steam juicer. Fill the bottom pan with water and steam for 30 minutes. Remove from heat and let stand for another 30 minutes. Drain juice from steamer and measure. There should be 3 cups of strawberry juice. Adjust the amount of juice using the previous instructions if necessary.

Note: You will need a steam juicer for the second juicing technique. Two quarts of prepared strawberries will weigh about 2½ pounds. Strawberries are currently sold in two formats: small, green 12-ounce baskets and the 1-pound clear plastic clamshell containers.

STRAWBERRY JELLY
(Makes 4 half-pints)

3 c. strawberry juice from above   *3 c. sugar*
1 (1.75 oz.) box powdered fruit
*   pectin*

Place the 3 cups of strawberry juice from the above recipe in a tall pot. Stir in the powdered pectin. Cook over medium-high heat and bring to a full boil while stirring frequently. Add sugar and return to a rolling boil. Boil hard for 1 minute. Remove from heat, skim foam, pour into hot, sterilized jars, and seal. Process 10 minutes in a boiling water bath.

QUINCE JUICE FOR MAKING JELLY
(Makes 3 ⅓ to 5 cups of juice)

TRADITIONAL BOILING METHOD

6 lbs. quince   **3 qt. water**

Remove the stems from the quince, wash, and drain. Some cooks recommend that you remove the fuzz from the quince. This can be very time consuming and is not really necessary. Cut quince into 1 to 1½-inch cubes. You should have about 4 quarts of prepared fruit when done. In a 6-quart pot, combine the quince and 3 quarts water. Bring the fruit to a boil over medium-high heat. Reduce heat when water begins to boil, and simmer gently with the pot covered for 1½ hours. Stir the quince occasionally so that they cook evenly. Place a colander over a 3-quart or larger pot. Line the colander with a large cotton pressing cloth that is at least 20 inches square. Pour the cooked quince into the colander so that the juice is collected in the large pot below the colander. Let stand for about 30 minutes or until juice stops dripping. This method will produce 4 to 5 cups of juice. This juice is delicious but slightly cloudy when compared to the next two methods.

QUINCE JUICE FROM EXTRACTION JUICER

6 lbs. quince

Wash, drain and cut quince into small pieces that will fit into your juicer. Run the quince pieces through your extraction juicer. Since the juice will contain some small amount of pulp, you must heat the juice in a 2-quart saucepan until it just begins to simmer. Remove from heat and strain the juice through a colander lined with a pressing cloth. This method will produce about 3⅓ cups of juice.

QUINCE JUICE FROM STEAM JUICER

6 lbs. of quince

Wash, drain, and cut quince into 1 to 1½-inch cubes. You should have about 4 quarts of prepared fruit when done. Place in the top basket of a steam juicer. Fill the bottom pan with water, place over medium heat, and simmer for about 2 hours. Turn off heat and let stand for 30 minutes or until juice stops dripping from top basket. You should have about 3⅓ cups of juice. The amount of juice collected varies greatly depending on how much moisture is in the quince. The size of the fruit also makes a difference. Smaller quince tend to be drier than the larger ones.

Note: You will need the following supplies: a 6-qt. or larger pot, a 3-qt. saucepan, a pressing cloth at least 20 inches square, and a colander. This juice will be used in the following recipes for quince jelly. You do not have to peel or core the quince when preparing these recipes.

QUINCE JELLY
(Makes 5 half-pints)

3⅓ c. quince juice from previous   3⅓ c. sugar
   recipe
1 (1.75 oz.) box powdered fruit
   pectin

Combine 3⅓ cups quince juice and powdered pectin in a tall pot. Bring to a full boil while stirring frequently to make sure that the powdered pectin is dissolved. Stir in the sugar and return to a rolling boil. Continue to boil hard for 2 minutes. Remove from heat, skim foam, pour into hot, sterilized jars, and seal. Process for 10 minutes in a boiling water bath.

QUINCE-APPLE JELLY
(Makes 5 half-pints)

1⅔ c. quince juice   3⅓ c. sugar
1⅔ c. apple juice
1 (1.75 oz.) box powdered fruit
   pectin

Measure quince and apple juice into a tall pot. Stir in powdered pectin and bring to a full boil while stirring frequently. Add sugar and return to a full rolling boil for 1 minute. Remove from heat, skim foam, pour into hot, sterilized jars, and seal. Process in a boiling water bath for 10 minutes.

Note: Please refer to previous recipes in this chapter for preparing quince juice and apple juice. This recipe allows you to make quince jelly even when quince juice is at a premium. Commercial unsweetened apple juice can be used in this recipe in place of homemade juice.

IF YOUR JELLY (OR JAM) DOES NOT SET UP

Soft jelly (or jam) that did not gel   **Powdered fruit pectin**
Water   **Sugar**

If your jelly does not set up right away, let it stand for a week or two before you try this method. Sometimes jelly will set up after resting for a while. Measure the jelly to be recooked and put in a tall pot. For each quart of soft jelly, measure and put aside ¼ cup water, 4 teaspoons powdered pectin and ¼ cup sugar. Combine the water and pectin in a 1-quart saucepan. Heat and stir until it begins to simmer. Add this to the pot of jelly along with the sugar that you put aside. Bring the mixture to a full rolling boil over high heat while stirring constantly. Boil hard for 30 seconds. Remove from heat, skim foam, pour into hot, sterilized jars, and seal. Process in a boiling water bath for 10 minutes. If the jelly does not thicken as hoped for, then use it as a syrup for pancakes or waffles. This method can also be used on jam and marmalade.

Note: There may come a time when your jelly or jam doesn't gel. This can be caused by a number of issues including, over-ripe fruit, not enough pectin, inaccurate measuring, undercooking, overcooking, or not enough pectin when doubling a recipe. Here is a recipe that may help you to salvage your hard work. For your information, soft jelly has less sugar than traditional syrup.

Jams

APRICOT JAM
(Makes 4 half-pints)

2 lbs. fresh apricots   **2 Tbs. lemon juice**
1 (1.75 oz.) box powdered fruit   **3 c. sugar**
  pectin

Wash, pit, and do not peel the apricots. Chop into small pieces. Mash the apricots in a large bowl to help release some of the juice and measure. You should have 2¾ cups of prepared apricots. In a 3-quart saucepan, combine apricots, powdered fruit pectin, and lemon juice. Cook over medium heat while stirring frequently until it begins to simmer. Stir in the sugar and continue stirring over medium-high heat until it reaches a full rolling boil. Boil hard for 1 minute. Remove from heat, skim foam, pour into hot, sterilized jars, and seal. Process 10 minutes in a boiling water bath.

Note: This jam may take up to 2 weeks to set. To make jam from dried apricots, see the next recipe.

APRICOT JAM FROM DRIED APRICOTS
(Makes 5 half-pints)

1 c. dried apricots (about 6 oz. net wt.)
3 c. water
2 Tbs. lemon juice

1 (1.75 oz.) box powdered fruit pectin
3 ⅓ c. sugar

Dice the dried apricots into small pieces. Pour 3 cups water over the apricots in a 3-quart saucepan. Bring to a boil and remove from heat. Cover and let stand for 1 hour. Mash the apricots with a potato masher. Return to heat, simmer gently for 10 minutes, and measure. You should have 3 ¼ cups of reconstituted apricots. Cook down or add water until you have the correct amount. Add the lemon juice and powdered fruit pectin to the apricots. Cook over medium heat while stirring frequently until it begins to boil. Stir in the sugar and continue stirring over medium-high heat until it reaches a full rolling boil. Boil hard for 1 minute. Remove from heat, skim foam, pour into hot, sterilized jars, and seal. Process 10 minutes in a boiling water bath.

Note: If you run out of apricot jam and would like to make more before they are available in the Spring, you can use this recipe to make a fresh batch from dried apricots.

APRICOT-PINEAPPLE JAM
(Makes 4 half-pints)

1 ¼ lbs. fresh apricots
1 (8 oz.) can pineapple slices
2 Tbs. lemon juice

1 (1.75 oz.) pkg. powdered fruit pectin
2 ¾ c. sugar

Wash, pit, and do not peel apricots. Chop or grind into small pieces and measure. You should have 2 cups of firmly packed, prepared apricots. Drain, finely chop, and measure the canned pineapple slices. There should be ½ cup of chopped pineapple. Combine apricots, pineapple, lemon juice, and powdered fruit pectin in a 3-quart saucepan. Stir frequently over medium heat and bring to a full boil. Add sugar and continue to stir over medium-high heat until it reaches a full rolling boil. Boil hard for 1 minute. Remove from heat, skim foam, pour into hot, sterilized jars, and seal. Process for 10 minutes in a boiling water bath.

Note: The addition of pineapple to this recipe makes the jam sweeter for those who find regular apricot jam a little bit too tart. This jam may take 2 weeks to set. An 8 ounce can of pineapple contains 4 rings.

FIG JAM
(Makes 6 half-pints)

3 (16 oz.) baskets of fresh figs
3 ½ c. sugar
2 Tbs. lemon juice

Finely grated rind of one lemon (1 to 1 ½ tsp.)

Wash figs and drain. Remove stems and chop figs into small pieces. You should have about 5 cups of chopped figs. Transfer figs to a 3-quart saucepan. Add the sugar, lemon juice, and grated lemon rind. Cook slowly over medium heat until thickened, about 1 hour. Stir frequently, and slowly reduce heat while cooking. This will help to keep the jam from sticking to the pot. Place a small quantity on a saucer. When no rim of liquid appears around the edge of the jam, it is done. If not done, continue cooking and test again every 5 to 10 minutes. When done, place in hot, sterilized jars, and seal. Process for 10 minutes in a boiling water bath.

Note: You will need to purchase 3 pounds of fresh figs to prepare this recipe. This jam does not require the addition of powdered fruit pectin. You can cook it for a longer period of time to make it thicker, but this will reduce the final amount of jam.

PEACH JAM
(Makes 5 half-pints)

3 to 4 lbs. peaches
1 Tbs. lemon juice
¼ c. water

1 (1.75 oz.) box powdered fruit pectin
3 ⅓ c. sugar

Pit, peel, and finely chop peaches. Mash with a potato masher and measure. There should be 3 cups of prepared fruit. Combine peaches, lemon juice, water, and powdered pectin in a 3-quart saucepan. Place over medium heat and stir frequently until mixture comes to a boil. Stir in sugar and return to a hard boil for 1 minute. Remove from heat, skim foam, pour into hot, sterilized jars, and seal. Process in a boiling water bath for 10 minutes. Gently shake the jars after 1 hour and 2 hours to keep the chunks of fruit from rising to the top.

240812-16

PLUM JAM
(Makes 6 half-pints)

3 lb. fresh plums
½ c. water
1 (1.75 oz.) box powdered fruit
  pectin

4 c. sugar

Wash, pit, and do not peel plums. Chop into small pieces or briefly run in a food processor. There should be 3½ cups of prepared plums that weigh about 2 pounds. Add ½ cup water to plums in a 4-quart pot. Place lid on pot and simmer gently for 5 minutes. Stir in powdered pectin and bring to a full boil. Add sugar and return to a rolling boil. Boil hard for 2 minutes. Remove from heat, skim foam, pour into hot, sterilized jars, and seal. Process in a boiling water bath for 10 minutes.

RASPBERRY JAM
(Makes 6 half-pints)

6 (6 oz.) baskets raspberries
1 (1.75 oz.) box powdered fruit
  pectin

4 c. sugar

Rinse and drain raspberries. Mash with a potato masher and measure. You should have 4 cups of mashed fruit. Place in a 4-quart pot and stir in the powdered pectin. Bring to a boil over medium heat while stirring frequently. Add sugar and return to a full rolling boil that cannot be stirred down. Boil hard for 2 minutes. Remove from heat, skim foam, pour into hot, sterilized jars, and seal. Process in a boiling water bath for 10 minutes.

RASPBERRY-FIG JAM
(Makes 4 half-pints)

1½ c. raspberry juice
1½ c. finely chopped figs
2 Tbs. lemon juice

1 (1.75 oz.) box powdered fruit
  pectin
3 c. sugar

In a 3-quart saucepan combine the raspberry juice, figs, lemon juice, and powdered pectin Stir continuously over high heat and bring to a full boil. Add sugar and return to a rolling boil over medium-high heat. Boil hard for 1 minute. Remove from heat, skim foam, pour into jars, and seal. Process 10 minutes in a boiling water bath.

Note: You will need about 4 (6 oz.) baskets of raspberries to get 1½ cups of raspberry juice. Follow the first recipe in this chapter (Blackberry Juice for Making Jelly) to extract the juice from the raspberries. You will also need 16 oz. (1 pound) of fresh figs to get the required 1½ cups of chopped figs.

STRAWBERRY JAM
(Makes 5 half-pints)

4 (12 oz.) baskets strawberries --- (3 lbs.)
1 (1.75 oz.) box powdered fruit pectin

3½ cups sugar

Rinse and drain strawberries. Remove stems, cut into quarters, mash, and measure. You should have 3½ cups of mashed strawberries that weigh 30 ounces. Pour into a 3-quart saucepan and stir in powdered fruit pectin. Bring to a full boil over medium heat while stirring frequently. Add sugar and return to a rolling boil that cannot be stirred down. Boil hard for 2 minutes. Remove from heat, skim foam, pour into hot, sterilized jars, and seal. Process 10 minutes in a boiling water bath. Gently shake after 1 hour and 2 hours of cooling to help prevent all of the fruit from rising to the top of the jar. Allow 24 hours for jam to set up.

Note: If you get your strawberries in the clear 1-pound clamshell baskets, then you will need to get three (1-pound) clamshells of strawberries.

STRAWBERRY-FIG JAM
(Makes about 4 half-pints)

1 lb. strawberries
12 oz. fresh figs (about 12 figs)
1 Tbs. lemon juice

1 (1.75 oz.) box powdered fruit pectin
2¾ c. sugar

Rinse and drain strawberries. Remove stems, cut into quarters, mash, and measure. You should have about 1½ cups of strawberries when done. Wash figs, drain, and finely chop. This should make about 1¼ cups of figs when done. Mix the strawberries and figs together in a bowl and measure the combined fruit. You should have 2¾ cups of fruit. Place the fruit in a 3-quart saucepan. Stir in powdered fruit pectin. Bring to a full boil over medium heat while stirring frequently. Add sugar, increase to medium-high heat, and return to a rolling boil. Boil hard for 2 minutes. Remove from heat, skim foam, pour into hot, sterilized jars, and seal. Process 10 minutes in a boiling water bath. Gently shake jars after resting for 1 hour and 2 hours to help keep all of the fruit from rising to the tops of the jars.

240812-16

Marmalades

GRAPEFRUIT MARMALDE
(Makes 7 half-pints)

PREPARING THE FRUIT

3 medium white grapefruit	*2 ½ c. water*
2 lemons (8 to 10 oz. total wt.)	*⅛ tsp. baking soda*

To prepare fruit, use a zesting tool to remove as much zest as possible from the rinds of the grapefruit and lemons. There should be about 1 cup of zest when finished. Peel the remaining rind from fruit and discard. Combine the zest, 2 ½ cups water, and ⅛ teaspoon baking soda in a covered 4-quart pot. Simmer for 10 minutes. Cut the peeled grapefruit and lemons into quarters and remove seeds. Combine the grapefruit and lemons in a blender and whirl at a slow speed for 30 seconds. Add this fruit to the zest in the pot and simmer for an additional 10 minutes. Measure the contents of the pot. There should be 4 cups of prepared fruit. If there is too much, then remove some of the liquid or cook it down until you have the right amount. If there is not enough, then add water to make up the difference.

CANNING THE MARMALADE

1 (1.75 oz.) box powdered fruit pectin	*5 ½ c. sugar*

Stir the pectin into the fruit and bring to a boil while stirring frequently. Add the sugar and continue to stir until all of the sugar is dissolved. Return to a hard rolling boil for 1 minute. Remove from heat, skim foam, pour into hot, sterilized jars, and seal. Process in a boiling water bath for 10 minutes. Remove jars from pot and place on a dry towel to cool. Gently shake jars after 30 minutes and 1 ½ hours to help prevent all of the rind from floating to the top.

Note: You will need a zesting tool to prepare this marmalade. Traditional marmalade recipes include large pieces of grapefruit peel in the final product. This recipe, just like the recipe for Orange Marmalade, calls for the use of a zesting tool that creates smaller pieces of peel that are easier to spread on toast, etc.

ORANGE MARMALADE
(Makes 7 half-pints)

PREPARING THE FRUIT

5 oranges (about 3 lbs.)
2 lemons (8 to 10 oz. total wt.)

2 ½ c. water
⅛ tsp. baking soda

Use a zesting tool to remove as much zest as possible from the rinds of 5 oranges and 2 lemons. There should be 1 cup of zest when finished. Peel and discard the rind from 4 of the oranges and the 2 lemons. Cut the orange and lemon fruit into quarters and remove any seeds. The extra orange should be set aside and refrigerated until ready to eat. Combine the orange zest, lemon zest, 2½ cups water, and ⅛-teaspoon baking soda in a 4-quart pot. Cover and simmer for 10 minutes. Place the prepared orange and lemon fruit in a blender. Whirl at a low speed for 30 seconds. Add this fruit to the zest in the pot. Simmer for an additional 10 minutes and measure. There should be 4 cups of prepared fruit. If there is too much, then remove some of the liquid or cook it down until you have the right amount. If there not enough, then add water to make up the difference.

CANNING THE MARMALADE

1 (1.75 oz.) box powdered fruit pectin

5 ½ cups sugar

Stir the pectin into the fruit and bring to a full boil. Add the sugar and continue to stir until all of the sugar is dissolved. Return to a hard rolling boil for 1 minute. Remove from heat, skim foam, pour into hot, sterilized jars, and seal. Process for 10 minutes in a boiling water bath. Place the jars on a dry towel to cool. After 30 minutes and 1 ½ hours, shake the jars gently to prevent all of the rind from floating to the top.

Note: You will need a zesting tool to prepare this marmalade. Traditional marmalade recipes include large pieces of orange peel in the final product. This recipe calls for the use of a zesting tool that results in smaller pieces of peel that are easier to spread on toast, etc. There will also be a leftover, peeled orange that can be used for eating later.

240812-16

TANGERINE MARMALADE
(Makes 7 half-pints)

PREPARING THE FRUIT

6 to 8 tangerines, about 1 ¼ lb.
1 lrg. lemon (4 to 5 oz.)

2 ½ c. water
⅛ tsp. baking soda

Cut the lemon from top to bottom into quarters. Remove the fruit from each quarter, remove any seeds, and reserve the fruit. Use a spoon to remove as much white pith from the lemon peel as possible. Slice the remaining lemon peel crosswise into strips about ⅛ inch wide. Peel the tangerines and remove any seeds in the fruit. Slice the tangerine peel into strips ⅛ inch wide. Since the tangerine peel is fairly thin, you can slice it without removing any of the white pith. Combine the lemon and tangerine peels and measure. There should be 1 ½ to 2 cups. Place the sliced peels in a 4-quart pot and add the 2 ½ cups water and ⅛ teaspoon baking soda. Cover, bring to a boil, and simmer for 20 minutes. While the sliced peel is simmering, combine the lemon and tangerine fruit in a blender. Run the blender at a low speed for about 1 minute. There should be about 2 cups of blended fruit when done. Add the blended fruit to the rind when it is done simmering. Return to a boil and simmer gently, uncovered, for 10 more minutes. Measure the fruit in the pot. There should be 4 cups. If there is too much, then remove some of the liquid or continue to cook until reduced to 4 cups. If there is not enough, then add some water to make up the difference.

CANNING THE MARMALADE

1 (1.75 oz.) box powdered fruit pectin

5 ½ c. sugar

Stir the powdered fruit pectin into the 4 cups of fruit in the pot and bring to a full boil while stirring frequently. Add the sugar, continue to stir until all of the sugar is dissolved, and return to a hard boil for 1 minute. Remove from heat, skim foam, pour into hot, sterilized jars, and seal. Process for 10 minutes in a boiling water bath. Place the jars on a dry towel to cool. Gently shake the jars after 1 hour and 2 hours, to prevent all of the rind from floating to the top.

KUMQUAT MARMALADE
(Makes 7 half-pints)

PREPARING THE FRUIT

1 ½ lbs. kumquats (about 5 c.)   2 ½ c. water
1 lrg. lemon (4 to 5 oz.)   ⅛ tsp. baking soda

Cut the lemon from top to bottom into quarters. Remove the fruit from each quarter, remove any seeds, and reserve the fruit. Use a spoon to remove as much white pith from the lemon peel as possible. Slice the remaining lemon peel crosswise into thin strips about ⅛ inch wide. Cut about ¼ inch off of the stem end of the kumquats and cut in half lengthwise. Scoop the fruit from the rinds with a teaspoon. Remove all of the seeds from the kumquat fruit and set aside. Lay the sections of kumquat rind flat, slice crosswise into strips ⅛ inch wide, and add to the sliced lemon rind. There should be a total of 2 cups of sliced rind and 1 cup of kumquat fruit when finished. Combine the lemon rind, kumquat rind, 2 ½ cups water, and ⅛ teaspoon baking soda in a 4-quart pot. Cover pot and simmer for 10 minutes. Combine the kumquat fruit and lemon fruit in a blender. Whirl the fruit in the blender at a slow speed for about 1 minute. Add the fruit to the rind in the pot. Simmer for 10 more minutes and measure the contents of the pot. There should be 4 cups of prepared fruit. If there is too much, then remove some of the liquid, or cook it down until you have the right amount. If there is not enough, then add water to make up the difference.

CANNING THE MARMALADE

1 (1.75 oz.) box powdered fruit   5 ½ c. sugar
   pectin

Stir the pectin into the fruit and bring it to a full boil while stirring frequently. Add the sugar and continue to stir until all of the sugar is dissolved. Return to a hard rolling boil for 2 minutes. Remove from heat, skim foam, pour into hot, sterilized jars, and seal. Process for 10 minutes in a boiling water bath. Place jars on a dry towel to cool. Gently shake the jars after 1 hour and again after 2 hours to prevent all of the rind from floating to the top.

Note: Preparing this marmalade is time consuming and a lot of work, but it has a unique flavor that sets it apart from other marmalades.

240812-16

Fruit Butters

APRICOT BUTTER
(Makes 5 to 6 half-pints)

4 lbs. fresh apricots
¼ c. water
3 to 4 c. sugar

¾ tsp. cinnamon
¼ tsp. cloves

Wash, do not peel, pit, and cut apricots in half. You should have a minimum of 2 quarts of apricots. In a 3-quart saucepan combine the apricot halves and ¼ cup water. Cook over medium heat until soft. Stir occasionally to prevent scorching. Run through a strainer or food mill and measure the resulting apricot pulp. For each cup of pulp add ½ cup of sugar. Stir in the cinnamon and cloves. Cook for ¾ to 1 hour while stirring frequently. Test by placing a small quantity on a saucer. When no rim of liquid appears around the edge of the butter, it is done. This could take up to 2 hours. Pour into hot, sterilized jars, and seal. Process for 10 minutes in a boiling water bath.

PEACH BUTTER
(Makes 5 to 6 half-pints)

4 lbs. peaches
3 to 4 c. sugar
1 Tbs. lemon juice

1 tsp. ground cinnamon
½ tsp. whole cloves, tied in a
cheesecloth bag (spice bag)

Pit, peel and slice peaches. Measure into a 3-quart pot. You should have at least 2 quarts of sliced peaches. Cook in their own juice until soft. If peaches are not juicy, add ½ cup water to prevent scorching. Run the cooked fruit through a fine strainer or food mill. Measure pulp and place in a 3-quart pot. There should be at least 6 cups of pulp. For each cup of pulp, add ½ cup sugar. Stir in lemon juice, cinnamon, and clove spice bag. Cook slowly until sugar is dissolved. Continue to cook over medium heat and stir frequently for about 45 minutes. To test, place a small quantity on a saucer. When no rim of liquid appears around the edge of the butter, it is done. This could take up to 2 hours. Remove cheesecloth bag. Pour into hot, sterilized jars, and seal. Process for 10 minutes in a boiling water bath.

APPLE BUTTER
(Makes 4 pints)

Start with 5 lb. apples; Fuji, Gala, Granny Smith or any other good tart apple
2 ½ c. water

3 ½ c. sugar, minimum
1 ¼ tsp. cinnamon
½ tsp. cloves
¼ tsp. allspice

Wash apples thoroughly. Remove stems, quarter, core, and do not peel the apples. You should have about 4 pounds of prepared apples when done. Place the apples in a 6 to 8-quart pot and add 2 ½ cups of water. Cook slowly over medium heat until soft. This will take from 1 to 1 ½ hours. Stir occasionally to keep apples from sticking to pot. Put fruit through a food mill or fine strainer and measure into a 4-quart pot. There should be about 7 cups of pulp when done. For each cupful of pulp, add ½ cup of sugar. Add the cinnamon, cloves, and allspice. Stir and cook over medium-high heat, until butter begins to bubble. Reduce heat as butter thickens to prevent scorching. Cook gently for 30 minutes. Place a small quantity on a saucer. When no rim of liquid appears around the edge of the butter, it is done. This could take from 30 minutes to 2 hours. The longer you allow the apple butter to simmer, the thicker it will be. Pour into hot, sterilized jars, and seal. Process for 10 minutes in a boiling water bath.

Note: You will need a 6 to 8-quart pot and a 4-quart pot. A food mill will be very helpful in preparing this recipe. It will separate the skins from the pulp when the apples are done cooking. You can use a fine strainer as a substitute, but it will take longer and require more work. Press the cooked apples through the strainer with the back of a spoon.

APPLE BUTTER MADE FROM CANNED APPLESAUCE
(Makes 3 pints)

4 (15 oz.) cans applesauce (6 c.)
3 c. sugar
1 tsp. cinnamon

½ tsp. cloves
¼ tsp. nutmeg
Pinch of allspice

In a 3-quart saucepan combine the applesauce, sugar, cinnamon, cloves, nutmeg, and allspice. Stir and cook over medium-high heat, until butter begins to boil. Reduce heat as apple butter thickens to prevent scorching. Cook gently for 10 minutes. Place a small quantity on a saucer. When no rim of liquid appears around the edge of the butter, it is done. This may take up to an hour. Pour into hot, sterilized jars, and seal. Process for 10 minutes in a boiling water bath.

Note: When you do not have time to make apple butter from scratch, you can use this recipe to make some that tastes better than any commercial variety.

240812-16

Candy

Candy

Making your own candy can be challenging. It hardly seems practical to make candy when it can be purchased at a local store at a very reasonable price. Most of the candy we make is used as gifts for special occasions, especially during the holidays. Homemade candy is also a good gift for that person who has everything.

Notes on Candy making

Chocolate: Real chocolate can be difficult to work with. The kitchen should a certain temperature. Chocolate also has to be tempered before it is used for dipping. This keeps the chocolate from streaking when it is done. The best chocolate to use for the occasional chocolate maker is what is called chocolate compound which comes in the form of small wafers or discs. Unlike real chocolate, chocolate compound does not have cocoa butter. The cocoa butter has been removed and replaced with coconut oil.

Caramels: When using caramels for making candy, find a brand that is easy for you to acquire and stick with it for all of your candy making. Different brands are softer than others, so you want to stick with the same brand so you have consistent results.

Equipment Suggestions

Here are a few pieces if equipment that you will find helpful if you plan to become a serious candy maker.

Double Boiler: This is almost a necessity. It will be used for melting chocolate and caramel. Some cooks melt their chocolate in a microwave oven, but I have found it to be unreliable and inconsistent.

Candy Thermometer: This will come in very handy. Some recipes explain how you can test candy for doneness by dropping a small amount in some cold water. The only problem is that by the time you are done with the test, the temperature of the candy may have risen so high that the candy may be ruined.

Plastic Candy Molds: You can get these at baking/candy supply stores. They are also available on the internet. You will need candy molds to make peanut butter cups and any candy that has a soft filling, like Marshmallow Creme.

Colored Candy Foils: These can also be purchased at a candy supply store or on the internet. They are very handy for wrapping individual pieces of candy and are very attractive. While they come in several sizes, the 4-inch square foils are the most useful.

Teflon® Pans: While you may be tempted to use a Teflon® pan when making candy, it really is not a good idea. The high temperatures needed for making some candies could adversely effect the Teflon® coating.

CANDY

ENGLISH TOFFEE
(Makes 1 ⅓ pounds of random size Toffee pieces)

PREPARING THE TOFFEE

½ c. coarsely chopped dry
  roasted almonds
½ c. butter (1 cube) do not use
  substitutes

1 c. sugar
2 Tbs. water
Non-stick spray

Prepare the coarsely chopped almonds ahead of time. Prepare a large cookie sheet by coating the bottom with a thin layer of non-stick spray. Combine the butter, sugar, and water in a 2-quart saucepan with a heavy bottom. Cook over medium heat until butter is melted. Do not stir once butter is melted so that the toffee does not become grainy. Increase to high heat and quickly bring to a boil. Continue to cook, without stirring, until the syrup reaches the light crack stage, 275°. Reduce the heat slowly as the temperature approaches 275° in order to help prevent the candy from burning. Remove from heat and quickly stir in the ½ cup of coarsely chopped almonds. Pour the candy onto the prepared cookie sheet and spread to about ¼-inch in thickness. The candy will not go to the edges of the cookie sheet. Set aside and let cool to room temperature. Wipe the top of the candy with a paper towel to remove any melted butter that would keep the chocolate from adhering to the toffee.

ADDING THE CHOCOLATE COATING

¼ c. finely chopped or ground
  dry roasted almonds

8 oz. milk chocolate

Prepare the finely ground almonds. Melt the chocolate in the top of a double boiler. The water should be hot but not boiling. Spread the melted chocolate evenly over the top and down the sides of the candy. Sprinkle the ¼ cup of finely ground almonds over the chocolate. Gently press the almonds into the chocolate with the back of a large spoon so that the almonds do not fall off the candy when it is cool. Break the candy into pieces when it is thoroughly cooled. Store in an airtight container.

Note: You will need a large cookie sheet and an accurate candy thermometer. Hershey's® milk chocolate or any other brand will work just fine. The almonds do not have to be roasted but the dry roasted almonds have a better flavor. You can use a knife to coarsely chop the almonds. You can use a knife or blender to prepare the finely chopped almonds.

BITE-SIZE ENGLISH TOFFEE
(Makes 45 pieces or 1 ½ pounds)

MAKING THE TOFFEE CENTERS

½ c. coarsely chopped dry
  roasted almonds
Non-stick spray
½ c. butter (1 cube) do not use
  substitutes

1 c. sugar
2 Tbs. water

Prepare the coarsely chopped almonds ahead of time. Coat the bottom and sides of an 8 x 8 x 2-inch baking pan with a thin layer of non-stick spray. Combine the butter, sugar, and water in a 2-quart saucepan with a heavy bottom. Cook over medium heat until butter is melted. Do not stir once the butter is melted so that the toffee does not develop a grainy texture. Increase to medium-high heat and quickly bring to a boil. Continue to cook until the syrup reaches 275°. Reduce the heat slowly as the temperature approaches 275° in order to help prevent the candy from burning. Remove from heat and quickly stir in ½ cup of coarsely chopped almonds. Pour the candy into the 8-inch square pan and spread out to an even thickness. The candy will go all of the way to the sides of the pan. Let the candy rest for 7 to 8 minutes at the most. If you wait too long the candy will harden and be impossible to cut into pieces. Turn out onto a cutting board with the top side down. Cut into pieces that are about ¾ x 1 ¼-inches. You should have about 9 rows by 5 rows of toffee centers when cut. Allow the toffee centers to cool before dipping in chocolate.

ADDING THE CHOCOLATE COATING

1 c. finely chopped or ground dry
  roasted almonds

¾ lb. (12 oz.) milk chocolate

Prepare the finely ground almonds. Melt the chocolate in the top of a double boiler. The water should be hot but not boiling. Turn off the heat once the chocolate is melted. Spread about half of the finely chopped almonds about ¼-inch thick on a piece of wax paper. Working with one piece at a time, dip a toffee center in the chocolate until it is completely covered and put it on the finely ground almonds. Move on to the next piece and dip it in chocolate and put it on the ground almonds. The dipped pieces should be at least 1 inch to 1 ½ inches apart. Continue until you have about 12 pieces that have been dipped in chocolate. Go back to the first piece and turn it over to coat the top. Use a fork to press almonds up against the sides of the piece of candy. Continue until all 12 pieces have been coated with almonds. Remove the pieces with a fork and set on another piece of clean wax paper to allow the chocolate to finish hardening. Add more ground almonds to replace what has been used on the wax paper. Repeat for the remaining pieces of toffee.

(continued)

Note: You will need an 8 x 8 x 2-inch baking pan and wax paper for this recipe. This has the same ingredients and instructions, with some variation in quantities, as the previous recipe. The greatest difference is that the brittle is poured into an 8-inch square pan and then cut into bite-size pieces to be coated with chocolate and finely ground almonds.

PEANUT BUTTER CUPS
(Makes 36 to 42 medium cups or 1 1/3 pounds)

PREPARING THE FILLING

½ c. creamy peanut butter
1 c. powdered sugar

¼ c. (½ cube) margarine, softened

In a medium bowl, stir together the peanut butter and margarine until well blended. Sift powdered sugar into the peanut butter and mix well. Take a level teaspoon of this filling and roll it into a ball. Place on a sheet of wax paper. Repeat until all of the filling is used.

FILLING THE PEANUT BUTTER CUPS

1 ¼ lb. milk chocolate wafers

Melt the chocolate wafers in the top of a double boiler. Fill a candy mold about ¼ full of melted chocolate. Use a small brush, about ¼ inch wide, to coat the sides of the candy molds with the chocolate from the bottom of the mold. Place the mold in the freezer for 5 minutes to harden. Remove from the freezer and hold the mold up to a light source to look for thin spots in the chocolate coating the molds. Paint the thin spots with more melted chocolate and return them to the freezer for another 3 minutes. When placing the molds in the freezer, you do not want the chocolate to freeze, only harden. You could leave the molds at room temperature to harden, but it will take much longer. Place one of the peanut butter balls in a mold coated with chocolate and press down so that it fills the mold. Flatten the top so that it is level. The peanut butter filling should come up to about ⅛ inch below the top edge of the mold. Remove or add filling as necessary. Place a small amount of chocolate on top and spread to the edges of the peanut butter cup. Gently spread with back of spoon until top of candy is smooth. Repeat until the tray is full. Place in freezer again until top of candy has hardened, about 5 minutes. Place mold upside-down on a sheet of wax paper on a counter top and tap gently until all of the candy is removed from the mold. Use a paring knife to remove any excess chocolate around the top edges of the finished peanut butter cup.

Note: You will need a small brush about ¼-inch wide. Look for clear plastic peanut butter cup molds at candy supply stores. Medium sized candy molds come in a tray that is about 8 x 10-inches. They usually have 11 or 12 cavities. The finished cups are 1 ¼-inches in diameter and ¾-inches tall. There are also molds for making smaller and larger peanut butter cups.

MARSHMALLOW CREME
(Makes 2 ¼ cups)

SIMPLE SYRUP

⅔ c. sugar   ⅓ c. water

Combine the water and sugar in a 1-quart saucepan. Cook and stir over medium heat until all of the sugar is dissolved and the syrup begins to bubble. Set aside until ready to use. Simple syrup is basically two parts sugar and one part water. This recipe will make a little more than ⅔ cup, which is just enough for the marshmallow creme.

MARSHMALLOW CREME

⅔ c. Simple Syrup (see above),   ⅔ c. light corn syrup
   divided (⅓ c. + ⅓ c.)
1 Tbs. + 1 tsp. dried egg white
   powder

Prepare the simple syrup ahead of time and allow to return to room temperature before using. Pour ⅓ cup of the simple syrup into the mixing bowl of an electric mixer and add the egg white powder. Beat at low speed in order to blend together and set aside. In a 1-quart saucepan, combine the remaining ⅓ cup of simple syrup and ⅔ cup corn syrup. Heat and stir to 220° and then remove from heat. Turn the mixer with the egg whites on to high speed. Slowly add the heated syrup in a thin stream. Continue beating the egg whites while you add all of the syrup in a continuous slow stream. Continue beating even after all of the syrup has been added. The egg whites should look like a thick meringue. When the motor begins to drag and slow down under the strain of the thickening creme, then turn it off. This could take 2 to 3 minutes. If you do not plan to use the marshmallow creme right away, then store in an airtight container until ready to use. It should keep this way, at room temperature, for at least 2 weeks. This makes a little more marshmallow creme than you will need for the following Honey Nougat recipe

Note: You will need a sturdy electric stand mixer and candy thermometer to prepare this recipe. You can get the dried egg white powder from a baking supply store or on the internet. The Marshmallow Creme (a.k.a. Fluff) is used in making the following recipes for Honey Nougat and Marshmallow Creme Filled Chocolates. In spite of its name (marshmallow), it does not contain gelatin.

HONEY NOUGAT
(Fills one 8 x 8 x 2-inch baking pan)

Nonstick spray
1 ½ c. Marshmallow Creme (see
   previous recipe)
⅔ c. sugar
⅓ c. light corn syrup

3 Tbs. honey
3 Tbs water
1 Tbs. vegetable shortening
2 Tbs. confectioners sugar, sifted

Spray the bottom and sides of an 8 x 8 x 2-inch baking pan with non-stick spray and set aside. Measure the Marshmallow Creme ahead of time so that it is ready to use as soon as the syrup mixture is finished cooking. In a 2-quart saucepan, combine the sugar, corn syrup, honey, and water. Cook over medium heat until it begins to boil. Watch carefully and adjust the heat so that the syrup mixture does not boil over. Increase the heat slightly and cook until the syrup reaches 272°. Remove from heat and let stand for exactly 5 minutes. Stir in the shortening until all of it has melted, not more than 1 minute. Add the marshmallow creme and stir with a large spoon until the syrup and Marshmallow Creme are thoroughly blended. Gently stir in the confectioners sugar. Spread the nougat out evenly in the baking pan and let stand for 24 hours. This last step cannot be rushed.

Note: You will need an 8 x 8 x 2-inch baking pan, a 2-quart saucepan with a heavy bottom, and a candy thermometer. This is the first step for making the Miniature Candy Bars on the next page.

HOW TO MELT CHOCOLATE WAFERS

At least ½ lb. chocolate wafers or
   flavored coatings

Place the chocolate wafers in the top of a double boiler and set aside. Place the bottom of the double boiler, which should be about half full of water, over high heat and bring to a boil. Remove from heat and place the top of the double boiler with the chocolate over the water. Stir occasionally until the chocolate is melted, about 3 to 5 minutes. Remove the top of the pan and allow the chocolate to cool for 15 to 20 minutes. You can also place the pan in cool, not cold, water and stir until it thickens slightly. Add cold water to the hot water in the bottom pan to make the water warm. Place the chocolate over the warm water and it is ready to dip.

Note: "Real" chocolate must be tempered before being used to coat candy. Tempering gives it a shiny surface and prevents white streaks. Chocolate wafers or coatings, which are used for most of the recipes here, are made with coconut oil instead of cocoa butter which makes it easier to melt properly. Since chocolate burns easily, it should never be heated over 110°.

MINIATURE CANDY BARS
(Makes 2¼ pounds or 64 pieces)

Honey Nougat from previous
  recipe
½ lb. Kraft® caramels (about 28
  pieces)

1 Tbs. canned milk
1 lb. milk chocolate wafers,
  melted in a double boiler

Prepare the Honey Nougat in the previous recipe and allow it to stand for 24 hours before continuing. Remove the wrappers from the caramel candy and place in the top of a double boiler over simmering water. Add the canned milk and stir until all of the caramel has melted. Remove from heat and pour over the honey nougat in the pan. Spread the caramel to an even thickness. Allow to rest for at least another 12 hours. When you are ready to cut the candy into small pieces, melt the chocolate in the top of a double boiler over simmering water. Stir until smooth. Remove from heat while you cut the, pieces of candy. Turn the nougat out onto a piece of wax paper that is on top of a cutting board. The candy should be top side down so that the caramel is resting on the wax paper. This will make the candy easier to cut. Cut the candy, using a large knife, into ⅞-inch squares. Once all of the pieces have been cut, you can start dipping them in the melted chocolate. Place on wax paper while the chocolate hardens. Please note that once you cut the candy into pieces, you should dip all of them in chocolate as soon as possible. If they are allowed to stand, even for a few hours, they could begin to flatten and lose their square shape.

Note: You will need a double boiler for melting the caramel and chocolate. This candy starts with the Honey Nougat from the previous recipe. Caramel is spread over the nougat, it is cut into pieces and then dipped in chocolate. You can omit the caramel if you like. If you are fond of caramel, you can double the amount of caramel that you spread on top.

SUGARED WALNUT NIBBLES
(Makes 1 quart)

1 c. white sugar
1 c. brown sugar
½ c. sour cream

½ tsp. vanilla
¼ tsp. cinnamon
4 c. shelled walnuts (about 1 lb.)

In a 2-quart saucepan combine the white sugar, brown sugar, and sour cream. Place over medium heat and stir until it begins to boil. Reduce heat and let simmer gently for 5 minutes. Remove from heat and quickly stir in the vanilla and cinnamon. Add the walnuts and stir until all are coated. Spread out on a large cookie sheet covered with wax paper. Let cool and then break into pieces. Store in an airtight container.

240812-16

MARSHMALLOW CREME FILLED CHOCOLATES
(Makes 48 pieces or 1 pound)

1 c. Marshmallow Creme (see recipe earlier in this chapter)

1 lb. dark chocolate wafers

Melt chocolate wafers in the top of a double boiler. Fill the molds about ¼ full with chocolate. Using the small brush, coat the sides of the molds with the chocolate from the bottom. Place in a freezer to harden, about 5 minutes. Remove from the freezer and hold up to the light. Brush any thin spots with more chocolate. Return to freezer for about 3 minutes to harden. Remove from freezer. Place a small round tip on the decorating tool or pastry bag and fill with marshmallow creme. The tip should be about ⅛ inch in diameter. Use the cake decorating cylinder or pastry bag to fill the chocolate molds with marshmallow creme to within ⅛ inch of the top. You can use a spoon to fill the molds, but using the decorating tool or pastry bag is much faster. Let the candy stand for 3 to 5 minutes to let the marshmallow creme settle and level off. Do not let the marshmallow creme filling touch the top edge of the mold or it will not seal properly. Fill the top of the candy with melted chocolate and smooth with the back of a spoon to make level. Return to freezer for 5 minutes or until the top of the candy has hardened. Place mold upside-down on a sheet of wax paper on a counter top and tap gently until all of the candy is removed from the mold. Use a paring knife to remove any excess chocolate around the edges of the candy. Handle carefully because these are very delicate. You can wrap these in candy foil if you like.

Note: This candy is an excellent way to use leftover marshmallow creme. You will need a cake decorating plunger-style cylinder or pastry bag with a plain round nozzle. You will also need clear plastic molds and a ¼-inch wide brush. The molds should be about 1-inch in diameter, ¾-inch tall, and have a rounded top. The molds usually come in a tray that has 11 or 12 cavities.

WALNUT CHEWS
(Makes 70 pieces or 1 ½ pounds)

Heaping 2 c. walnut halves; about
  70 pieces or ½ pound
½ lb. Kraft® caramels (about 28
  pieces)

1 Tbs. canned milk
12 oz. dark chocolate wafers

Remove the wrappers from the caramels and place the caramels in the top of a double boiler. Add the 1 tablespoon of canned milk. Bring the water in the double boiler to a gentle simmer. Stir the caramels until they are completely melted and all of the milk has been mixed in. This could take several minutes. Allow to cool for about 15 minutes. Gently dip a walnut half upside down in the caramel until only the top of the walnut is coated. Do not dip the entire walnut in the caramel. You only want the soft caramel on the top of the walnut. Place on a sheet of wax paper, right side up so that the caramel is not touching the waxed paper. Repeat for all of the remaining walnuts. Allow to cool for at least 2 to 3 hours while the caramel hardens. Wash the double boiler and use it to melt the chocolate wafers. Dip each caramel-coated walnut half in the melted chocolate until it is completely covered and set aside on another sheet of wax paper. After the chocolate has hardened, store in an airtight container or wrap each piece in a candy foil wrapper.

Note: You will need a double boiler for this recipe to melt the caramels and chocolate. Pecan halves can be used in place of the walnuts. Since pecans are smaller than walnuts, a half pound of pecans should yield 110 to 120 pecan halves.

BLANCHED WALNUTS
(Makes 4 cups)

4 c. shelled walnut pieces and/or
  halves (about 1 lb.)

1 ½ qt. water

Pick through the walnuts and remove any pieces of shell that may have been missed during the packaging process. Fill a 3-quart saucepan with 1 ½ quarts water. Place over high heat and bring to a boil. Add the walnuts to the pot of boiling water. Simmer gently for 5 minutes, stirring once or twice while cooking. Drain and rinse thoroughly. Spread on a cookie sheet and dry in a preheated 275° oven for 1 ½ hours. Store in an airtight container.

Note: Blanching and roasting walnuts helps to remove some of the tannin that is in the walnuts. This gives the walnuts a milder flavor and makes them more tender. Blanched walnuts do not keep as well as unblanched, so they should be used within a week or two.

PENUCHE
(Makes 5 pounds)

5 c. granulated sugar
1 (12 oz.) can evaporated milk
1 c. butter (2 sticks) do not use
  substitutes
1 tsp. vanilla

1 ½ (11 oz.) pkg. butterscotch
  morsels (2⅔ c.)
½ tsp. salt
2 to 3 c. chopped walnuts
Nonstick spray

Combine sugar, milk, and butter in a 3-quart saucepan with a heavy bottom. Cook over medium heat while stirring constantly. When the mixture begins to boil, reduce heat slightly so that it does not scorch. Do not stir once boiling begins. Let boil for 7 ½ minutes and remove from heat. Quickly add the 2⅔ cups of butterscotch morsels, vanilla, and salt. Stir briskly until all of the butterscotch has melted. This could take 4 to 5 minutes. Stir in the walnuts and pour into a 13 x 9 x 2-inch baking pan that has been lightly coated with nonstick spray. Let cool before cutting into pieces.

Note: You will need a 13 x 9 x 2-inch baking pan for this recipe. This is also known as butterscotch fudge. You can follow this recipe to make regular chocolate fudge by using an equal amount of chocolate morsels in place of the butterscotch morsels. For a smaller amount, use an 8-inch square pan and prepare half of this recipe.

PEANUT BRITTLE
(Makes 1 pound)

Non-stick spray
1 c. white sugar
½ c. light corn syrup
¼ c. water

1 ½ c. salted peanuts (½ lb.)
1 Tbs. butter
1 tsp. baking soda

Prepare a large 15 x 10-inch cookie sheet by coating it with a thin layer of non-stick spray. Measure all of the ingredients ahead of time. Once you begin to cook this recipe everything will come together very quickly. Combine sugar, corn syrup, and water in a 2-quart saucepan. Cook and stir over medium-high heat until it reaches 250°. Stir in the peanuts. Continue to cook and stir until the candy reaches 295°. Remove from stove and stir in the butter until it has melted. This should only take a few seconds. Quickly stir in the baking soda. The candy mixture will foam up after the baking soda has been added. Pour onto the prepared cookie sheet before the foaming subsides. The foaming makes the brittle more tender. Break into pieces when cool. Store in an airtight container.

Note: You will need a large 15 x 10-inch cookie sheet. If you would like to make brittle for someone who is allergic to peanuts, you can use cashews in place of the peanuts. Stir the cashew mixture a little more often once they have been added because they tend to scorch more easily than peanuts.

CRANBERRY CLUSTERS
(Makes ¾ lb. or 16 to 24 clusters)

½ lb. white chocolate wafers   ¼ lb. dried cranberries

Melt the white chocolate wafers in the top of a double boiler. As soon as the chocolate is melted, remove from the heat and stir in the dried cranberries. Drop by spoonfuls onto wax paper. You can also drop them into molds, like those used for peanut butter cups, for a neater appearance.

USING LEFTOVER CHOCOLATE

Your choice of dried fruit and/or   Leftover melted chocolate
  nuts

This same technique can be used for leftover chocolate from any of the recipes in this chapter. Stir the dried fruit and/or nuts into the leftover melted chocolate and spoon onto wax paper or into candy molds.

CARAMEL CORN WITH CASHEWS
(Makes 3 quarts)

3 qts. popped popcorn (about ---   ⅛ tsp. cream of tartar
  ½ c. uncooked)   ¼ tsp. salt
1 c. sugar   ½ tsp. baking soda
¼ c. light corn syrup   1 c. cashew halves and/or pieces
½ c. butter   Non-stick spray

Start with a heaping ½-cup of unpopped corn. Pop the popcorn according to the package directions and measure to make sure that you have about 3 quarts. Set aside in a very large bowl until needed. In a 2-quart saucepan, combine sugar, corn syrup, butter, cream of tartar, and salt. Stir until sugar is dissolved. Do not stir once the butter is melted. Boil rapidly over medium-high heat until mixture reaches 260°. Remove from heat and quickly stir in baking soda and cashews. Immediately pour over popcorn in a very large bowl, stirring until well coated. This may take several minutes to get the caramel evenly distributed in the popcorn. Spread evenly on a large cookie sheet that has been lightly coated with non-stick spray. Bake caramel corn for 1 hour in a preheated 200° oven, stirring once or twice. You may have to bake in 2 batches or use 2 cookie sheets. Store in a tightly covered container. If it becomes sticky, place in a preheated 200° oven again for 10 to 15 minutes.

Note: You will need a very large bowl to mix the caramel corn together at the end. The bowl should be large enough so that you can stir the popcorn without it spilling out of the bowl. If you don't have a bowl large enough, then a large pot will work just as well.

This and That

This and That

Four of the recipes in this chapter require a boiling water bath. Please see the Introduction for detailed instructions on how to use a boiling water bath.

This chapter is a collection of recipes that could not find a home in any of the other chapters. Some of these are used as ingredients in other recipes: Toasted Bread Crumbs, Cinnamon Sugar, and Hickory Salt are good examples. While some of these can be purchased at a grocery store, the homemade versions will usually cost less and taste better.

Most of the remaining recipes can stand alone: Red Pepper Relish, Yogurtnanda, and Cheese Blintzes to name a few.

THIS AND THAT

HICKORY SALT
(Makes 1 cup)

½ c. salt
2 Tbs. Liquid Hickory Smoke
  Flavor

½ c. nutritional yeast

The salt that you use for this recipe can be table salt, sea salt, kosher salt or whatever kind of salt you prefer. Place the salt in a ceramic, glass, or stainless steel bowl and stir in the liquid smoke. Avoid using a plastic bowl because it could absorb some of the liquid smoke flavor and be difficult to remove. Spread the salt evenly in the bottom of a 13 x 9 x 2-inch baking dish. Place the dish in a 225° oven for 1½ hours. Remove the salt from the oven and let cool. Sift the salt through a large wire strainer to remove any lumps. Stir in the nutritional yeast. The nutritional yeast is added as a filler to keep the hickory salt from being too salty. Place the salt for immediate use in a small jar or shaker. Store the remaining hickory salt in a jar with a tight fitting lid. Be advised, when you make this hickory salt, it will fill your kitchen with a strong smoky aroma that will take almost 24 hours to dissipate.

SUBSTITUTION:

1 tsp. imitation bacon bits

Although this is not a great substitute for hickory salt, it usually works when you are in a bind. Place the bacon bits on a cutting board and crush them with the back of a large spoon like a soup spoon. As an alternative you can use a mortar and pestle. You should have a fine powder when done. Crushing the bacon bits does not reduce their volume. One teaspoon of whole bacon bits will yield one teaspoon of crushed imitation bacon bits.

Note: You will need a 13 x 9 x 2-inch baking dish for this recipe. There are several recipes in this book that call for hickory salt which can be hard to find at your local grocery store. Hickory salt makes it possible to add a mild hickory smoked flavor to recipes which can be difficult to do with the intense flavor of liquid smoke.

YOGURTNANDA
(Makes 1 quart)

¾ c. (6 fl. oz.) frozen limeade
  concentrate (i.e. half of a 12 oz.
  container)
1 lb. plain yogurt (1⅔ c.)

1⅓ c. milk (anything from nonfat
  to whole milk will work)
6 ice cubes

Place the limeade, yogurt, milk, and ice cubes in a blender. Hold the blender lid in place while blending so that one of the ice cubes does not bounce up and knock the lid off. Blend at medium speed for 20 to 30 seconds. Serve immediately or keep chilled until ready to serve. Gently stir refrigerated yogurtnanda before serving. Makes about 1 quart or four 8-ounce glasses.

SINGLE (8 oz.) SERVING OF YOGURTNANDA

⅓ c. yogurt
3 Tbs. frozen limeade concentrate

⅓ c. milk
2 ice cubes

Follow the same directions as outlined above. Will make about one 8-oz. glass of yogurtnanda.

Note: Yogurtnanda is a distant cousin to the fruit smoothie. While this recipe originally used limeade, you can substitute an equal amount of any frozen fruit juice concentrate. Orange juice, lemonade, or cranberry juice will all work. "Nanda" is a Sanskrit suffix that means "bliss," so yogurtnanda means "blissful yogurt."

BLUEBERRY SMOOTHIE
(Makes one 8-ounce glass)

½ c. fresh or frozen blueberries
½ banana, sliced (⅓ cup)

½ c. milk
1 ice cube (opt.)

Place the blueberries, sliced banana, milk, and optional ice cube in a blender. Mix in blender at medium speed for 20 to 30 seconds. Serve.

Note: An equal amount of frozen strawberries can be used in place of the blueberries. For a richer, decadent smoothie, add one large scoop of vanilla ice cream.

240812-16

CRANBERRY SMOOTHIE
(Makes one large 12-ounce glass)

⅓ c. jellied cranberry sauce (a ¾-
   inch slice from can)
½ banana, sliced

½ c. milk
½ tsp. sugar or honey

Combine the sliced banana, milk, jellied cranberry sauce, and sugar in a blender. Whirl in blender at medium speed for 20 to 30 seconds. The addition of the sugar keeps this smoothie from being too tart.

Note: This recipe was created as a way to use up the extra cranberry sauce that is frequently left over from the holidays.

TOASTED BREAD CRUMBS
(Makes 3 to 4 cups)

MELBA TOAST

**Bread slices and/or hamburger/
   hot dog buns, about 1 pound**

Place the bread slices and/or buns on a cookie sheet. They can touch each other but should not overlap. Place in a 275° oven and bake for one hour. Turn off oven and leave the toast in the warm oven for an additional 15 minutes. This toast keeps well in an airtight container. In addition to making bread crumbs it can be used in place of crackers for snacks.

TOASTED BREAD CRUMBS

Melba Toast from above

Break the Melba toast from above into pieces. Place a few pieces of the Melba toast in a plastic bag and seal. Put the bag on a counter top and crush with a rolling pin. Repeat until all of the Melba toast has been used. Another option is to whirl some of the broken pieces in a blender for about 30 seconds. Sift the crumbs through a colander to remove any large pieces. Return the large pieces to the blender and repeat. Repeat for remaining toast. Store in an airtight container. For long term storage they can be kept in the freezer. The crumbs from the blender will have a finer texture and will not be as "crunchy" as the crumbs crushed in the bag. You can also use a food processor in place of the blender.

Note: These dried bread crumbs are essentially Melba Toast that has been crushed or ground up. Never throw out old bread or buns. Put them in a bag in the freezer and when you have a large collection, then thaw them out and use them in this recipe. This is not true "Melba Toast", which is generally much thinner.

SEASONED TOASTED BREAD CRUMBS
(Makes 2 cups)

2 c. Toasted Bread Crumbs (see
   previous recipe)
2 Tbs. Parmesan cheese
1 Tbs. dried parsley flakes
1 tsp. salt
1 tsp. paprika

1 tsp. sugar
1 tsp. onion powder
1 tsp. dried oregano, crushed
½ tsp. garlic powder
½ tsp. black pepper
Dash cayenne pepper (opt.)

Place the Toasted Bread Crumbs in a large bowl. Add the Parmesan cheese, parsley flakes, salt, paprika, sugar, onion powder, oregano, garlic powder, and black pepper. Add the dash of cayenne pepper if you would like a spicier flavor. Stir everything together until well blended. Store in a jar with a tight fitting lid until ready to use.

ROASTED ALMONDS
(Makes 1 quart)

1 qt. shelled almonds, about -----
   1 lb. plus 6 oz.

Spread almonds evenly on a cookie sheet or large baking pan. Bake at 275° for 1 ½ hours. Stir two or three times with a spatula during baking to make sure that almonds are evenly roasted. Remove from oven and let cool to room temperature. Store in a jar with a tight fitting lid.

Note: Roasting almonds improves their flavor immensely. Most commercially roasted almonds have been fried in oil. Almonds that have been roasted at home in the oven not only taste better but are better for you. Most of the recipes in this book that use almonds recommend that you use roasted almonds. One pound almonds measures 2 ¾ cups.

CINNAMON SUGAR
(Makes 1 cup)

1 c. sugar
1 Tbs. ground cinnamon

½ tsp. nutmeg

Combine sugar, cinnamon, and nutmeg in a bowl. Stir together until thoroughly mixed, and place in a shaker. Use in any recipe that calls for cinnamon sugar.

Note: You will need a shaker with a capacity of one cup. By having a shaker filled with cinnamon sugar on hand, you can have cinnamon toast at a moments' notice. It's also handy for those baking recipes that call for cinnamon sugar such as cinnamon rolls, raisin bread and the like. It can also be sprinkled over an apple or peach pie crust just before baking.

240812-16

SOFT CREAM CHEESE SPREAD
(Makes 1 ¼ cups)

1 (8 oz.) pkg. cream cheese   *3 Tbs. whole milk*

Allow cream cheese to reach room temperature. Mash with a fork and beat in milk until smooth. Chill and serve on waffles and top with apple butter. This will keep for about 7 to 10 days in the refrigerator.

Note: Although this spread is used mostly on waffles, it can also be used on bagels, etc. It is essentially a homemade version of the soft spread that you buy in tubs at the market.

SPANISH OLIVE CHEESE SPREAD
(Makes 1 cup)

1 (8 oz.) pkg. cream cheese   *12 queen size pimiento stuffed*
2 Tbs. milk   *Spanish olives*

Let the cream cheese stand at room temperature for about 1 hour. In a large bowl, beat together the cream cheese and milk until smooth and free of lumps. Chop the Spanish olives into small pieces. There should be ½ cup when done. Stir the olives into the cream cheese and refrigerate for at least one hour before serving. Serve on crackers or use as a spread for sandwiches.

CREAM CHEESE SANDWICH SPREAD
(Makes 1 ¾ cups or enough for 6 sandwiches)

1 (8 oz.) pkg. cream cheese at   *¼ c. sliced or chopped pimiento*
*   room temperature*   *   stuffed Spanish olives*
⅓ c. sour cream   *⅓ c. chopped walnuts*
½ c. sliced pitted black olives

Mash the cream cheese and sour cream together with a fork. Add the black olives, Spanish olives and chopped walnuts. Stir together until evenly blended. Refrigerate until ready to use. Serve on crackers or sandwiches made with toasted white bread.

Note: This is similar to the previous Spanish olive spread recipe but has enough variation to merit its own instructions.

FRESH REFRIGERATOR PICKLES
(Makes 1 quart)

3 cucumbers (1 lb.)
1 med. green pepper
1 med. red or yellow onion
2 Tbs. crushed celery seed (opt.)

1 Tbs. salt
¾ c. sugar
½ c. vinegar

Peel and cut cucumbers into ⅛-inch thick slices. Thinly slice green pepper and onion. Mix together with salt and celery seed. Let stand for 1 hour. Combine the sugar and vinegar in a 1-quart saucepan. Stir over medium heat until sugar is dissolved. Remove from heat and allow to cool. Pour over vegetables and mix well. Cover and refrigerate. Pickles are ready to eat in about a day.

Note: This recipe comes in handy during the summer when there is an abundance of cucumbers from the garden. Pickling cucumbers and Armenian cucumbers do not have to be peeled.

BREAD AND BUTTER PICKLES
(Makes 4 pints)

4 Armenian cucumbers (4 lbs.)
2 c. chopped yellow onion
1 c. chopped red bell pepper
½ c. rock salt
2 qt. ice water
2 c. sugar
2 c. cider vinegar

2 tsp. whole celery seed
2 tsp. whole mustard seed
1 tsp. ground ginger
1 tsp. cornstarch
½ tsp. ground turmeric
½ tsp. ground black pepper

Wash and cut the cucumbers crosswise into about ⅛-inch slices. You should have about eight cups of sliced cucumbers when done. In a large bowl combine the cucumbers, yellow onion, and bell pepper. Sprinkle rock salt over the top. Add ice water to cover and stir to dissolve salt. Let soak in brine for 2 hours. Drain into a colander and rinse thoroughly in cold water. In a large pot (not copper or iron) combine the sugar, vinegar, celery seed, mustard seed, ginger, cornstarch, turmeric, and black pepper. Stir and cook over medium heat until it begins to simmer. Add drained cucumber mix. Cook over high heat until mixture begins to boil. Stir frequently to keep vegetables toward the bottom of the pot from being over-cooked. Boil for 1 minute. Pack into hot, sterilized pint jars, and seal. Process 10 minutes in boiling water bath.

Note: Armenian cucumbers are firm, crisp, dry cucumbers that are ideal for making these pickles. They retain their crispness after they have been heated. While Armenian cucumbers are a favorite of home gardeners, they may be difficult to find at your local market or even a farmer's market. If you can't find any, then you can use regular pickling cucumbers instead.

240812-16

RED PEPPER RELISH
(Makes 4 to 5 half-pints)

12 red bell peppers (about 5 lbs.)   2 c. white vinegar
1 Tbs. salt   3 c. sugar

To prepare peppers, remove stems, cut in half lengthwise, and remove the seeds and white pulp from inside of the peppers. Grind or finely chop and measure the peppers. You should have 7 cups. Place in a large bowl, sprinkle salt over top, and mix well. Let stand for 6 hours. Pour peppers into a colander lined with a clean, sturdy cloth. Allow to drain over a sink or a bowl for 10 to 15 minutes. Discard the liquid. Combine the peppers, vinegar, and sugar in a 3-quart pot. Cook over high heat until mixture begins to boil. Reduce heat and simmer for about 1 hour. Pour into hot, sterilized jars and seal. Process for 10 minutes in a boiling water bath.

Note: You can substitute yellow or orange peppers for the red peppers. The most popular way to serve this relish is on crackers that have been covered with soft cream cheese.

SWEET PICKLE RELISH
(Makes 3 pints)

3 qt. finely chopped pickling
   cucumbers
1 c. finely chopped red bell
   peppers
1 c. finely chopped yellow onions
3 Tbs. pickling salt
2 c. cold water

1 ½ c. sugar
1 ½ c. white vinegar
1 ½ Tbs. whole mustard seed
¾ tsp. ground ginger
½ tsp. ground turmeric
½ tsp. ground cinnamon
¼ tsp. ground mace

In a very large bowl, combine chopped cucumbers, bell peppers, onions, and salt. Stir together until salt is thoroughly mixed into vegetables. Let stand for at least 2 hours or overnight. Next morning, place vegetables in a colander lined with a pressing cloth and force out some of the brine. Pour 2 cups cold water over the vegetables to remove some of the salt. Join the four corners of the cloth together over the colander and twist to close. Squeeze out as much brine as possible. In a 3-quart pot combine the sugar, vinegar, mustard seed, ginger, turmeric, cinnamon, and mace. Bring to a boil and stir over medium heat. Add the chopped cucumber mixture. Continue to cook and stir over high heat. When relish begins to boil, reduce heat and allow to simmer for 3 minutes. Quickly pack into hot, sterilized jars, and seal. Process in a boiling water bath for 10 minutes.

Note: If you are a home gardener, this is a good way to use those funny shaped and large cucumbers that "got away from you." You can also use Armenian cucumbers. Scoop the seeds out of large cucumbers before chopping. You can chop the cucumbers by hand or use a food processor.

LEMON SYRUP FOR MAKING LEMONADE
(Makes 1 pint which will make 2 quarts lemonade)

CANNING THE LEMON SYRUP

2 lb. fresh lemons (about 8   *1 ½ c. sugar*
medium lemons)

Sterilize two half-pint jars for 15 minutes in a pot of boiling water. Juice the lemons and strain the juice to remove any seeds. There should be about 1 ¼ cups of lemon juice. In a 1-quart saucepan combine the lemon juice and sugar to make the lemon syrup. Heat to 185°. The lemon syrup should just be starting to simmer. Pour into the empty hot sterilized jars and seal. Return the jars to the pot that they were sterilized in. Process in a boiling water bath for 10 minutes. Remove from pot and allow to cool to room temperature.

PREPARING LEMONADE

1 half-pint jar of lemon syrup
from above

To make lemonade, combine one half-pint jar of lemon syrup and three cups water in a large pitcher or other container. Add ice cubes. Add more water if the lemonade is too strong. Enjoy.

FROZEN STRAWBERRIES
(Makes 1 quart)

2 (12 oz.) baskets fresh   *⅔ c. sugar*
strawberries (1 ½ lb.)

Wash the red, ripe, strawberries and drain. Remove caps, cut into large pieces or slice, and measure. There should be one quart (about 1 ¼ pounds) of prepared strawberries. Stir in the sugar and let marinate until all of the sugar is dissolved. The sugar will form a thick syrup in about 15 to 20 minutes. Stir 2 or 3 times to help the sugar dissolve. Place in plastic containers and freeze.

Note: Strawberry season is fairly short for the home gardener. Here is a way to freeze them so that they are available during those winter months when the selection of fresh juicy fruit is limited. These strawberries can be used to make strawberry shortcake or smoothies.

240812-16

PANCAKE SYRUP
(Makes 3 cups)

2 c. sugar
¾ tsp. Mapleine® Imitation Maple
  Flavor

1 c. water
½ c. Karo® dark corn syrup
½ c. honey

Place sugar and Mapleine® imitation maple flavor in a 2-quart saucepan. Add one cup water, place over high heat, and stir until sugar is dissolved. Add Karo® Dark Corn Syrup and honey. Lower heat and continue stirring until syrup begins to boil. Be careful that syrup does not boil over. Serve warm or at room temperature. Extra syrup should be refrigerated.

CRANBERRY PANCAKE SYRUP
(Makes 1 ½ cups)

1 (14 oz.) can jellied cranberry
  sauce

⅝ c. sugar (½ c. plus 2 Tbs.)
5 Tbs. water (¼ c. plus 1 Tbs.)

Mash the jellied cranberry sauce in a 1-quart saucepan. There will be about 1 ¼ cups. Stir in sugar and water. Heat to a gentle simmer. Place in a blender and whirl at a low speed for 20 to 30 seconds. Return to pan and simmer for 1 minute. Cool and serve. This will keep for at least one week in the refrigerator.

SYRUP MADE FROM LEFTOVER CRANBERRY SAUCE

½ c. jellied cranberry sauce (a 1-
  in. slice from the can)

¼ c. sugar
2 Tbs. water

Can you see the pattern here? Just follow the "Half Rule" when using leftover jellied cranberry sauce. Mash the cranberry sauce and measure. Then add half as much sugar as there is cranberry sauce and half as much water as there is sugar. Follow the cooking directions from above. A ½ cup of cranberry sauce makes about ⅔ cup of syrup. The formula will work for any amount of leftover cranberry sauce that you may have.

Note: Here is a method for using some of that jellied cranberry sauce left over from the holidays. It is also good on French Toast. Be sure to look at the recipes for Cranberry Smoothie (in this chapter) and Cranberry Bars (Chapter: Desserts; Cookies and Bars) for more ways to use leftover jellied cranberry sauce. This syrup will be thicker than your traditional maple syrup.

CHEESE BLINTZES
(Makes 20 to 22 blintzes)

COTTAGE CHEESE FILLING

1 lb. cream style cottage cheese   *2 Tbs. sugar*

Place the cream style cottage cheese in a large fine-mesh strainer and rinse in the sink under cold water to remove the cream. Set aside to drain for 5 minutes. In a small bowl, mix together the drained cottage cheese and two tablespoons of sugar. Set aside until ready to cook blintzes.

BLINTZ BATTER AND COOKING INSTRUCTIONS

1 c. all-purpose flour
¼ tsp. salt
1 ¼ c. milk
8 eggs, lightly beaten
2 Tbs. butter, melted

½ c. butter (1 stick), melted --- or
non-stick spray
8 oz. sour cream
Strawberry jam

In a large bowl combine the flour and salt and slowly stir in the milk until smooth and free of lumps. Stir in the beaten eggs and two tablespoons melted butter. Place in a 4-cup measuring cup to make it easy to pour the batter into the frying pan. You should have about 3½ cups of batter. Place the omelet pan or Teflon® skillet over medium heat. Add about 1 teaspoon of the melted butter and tilt the pan in a circular motion to cover the bottom of the pan. A spritz of non-stick spray can be used in place of the butter. Pour a scant ¼ cup of the batter in the center of the pan. Tilt the pan in a circular motion again until the batter evenly covers the bottom of the pan all of the way to the edge. When the batter begins to set, but is not stiff, place a level tablespoon of the sweetened cottage cheese in the center of the batter. Fold one edge of the blintz over the filling followed by the edge opposite the first fold. Fold the two ends that are perpendicular to the first folds, over the center of the blintz. The blintz should have a 2½ to 3-inch square or similar rectangular shape when completed. Continue to cook, turning once, until lightly browned on both sides. You can serve immediately or refrigerate for up to 24 hours before serving. Using two pans at once will speed up the cooking process considerably. To serve, place a teaspoon of sour cream on top of each blintz followed by a spoonful of strawberry jam. If the blintzes have been stored in the refrigerator for any amount of time, reheat the chilled blintzes in a frying pan with a small amount of butter or non-stick spray before serving.

MOZZARELLA FILLING

Blintz batter from above   *8 oz. Mozzarella cheese*

Prepare the Blintz Batter as directed in the above instructions. Cut the Mozzarella cheese into pieces about 1 inch square and ¼ inch thick.

(continued)

Follow the Cooking Directions from above and use the pieces of Mozzarella in place of the cottage cheese filling.

Note: You will need an omelet pan or 6-inch Teflon® skillet. If you are fortunate enough to have a source for dry cottage cheese, then you can use about ¾-pound dry cottage cheese in place of the washed cream style cheese. These can be served for breakfast or brunch.

DEVILED EGGS
(Makes 12 Deviled Eggs)

COOKING THE HARD BOILED EGGS

6 lrg. eggs   *½ tsp. salt*

Place the eggs in a single layer in a 2-quart saucepan. Fill with enough water so that there is 1 inch of water above the eggs. Remove the eggs from the saucepan. Add the ½ teaspoon salt to the water and place over high heat until water begins to boil. The salt will help to heal any eggs that become cracked during cooking. Return the eggs to the saucepan by gently lowering them into the water with a spoon. Begin counting the cooking time as soon as the last egg is in the water. Cover and let the water simmer gently for 15 minutes. Drain the saucepan of hot water and fill with cold water. Replace the water with fresh cold water after 5 and 10 minutes. Finally, remove the eggs from the saucepan and keep in the refrigerator until ready to use.

PREPARING THE DEVILED EGGS

6 hard boiled eggs from above	*Dash black pepper*
¼ c. mayonnaise	*Pinch cayenne*
¼ tsp. yellow mustard	*Paprika for garnish*
⅛ tsp. salt	

Peel the eggs and cut in half lengthwise. Gently remove the yolks from the eggs and place in a medium bowl. Mash the yolks with a fork. Add the mayonnaise, yellow mustard, salt, black pepper, and cayenne. Mix together thoroughly and spoon the yolk mixture into the egg whites. Garnish with paprika if desired. Refrigerate until ready to serve.

RICE FOR BREAKFAST
(Makes 2 large servings)

BASIC RECIPE

⅔ c. uncooked long grain rice
1⅓ c. water
1 hard boiled egg

½ tsp. salt
4 tsp. (2 patties) butter

Combine the rice and water in a 1-quart saucepan. Cook the rice according to the package directions. If you prefer, you can cook the rice in a rice cooker. This will make 2 cups of rice. The hard boiled egg can be cooking at the same time as the rice. Add the salt and butter to the cooked rice when done. Stir until butter is melted. Peel the hard boiled egg, chop into small pieces, stir into the rice, and serve.

BREAKFAST RICE VARIATION

1 MorningStar Farms® sausage
   patty
2 tsp. vegetable oil
2 hard boiled eggs, chopped

4 tsp. (2 patties) butter
2 Tbs. chopped parsley
1 clove garlic, finely minced
½ tsp. salt

Place the vegetable oil in a small saucepan and add the sausage patty. Cook over medium heat for 5 to 6 minutes while turning once, until lightly browned on each side. Chop the sausage into small pieces. Add the sausage, hard boiled eggs, butter, chopped parsley, minced garlic, and salt to the rice. Mix everything together and serve.

Note: If you like, you can use a scrambled egg in place of the hard boiled egg.

SOUTHERN FRIED GRITS
(Makes 2 to 3 servings)

½ c. quick grits
1 Tbs. butter
½ tsp. salt
1⅔ c. water
1 egg beaten with 1 Tbs. milk

⅔ c. toasted bread crumbs (see
   recipe earlier in this chapter)
vegetable oil, ¼-inch deep in
   frying pan
maple syrup or honey

Prepare grits a day ahead of time. Combine the grits, butter, salt, and 1⅔ cups water in a 1-quart saucepan. Cook according to package directions. Pour into a 9 x 5 x 3-inch bread pan and chill overnight. Cut into 6 equal pieces by cutting across the width of the pan. Dip each piece in egg and then bread crumbs. Fry in vegetable oil over medium-high heat or 350° in an electric skillet. Turn once so that the grits are golden brown on both sides. Serve warm with syrup or honey.

240812-16

INDEX OF RECIPES

240812-16

BREAD

Baking Powder Breads

Yeast Breads

243

Ordering Cookbooks

Cookbooks make great gifts for birthdays, anniversaries, weddings, showers, Christmas, Mother's Day, and other special occasions.

To order additional copies of this cookbook, detach and mail the order form below with a check or money order to:

**The Vichara Monastery
10049 Ernst Rd.
Coulterville, CA 95311**

**(209) 878-3398
vicharamonastery@gmail.com**

You can also contact the monastery directly by phone or email.

. . . .

Please send me _____ copies of:

**The Joy of an Empty Pot
The Vichara Monastery Vegetarian Cookbook**

at **$30.00** each plus **$5.00** s/h per book.
California residents must add 8.00% sales tax ($2.40) per book.

Enclosed is my check for $_____.

Mail book(s) to:

_____
Name

_____
Address

_____   _____   _____
City   State   Zip

(_____) _____   _____
Phone   E-mail